Heartland Heroes

Heartland Heroes

Remembering World War II

Ken Hatfield

University of Missouri Press
Columbia and London

University of Missouri Press, Columbia, Missouri 65201
Printed and bound in the United States of America

5 4 3 2 1 07 06 05 04 03

Library of Congress Cataloging-in-Publication Data

Hatfield, Ken. (Kenneth K.), 1955–
Heartland heroes : remembering World War II / Ken. Hatfield.
p. cm.
Includes bibliographical references.
ISBN 0-8262-1460-6 (alk. paper)
1. World War, 1939–1945—United States. I. Title.
D769 .H38 2003
940.54'0973—dc21 2003001786

♾™ This paper meets the requirements of the
American National Standard for Permanence of Paper
for Printed Library Materials, Z39.48, 1984.

Designer: Jennifer Cropp
Typesetter: Bookcomp, Inc.
Printer and binder: Thomson-Shore, Inc.
Typefaces: Minion, Americana, Bickley Script

To my parents,

Dean and Donna Hatfield,
to whom I owe everything

Contents

Preface

In 1984, I was working as a reporter at a small weekly newspaper in Liberty, Missouri, when I interviewed a guy named Bob Barackman. Mike Perrault, a friend and coworker who happened to be Bob's nephew, had told me "Uncle Bob" had lots of war stories from when he served with the U.S. Marines in the Pacific during World War II. So, on a warm and sunny spring day, I drove out to his home in Kansas City, Missouri, looking for a story.

I don't remember much about the actual interview. I do remember Bob was friendly, gracious, and extremely candid. He was only fifty-nine at the time and already retired because of arthritic knees, so he had lots of time on his hands. He had been telling his war stories for years, but, as it turned out, only certain ones. Some he had kept bottled inside for forty years, that is, until he told them to me.

I was with him for several hours, occasionally prompting him with questions, but mostly just listening. I'm sure dredging up some of those memories was painful, but I think it was ultimately beneficial. I think talking about it allowed him to get some of that poison out of his system and finally reconcile his feelings after all those years. That's my hope anyway.

It's hard to explain the effect his stories had on me. My own father was a marine veteran of World War II and had served in the Pacific but not in combat, so my impressions of war were shaped more by films and television. I also had grown up in the shadow of Vietnam, had seen the pictures of maimed and mutilated young men in *Life* magazine, actually had to sweat out a draft lottery during my senior year of high school. I may not have had any personal experience with war, but I also had no illusions about what it was like. I believed then as I believe now: There is no glory in war.

But listening to Bob bare his soul, I learned that war is more than simply good and evil, more than courage and unrelenting terror. War is also about patriotism, about sacrifice, about conquering fear. And perhaps most of all, it's about the guy in the foxhole next to you—about taking care of each other, protecting each other, loving each other: a camaraderie so intense only men who have been in combat can ever know what it's like.

Yes, most of all, war is about love.

Bob's stories touched a chord in me, and I realized that as a journalist I had a unique opportunity to preserve that little piece of history each veteran carries with him. The following year I did a series of stories on local World War II veterans. At the time, I wrote that the purpose of the series was to commemorate the fortieth anniversary of the war's end, but the truth was, I just wanted to talk to the veterans and tell their stories.

Over the last seventeen years, I've interviewed nearly one hundred World War II veterans. Most were living in the Kansas City metropolitan area when I interviewed them. Several were former residents now living elsewhere. Unfortunately, many are now deceased.

This "project" might not have gone any further than bound copies of yellowed newsprint and dusty rolls of microfilm but for an incident that took place in August of 2001. I lost my newspaper job. That's when I decided to do what I had been putting off for years: compile my war stories into a book and try to get it published. The book you hold in your hands is the fruition of that dream.

Writing this book has not been without challenges. Although most of the stories had been published previously in newspapers, none existed as computer files and so had to be typed into my database. Luckily I've been scrupulous about saving my clippings and was able to locate all my old stories; however, in order to present the stories in chronological order, I had to do quite a bit of rewriting. For example, if a veteran participated in more than one major battle, I usually broke his story down into several component chapters. A side benefit for me was the opportunity to rewrite and reedit many of my older stories, which upon rereading, I found showed my youthful inexperience as a writer and a journalist.

Although most of these veterans came from a small corner of the country, they actually represent a much larger geographic area. Many grew up in places other than Kansas City—Honolulu, Hawaii; Bonham, Texas; Provo, Utah; and Heidelberg, Germany, to name a few—before settling in the Heartland. Frankly, I think it makes little difference where they came from or ended up. The experiences of World War II veterans are universal.

These were not famous men and women. They were ordinary people who lived through extraordinary times. They were young men, barely out of high school, who were sent halfway around the world to fight and die for their country. They were young women who found new skills and independence as nurses caring for the wounded, as factory workers keeping the boys supplied overseas, as military personnel performing critical duties on the home front. They were patriotic minorities fighting for freedom in another country, when they didn't have equality in their own.

After the war, the men came home and adjusted to peace as best they could. Some took advantage of the GI Bill, went to college, and found careers. Many went back home, back to their old jobs, seemingly unaffected by what they had seen and done. Some couldn't escape the memories. There were no counselors, no psychologists, available to mend their hidden wounds. It would be years before they talked about the war. For many of them, healing came slowly. For some, the wounds healed, but the scars remained.

A word about the stories in this book. I've learned over the years that the most vocal critics of World War II memoirs are often the veterans themselves. They, perhaps more than anyone, know the fallibility of memory and the temptation to embellish the truth. But I will say this: Only a handful of those interviewed approached me to tell their stories. I usually sought them out. Some told their stories matter-of-factly. Some obviously relished the telling. And some found it an extremely painful experience. There were many tears.

Many of the veterans willingly lent me their priceless regimental and divisional histories to help me piece together their stories. They provided documentation on their medals and commendations, though practically every one of them downplayed his awards and exploits, saying he hadn't done anything special. The ones who should be honored, they all said, are the ones who didn't come home.

Read this book for what it is: personal memories, frozen in time, of a fading war and a disappearing generation. All too soon, these stories will be all we have left.

Heartland Heroes

Pearl Harbor

First Shots

Pearl Harbor, Hawaii, December 6, 1941—It was dark when the USS *Ward* fired up her boilers and headed into the channel leading out of Pearl Harbor. As usual, the sailors not on watch came to quarters on deck to salute the flags of ships passing into the harbor. One of those topside was S1c (Seaman First Class) Pat Flanagan. The eighteen-year-old from St. Paul, Minnesota, called up from the navy reserves in January of 1941, was enjoying being away from home for the first time.

The *Ward,* a four-stack destroyer, passed a long line of ships. "We're in a national emergency," a sailor next to Flanagan said. "Why do we have all these battleships in here? It doesn't make any sense." It was peacetime in America but not elsewhere in the world. By late 1941, the Nazis had conquered Western Europe and were besieging Leningrad and Moscow in the east. In North Africa, Rommel had Tobruk encircled but was meeting stiff resistance from the feisty British. The Japanese had occupied Manchuria, Korea, portions of the Chinese mainland, and French Indochina. In response, President Franklin Roosevelt had declared a national emergency, putting the armed forces in a high state of readiness. But not everyone was taking the emergency seriously. By the evening of Saturday, December 6, nearly a dozen battleships were moored side by side in the area of the harbor known as Battleship Row. Most of the planes at Hickam and Wheeler Fields were parked in neat rows.

That night the *Ward* was on routine patrol in the restricted waters outside Pearl Harbor. Flanagan went on watch at 0400 in the afterdeck house near the rear of the ship. About fifteen minutes earlier, the *Condor,* a minesweeper, had reported an unidentified submarine heading toward the entrance to Pearl Harbor and asked the *Ward* to investigate. General quarters were sounded about 0430, and Flanagan went to his battle station at gun number three. Flanagan was one of four loaders for the four-inch gun. Each round weighed ninety-eight pounds and had to be loaded by hand. Since it was Sunday morning, not everyone reported to his battle station. Some actually slept through the general quarters alarm.

The *Ward* was fitted with searchlights and sound instruments but no radar. The crew found no sign of the submarine. "We looked and looked, but we couldn't find nothin'," Flanagan said forty-five years later.

The sailors went back to their normal duties. Those who could, went back to sleep. Flanagan returned to his job of keeping a lookout for sailors who fell overboard.

Richard McBratney, a twenty-five-year-old water tender first class aboard the USS *Maryland,* a battleship moored on Battleship Row, was up early that warm, sunny Sunday morning. He didn't have duty that day and was looking forward to a planned shore leave. On shore, Pfc. Les LeTourneau also was up early. The lanky eighteen-year-old was a member of the regimental boxing team, which was preparing to leave for Honolulu for a tournament. LeTourneau was with the 251st Coast Artillery antiaircraft unit stationed at Camp Malakole on Barbers Point. Waking at dawn, he took a deep breath of the sun-washed tropical air. It looked like the beginning of another beautiful day in paradise.

At 0630, the USS *Antares,* a repair ship, reported something following it near the mouth of the channel. A PBY seaplane began circling the object and dropped a smoke bomb to mark its location. The *Ward* sounded her second general quarters at 0640. This time, nearly everyone reported to his battle station.

"I don't know why, but we did," Flanagan said. "[We] had a funny feeling. . . . We pursued this smoke bomb, and the sub came up. It was a wonder we didn't ram it. But still, when you stop to think about it, we didn't know if it was ours or someone else's. We wasn't at war, it could've been our own sub. But our own subs wouldn't come up in a restricted area. They knew better than that."

The *Ward*'s skipper, Lt. William Outerbridge, gave the order to load the guns and told the gunners to stand by. Meanwhile, Flanagan said, "we're bearing down on this darn sub." Rather than try to escape, the submarine headed straight for the *Ward* as if to ram the destroyer.

At 0645, gun number one opened fire at a distance of one hundred yards. "They really fired the first shots of World War II," Flanagan said. "And they missed." Moments later, gun number three was ordered to fire. "I could have picked up a can of beer and hit the darn thing," he said. Instead, "our gun three put a direct hit right into the conning tower."

The high-explosive shell hit the submarine just above the waterline. Almost immediately the sub rolled over and sank. Both the *Ward* and the PBY dropped several depth charges into the churning water, which in that area was about twelve hundred feet deep. The submarine didn't resurface. At 0653, the *Ward* radioed the commander of the Fourteenth Naval District that they had fired upon and apparently sunk an unidentified submarine near the net gate protecting the entrance to Pearl Harbor. Lieutenant Outerbridge asked for further orders. Headquarters asked for confirmation of the sinking.

There would be several more exchanges between the *Ward* and headquarters over the next hour. Lieutenant Outerbridge, who had taken command of the *Ward* only two days earlier, was concerned that the vessel might have been one of the Japanese midget submarines they had been warned to be on the watch for. The submarines were filled with explosives and used in suicide missions to sink Allied ships. And where you found one midget sub, there were usually others. However, naval command was reluctant to put the entire harbor on alert because of one unconfirmed incident. They refused to do anything until the sinking was confirmed. After all, the United States wasn't at war. "Our captain was pulling his hair out," Flanagan said. "He was extremely mad."

At about 0750, Flanagan heard someone say, "Hey, they're holding maneuvers." Flanagan looked up to see the sky filled with planes. "All of a sudden you could see smoke everywhere. It was terrible."

McBratney, who had been in the navy since 1934, was assigned to the *Maryland*'s firerooms, where the ship's boilers were located. "I was a glorified fireman," he said forty-four years later.

As McBratney finished breakfast, a sailor came running into the mess, shouting that the ship was on fire. Everyone immediately jumped to his feet and headed to his station. Almost simultaneously, they heard the sound of explosions and the general quarters alarm. McBratney's battle station was the number six fireroom on the third deck, twenty-eight feet below the waterline. Even down there he could hear the explosions on the surface.

The *Maryland* was moored to the quay, next to the USS *Oklahoma.* "We tried to move the ship, but the *Oklahoma* had us pinned in and we couldn't get out," McBratney said. "I don't know if it would have done us any good or not, 'cause the rest of them got hit anyway." The *Oklahoma,* which screened the *Maryland* from the Japanese torpedo bombers, took several hits. "She got the torpedoes that we would have got," he said. "We got two five hundred-pound bombs . . . hit on the bow. Blew the bow up."

After the attack, McBratney went topside and manned the hoses to keep the fire away from the *Maryland.* He also helped rescue seamen bobbing in the burning, oil-slicked water. Next to them, the *Oklahoma* had capsized. Only her masts, which were stuck in the harbor's muddy bottom, kept her from turning over completely. Despite the loss of her bow, the *Maryland* was still seaworthy; later, the bow was filled with concrete and the ship was sailed back to Bremerton, Washington, for repairs.

McBratney lost three buddies on the *Maryland.* They were members of a repair party stationed on the bow's second deck and were killed when the bow exploded. One of the men was found crushed beneath some lockers. "When we pulled him out," McBratney said grimly, "he was only half there."

LeTourneau stowed his gear in the back of the truck and watched as his buddy drove away to pick up the other members of the boxing team. He planned to pick up LeTourneau on the way back.

When he enlisted in the army in 1940, LeTourneau chose to be stationed in Hawaii rather than the Philippines. Eventually he was put in the 251st, a California National Guard unit. "It was the first National Guard outfit to go overseas," he said.

LeTourneau first knew that something was amiss that Sunday morning when someone told him that unidentified planes had attacked the camp and one of the sergeants had been hit while he was still in bed (it turned out the wound wasn't serious).

"The first thing we heard was that the sergeant was hit. We got strafed," LeTourneau said. "We didn't know what it was until we saw the Japanese planes."

LeTourneau's battle station was a three-inch antiaircraft gun at Pearl Harbor's West Loch ammunition dump, but there was no way to get there. "We were hemmed in because of the strafing," he said.

So they did the next best thing. "Everybody got rifles. I had a BAR [Browning Automatic Rifle, a portable machine gun]." Crouched behind a fifty-five-gallon water drum, he fired at the planes as they came in on their low-level strafing runs.

"Everybody was firing rifles. Never did get no machine guns or anything set up," he said. "I was firing on full automatic." LeTourneau thinks he helped shoot down at least one of the enemy planes. "One of 'em, when he turned off, he was smokin'."

Besides the wounded sergeant, the twelve hundred-man camp had only one other casualty, a lone pilot who had the misfortune to be in the air at the time of the attack. "We had one guy that was up in a private plane. We never heard from him," LeTourneau said. "I guess they [the Japanese] just shot him down."

After the attack, which lasted about two hours, LeTourneau was sent to his West Loch gun position, but by then there was nothing to shoot at. That night, however, nervous U.S. antiaircraft gunners opened fire on a group of navy fighters who had been diverted to Pearl Harbor from the USS *Enterprise.* LeTourneau saw one of the planes go down.

"There was nothing supposed to fly over the harbor," he said. "This pilot either got mixed up or something, but everything opened up on him."

So much changed when the bombs started falling at 7:55 A.M. on December 7. Flanagan feels that many of the twenty-four hundred men killed in the attack could have been saved if the navy had heeded the *Ward*'s warning. "We were in a national emergency. Germany was at war. They had plenty of time to fire up their boilers and get those ships out of Pearl Harbor.

"We sank that sub at quarter to seven," he said. "They had an hour and ten minutes to fire up those ships."

Although strafed and bombed during the attack, the *Ward* escaped damage and suffered no casualties. "They weren't after us," Flanagan said. "They were after those battleships. Which they got." After the attack, everyone was on high alert.

"Everybody was just fidgety as hell," Flanagan said. "All day we looked to the horizon for the invasion by the Japanese. . . . We just kept a-lookin.' They would have blown us out of the water. 'Course, we would have took some of them with us."

After Pearl Harbor, LeTourneau was sent to the Fiji Islands and later Guadalcanal. He ended his tour of duty in northern Bougainville.

McBratney spent the entire war on the *Maryland.* After his discharge, he reenlisted for a two-year stint on a fleet tanker during the Korean War.

Flanagan spent forty-four months in the Pacific before returning to the States. After the war, he stayed in touch with his former skipper, who retired as a rear admiral and died in 1986. "I want people to know Captain Outerbridge, as far as I'm concerned, could have saved thousands of lives," Flanagan said.

After the war, the *Ward*'s number three gun was enshrined on the grounds of the state capitol in St. Paul, where many of the recruits who served on her came from. It was removed from the destroyer later in the war when the *Ward* was converted to a high-speed troop transport. The *Ward* didn't survive the war. Late in 1944, she was en route from Leyte to Ormac Bay, part of a task force, when she was hit by a kamikaze. The commander of another ship in the task force, the USS *O'Brien,* was ordered to scuttle the crippled transport. The first salvo hit the *Ward*'s after magazine, and the ship exploded. Within minutes she disappeared into the sea.

The day was December 7, 1944. And Capt. William Outerbridge, the skipper of the *O'Brien,* wiped tears from his eyes.

Paradise Lost

On December 7, 1941, Dee Nicholson lost her island paradise. That was the day the planes came roaring over her home, spewing bullets and bombs, and plunged the world into war. Her life changed in an instant. Gone were the peaceful tropic evenings, the nighttime outings, the strolls on moon-washed beaches. Her new world was one of searchlights and air raid sirens, hours huddled in dank bomb shelters, once-pristine beaches now draped with barbed wire and guarded by machine gun emplacements. It was a time of paranoia and fear, of shortages and fierce patriotism. To a child growing up, the experience was as fearful as it was exciting, perhaps no less so for her parents.

Nicholson's father, Buddy Stagner, remembers that December morning like it was yesterday—the roar of the airplanes, the booming explosions; running out on his front lawn and standing there beside his six-year-old daughter, Dorinda—Dee for short—staring in disbelief at the burning cauldron that was Pearl Harbor.

Plans for the attack on Pearl Harbor had been in the works since the previous January when Adm. Isoroku Yamamoto, commander in chief of Japan's Combined Fleet, first diagrammed the idea. Although philosophically opposed to a war with the United States, Yamamoto—who spent a year at Harvard and knew the United States' industrial potential—felt it was his responsibility to knock out the sleeping giant before it awakened, and by so doing, bring a quick and early peace. His plan was daring—strike a crippling blow to the American Pacific Fleet, based at Pearl Harbor, and then wage all-out war until the U.S., wearied and demoralized by its losses, sought peace, leaving Japan its Asian conquests.

In the early morning hours of December 7, 1941, five two-man midget submarines, packed with explosives and manned by crews prepared to die for their emperor, were launched in the waters around Oahu, Hawaii's third largest island. This "Special Naval Attack Unit" was to sneak into Pearl Harbor and sink any ships it encountered.

The suicide submarines were only a small part of Japan's Advance Expeditionary Force, which was approaching Hawaii undetected from the north. The strike force, commanded by Vice Adm. Chuichi Nagumo, sailed from the Kurile Islands on November 26 and included six aircraft carriers, two battleships, three cruisers, and nine destroyers. Also, twenty-eight large submarines would operate off Oahu to sink any warships that managed to escape out to sea.

On the hangar deck of the flagship carrier *Akagi* was a plaster-of-Paris relief map of Pearl Harbor, which the pilots would use to identify their targets—the army airfields, Hickam and Wheeler; the Schofield army barracks; the naval air stations at Kaneohe and Ford Island; the marine base at Ewa; and, of course, the Pacific Fleet, moored bow to stern in tidy rows of military precision.

When the strike force was 200 miles from Hawaii, the carriers launched the first of two attack waves totaling 350 aircraft. Few if any of the airmen wore parachutes, preferring to die with honor rather than disgrace themselves by being captured.

At 0645 Hawaii time, the USS *Ward* sank one of the midget submarines at the mouth of the harbor. At 0702, Pvt. Joe Lockard, nineteen, and Pvt. George Elliott, twenty-three, were manning the U.S. Army Signal Corps' new radar station at Opana on the northern tip of Oahu when a large blip appeared on the screen. The men exchanged puzzled looks. It looked like a large flight of aircraft about 140 miles to the north. After ensuring that the equipment was working properly, they reported the sighting but were told it was probably a flight of B-17s coming in from California. At 7:39, the blip disappeared into the "dead zone" created by the surrounding hills.

The "blip," now less than twenty miles away, was actually the first wave of the Japanese attack. At 7:53 A.M., Cmdr. Mitsuo Fuchida shouted, "*Tora, tora, tora!*" into his radio—*tora,* which means tiger in Japanese, was the code word to tell the strike force that the Americans had been caught completely by surprise—and 187 Japanese warplanes screamed toward the peaceful harbor.

Stagner, who grew up in Independence, Missouri, was the branch superintendent for the Honolulu post office. He and his wife, Pansy, a Hawaiian native, had moved to Oahu in 1934. The two had met in Utah while he was stationed in Salt Lake City and she was attending the university there. Later, she returned to Hawaii, and he followed her after his four-year army stint was over.

They bought a home in an area called the Pearl City Peninsula, a spit of land jutting into the busy harbor. Nearby was Ford Island, where the Pacific Fleet was based. At the extreme southern tip of the peninsula was the Pan American Airways clipper base, where Pansy Stagner worked. As one of the few commercial airports on the island, the base also served the China Clipper seaplanes, which landed in the harbor and taxied to the pier like winged motorboats. Onboard were wealthy tourists from the States.

By 1941, the Stagners had two children—Dorinda and Ishmael, who was two. Dee, looking back fifty years, recalled idyllic days of fishing from the seaplane pier for big Samoan crabs. The navy ships were anchored just across the bay, and she could remember watching them move ponderously through the harbor like huge prehistoric beasts.

December 7 was a beautiful Sunday morning, and the family was up early, preparing for the walk to church. Pansy, dressed in a traditional muumuu, was fixing a breakfast of papayas, bananas, Portuguese sausage, rice, and eggs when they suddenly heard the sound of airplanes and explosions. Low-flying airplanes were nothing new to the Stagners. Hickam Field was on the east side of the harbor, and the marines' Ewa Field was just to the west.

"When the airplanes took off," Stagner recalled in 1991, "it sounded like they were coming in the bedroom window and going out the other side." The explosions weren't that unusual either, he said. "We figured that the army and navy were carrying on some damned realistic maneuvers. We were cursing [them]." When the noise didn't let up, curiosity got the best of Stagner, who went outside followed closely by his daughter. "We stood out in the front yard and watched the planes come over," Nicholson said. "They were so low we could see the pilots."

The planes were coming from the northwest through Kole Pass and flying directly over Ford Island. Explosions could be heard, and huge columns of smoke were rising from the harbor. "There was wave after wave after wave," Stagner said. Every so often there was a brief lull, then another group of warplanes would break through the pall, wings glinting in the sunshine, plummeting earthward through the puffs of antiaircraft fire. "We thought it was a maneuver," Nicholson said. "We didn't know it was the real thing."

The ships in the harbor weren't the only targets. The planes also strafed streets and houses. The Stagners' own home was hit several times with incendiary bullets, which ripped away part of their roof and scorched their kitchen wall. "Our roof was so full of bullets it leaked for months and months," Nicholson said.

"They machine-gunned cars on the road," Stagner said. "They shot at houses. They did all kinds of mischief."

Although he could plainly see the red sun emblem on the planes, Stagner refused to believe the evidence of his own eyes. He kept thinking it must be some terrible mistake. "Nobody had any fears of [the Japanese] attacking the Pacific Fleet," Stagner said. "Nobody, and that included the military. . . . They were utterly confident that Japan couldn't [threaten us]."

Fearing for their safety, Stagner ordered everyone into the family's black '39 Ford. He didn't know where he was going, but knew they had to get away from the harbor, which seemed to be the epicenter of the attack. When they rounded a turn, they suddenly had an unobstructed view of the harbor, and their worst fears were confirmed. The battle was over.

The USS *Utah,* a retired battleship that had been converted into a target ship, was on her side, already crippled by two torpedo hits. She later capsized, entombing fifty-five sailors. The ship had had some of her deck guns removed, and the Japanese pilots had mistaken her for an aircraft carrier. But most of the explosions were coming from Battleship Row, where much of the Pacific Fleet was berthed, including six battleships anchored side by side. Luckily, the fleet's three aircraft carriers were out to sea at the time.

The USS *Oklahoma,* ripped open by five torpedoes, had turned turtle; only the bottom of her hull showed. The *Arizona,* where more than a thousand sailors had died in a single hellish blast, was an inferno of fire and black smoke. The *West Virginia,* hit by six torpedoes, had settled into the harbor mud. As the family surveyed the desolation in stunned silence, a lone two-engine reconnaissance plane made pass after pass over the harbor. "That was a Japanese plane photographing the damage," Nicholson said.

Unsure what to do, Stagner tried to return home, but grim military policemen who streamed into the area refused to let the family by. So he drove to some nearby sugarcane fields, and the family hid there with other civilian refugees, including many of their Pearl City neighbors. They stayed there through the day, huddled around a shortwave radio. At nightfall, the military police evacuated the refugees to Waipahu, a plantation town ten miles away.

That night, six fighters from the USS *Enterprise,* searching for the Japanese carrier force that had spearheaded the attack, flew into Oahu when it became too dark to return to their carrier. Despite identifying themselves as Americans, they were attacked by antiaircraft gunners, who shot down all but one of the planes. Three of the pilots were killed.

Stagner and Nicholson remember watching the tracer-etched sky from their temporary home—the recreation hall of a sugar mill. "It was the most horrible fireworks I'd ever seen," Stagner said. Later, they found out one of the pilots had crashed just a block from their house in Pearl City. After a week, they were allowed to return home. Their house was damaged but repairable. Their yard was littered with antiaircraft shell casings, which they used as doorstops.

Things changed overnight in Hawaii. Rigid military control replaced the relaxed, peaceful tone of island life. "We lived under martial law," Nicholson said. "It went into effect December 7, which meant we were under military rule [the entire war]."

"The military took over and superseded all civilian activities," Stagner said. "They treated you like you were in a concentration camp."

Everyone on the island, including children, was fingerprinted and required to carry an ID card. The government also distributed personally fitted gas masks, which residents were required to take wherever they went.

"We were so sure that the Japanese would return and they would invade," Nicholson said. "And if they tried to invade, they would use poison gas first."

From 6 P.M. to 6 A.M. only essential government personnel were allowed to be outside. Stagner, as a postal superintendent, was considered essential and was one of the few civilians allowed on the darkened streets of Honolulu. He had to paint the headlights of his car with black enamel, leaving exposed on each only a tiny slit of light one inch wide and one-eighth of an inch high. Residents were required to install thick blackout curtains to ensure that no escaped light would give Japanese bombers a target. "They had patrols up and down the street to watch out for that," Stagner said.

"If the military police saw a light," Nicholson said, "they'd shoot [it] out."

On Hawaii, the U.S. government was particularly worried about spies and saboteurs. At the beginning of the war, 37 percent of the island's residents were of Japanese descent. That's why, unlike on the U.S. West Coast, most Japanese-Americans in Hawaii weren't interned in resettlement camps. In Hawaii, there were simply too many of them; however, Stagner recalls that some of their Japanese-American friends were sent to the States to spend the war in a resettlement camp in New Mexico. "We thought it was a damn shame because we knew those people were as American as we were." But after the attack on Pearl Harbor, many of those with close family ties to Japan were deported or returned voluntarily.

Stagner's job as postal superintendent included reading and censoring mail. "Every single piece of mail that came to or went from the island was read," Nicholson said. "Some letters looked like confetti after all the pieces were cut out."

Stagner said in Hawaii, even more than on the mainland, there was shock and anger at what the Japanese had done. "Everyone was just stunned to think such a thing could happen. . . . We felt the Japanese were our friends," he said. "You trusted them. If someone you trust turns on you, you hate them more than the ones who were always your enemy."

When the war began, the island was hit by shortages. Hawaii produces few necessities, and residents depend on imported goods, which soon were in short supply. Rice and meat were particularly hard to come by. "There were lines everywhere," Stagner said. "To this day I don't like standing in lines. If there's a line, I'll usually go someplace else."

Nicholson attended a private girl's school, the Sacred Hearts Convent, and remembers workers removing the jungle gyms and swings from the playground and replacing them with bomb shelters. The underground shelters were damp and smelly and often filled with water when it rained. "They were awful," she said.

But Nicholson doesn't remember the war as a time of hardship, except for when the authorities closed her school and converted it into a military hospital, forcing her to transfer to a school twenty miles away. "That was about the only hardship that I remember," she said. Other things—the curfew, the barbed wire, the air raid alerts—she took in stride. "To me, that was the way [it was]. It seemed . . . normal."

The things she remembers most are the feelings of pride and patriotism, of family togetherness, of shared adversity. Everyone took part in the war effort, from raising victory gardens to gathering scrap metal. One of her fondest memories is of her mother. A talented hula teacher, Pansy used to take her daughter along when she gave lessons at the naval housing. "She probably taught thousands of military wives how to dance the hula," Nicholson said.

Stagner and Nicholson went back to Hawaii in 1991 to take part in a ceremony on the fiftieth anniversary of the attack. The ceremony included a service aboard the USS *Arizona* Memorial, where the remains of nearly twelve hundred sailors remain entombed. That year, Stagner was asked what he thought about the Japanese.

"The Japanese now own about 90 percent of the island," he said. "And that's not the Hawaiian-born Japanese. That's the Japanese-born Japanese. . . . On the other hand, how much of New York City is owned by the Japanese?"

Does it bother him that the country that once tried to destroy the island is now its majority owner?

"It bothers me, but it's a frustration thing more than anything else," he said, "because there isn't a damn thing we can do about it."

The Fighting Six

Somewhere off the coast of Oahu, December 7, 1941—Navy Ens. Jim Daniels was in trouble. Having spent the day searching futilely for the Japanese strike force that had attacked Pearl Harbor that morning, his squadron of F4F Grumman Wildcats had tried to return to its aircraft carrier, the USS *Enterprise,* but found only an endless expanse of black ocean. He and his five fellow pilots were dangerously low on fuel.

Then he saw it—a meandering white trail in the blackness. The majestic ship was completely dark, but phosphorus churned up by the carrier's massive screws left a glowing tail. It was a comforting sight, but Daniels wasn't comforted for long. His squadron was notified that due to the possibility of enemy attack, the carrier's flight deck lights wouldn't be turned on. The six returning fighters were instructed to divert to the nearby naval base. The Wildcats banked away and headed toward the smoking ruin that was Pearl Harbor. The pilots did not realize what awaited them, and perhaps that's just as well. Within minutes, two of them would be dead and a third mortally wounded, all from friendly fire.

Daniels has an impressive resume. He served in three wars and flew 110 combat missions—55 during World War II and 55 in Korea. He commanded a fighter-bomber squadron in World War II, flew Panther jets and commanded an air wing during the Korean War, and was the commander of the aircraft carrier *Ticonderoga* in the early months of the Vietnam War.

As part of the fiftieth-anniversary commemoration of the attack on Pearl Harbor, Daniels, who had settled in Hawaii after the war, was asked to be on a panel of ten former U.S. and Japanese pilots who were in the air over Hawaii that day. Six years later, Daniels was the only one still alive. When President Bill Clinton attended ceremonies for the fiftieth anniversary of the end of World War II at the Punch Bowl Cemetery in Hawaii in 1995, he referred to Daniels—"the young Navy pilot born and raised on a farm in Missouri"—seven times in his speech.

"This is a great man. He's not just a guy," says Larry Nicholson, a Raytown, Missouri, photographer who met Daniels at the Pearl Harbor ceremony in 1991. Nicholson's wife, Dee, a six-year-old witness to the attack, also attended the ceremony with her father, Buddy Stagner. The Nicholsons returned to Hawaii in 1997 to videotape Daniels for a documentary about World War II.

"He is a genuine American hero," Larry Nicholson said. "There aren't many like him and he's one of the few left."

Daniels was born in 1915 and raised in the Kansas City area. His father, who was in the farm mortgage business, purchased a wheat farm west of Lee's Summit, Missouri, when Daniels was in grade school. "We used to spend our summers at the farm in Lee's Summit," he said. "I remember the chickens and the barn and the rest of it." He graduated from Pembrook Country Day School and attended the University of Kansas before enlisting in the navy in 1938. In September of '39 he received his wings and was assigned to Air Group Six based on the USS *Enterprise.* His home port was Pearl Harbor.

Daniel's fighter squadron (VF-6, also called the Fighting Six) included eighteen Grumman Wildcats, the standard carrier-based navy fighter at the beginning of the war. The single-seat, single-engine Wildcat had a top speed of three hundred miles per hour and was armed with fifty-caliber wing-mounted machine guns.

On November 28, 1941, the "Big E"—the flagship of Adm. William "Bull" Halsey—led her task group out of Pearl Harbor to deliver twelve Wildcats to Wake Island. On the way back, south of Midway, they ran into a storm, and Halsey ordered the group to slow down so the destroyers wouldn't take such a beating. So, instead of arriving at Pearl Harbor early on December 6, they would arrive later the next day. The delay meant the *Enterprise* and the rest of the task group would be one hundred fifty miles southwest of Pearl Harbor when the Japanese attacked on Sunday morning.

Daniels and his squadron had just returned from a routine patrol when messages started coming in about Japanese planes attacking Pearl Harbor. Halsey decided to keep his fighters on the *Enterprise* in case she, too, was attacked.

Later that afternoon, Halsey received a report of a Japanese carrier one hundred twenty-five miles to the southwest. Thinking they had located the Japanese fleet, he approved the launch of six scout planes, twelve torpedo bombers and six fighters to serve as a protective screen.

The planes searched the area, but no enemy ships were found. The Fighting Six continued the search until sunset and then headed for home. Flying with no lights and in radio silence, each pilot was able to stay in formation by keeping an eye on the faint glow of the red instrument panel lights in each cockpit and the white-hot exhaust manifold of the plane next to him. By dead reckoning, they made it back to the darkened carrier and her glowing phosphorus wake.

Lt. Fritz Hebel, the flight leader, asked for permission to land, but Halsey refused to risk turning on the carrier's landing lights. "He didn't know where the enemy was," Daniels said. "It wasn't just, 'No,' it was, 'Hell no!' " The fighter pilots, whose planes were already low on fuel, were ordered to proceed to the nearest air base on Ford Island, where dozens of exhausted antiaircraft gunners nervously searched the skies for the enemy.

The six Wildcats, still flying without lights or communications, passed over

Barber's Point and headed down Molokai Channel. The only lights visible on Oahu were the searchlight at Diamond Head and the fires still burning in the harbor. Passing over the devastation of Battleship Row, Hebel broke radio silence and requested permission to land. Howard Young, their group commander, was in the tower and told them to "make a normal carrier landing" on the airstrip. That meant Hebel would go in first with the other planes close behind.

Unfortunately, the tower on Ford Island was not in contact with any of the men in the gun-control stations, who had been told to shoot first and ask questions later. "As we came over the tower, we could see the battleships burning," Daniels said. Making their final approach, they cranked their wheels down—the Wildcat had no hydraulics—and turned on their running lights.

That's when "all hell broke loose," Daniels said. Antiaircraft guns and fifty-caliber machine guns at Hickam Field and Fort Shaftner, deck guns on the USS *Nevada,* aground off Hospital Point, and what seemed like every personal weapon in Pearl Harbor opened up on the Wildcats. "You could walk on it," Daniels said. "It was horrible."

Somehow Hebel made it through the curtain of lead and turned off toward Wheeler Field, an army fighter base ten miles to the north. There he was met by another fusillade of friendly fire. "He crashed on landing and was killed instantly," Daniels said. Herb Menges, Hebel's wingman, was shot down over the Pearl City Peninsula and crashed a block from where Dee Nicholson grew up. He, too, died instantly.

Gayle Hermann's plane was hit as he passed over Ford Island. "They put a five-inch shell through his engine," Daniels says. He crash-landed on a golf course near the runway and walked uninjured to the squadron hangar. Davey Flynn managed to get through the flak, but his plane ran out of gas over Barber's Point. He bailed out and landed in a cane field, breaking his leg. Eric Allen, Daniels's wingman, bailed out over Battleship Row. Unfortunately, navy gunners spotted Allen, a Naval Academy graduate with a beautiful tenor voice. "They put a fifty-caliber hole through his chest . . . as he came down in his parachute," Daniels said.

Only Daniels was left. Managing to evade the first hail of fire, he flew off into the dark, switching off his running lights. As he circled back to the harbor entrance, he called the tower and Young answered. The two men knew each other well, but it took a while for each to convince the other that he was who he said he was. By now, even Daniels wasn't sure.

"What's my middle name?" Daniels asked.

"Ganson," Young replied.

That convinced Daniels. "No Japanese in the world knows my middle name," he said.

Young told Daniels his only chance was to come in low and fast. Daniels cranked down his wheels and came in over Battleship Row. Once again, the air filled with bullets and tracers.

"I almost hit the *Nevada*," he said, "but got around it and landed successfully." He taxied to the north side of the field, where his squadron hangar was located. As he neared his normal parking spot, a marine in a sandbagged revetment opened fire on him with a tripod-mounted fifty-caliber machine gun. "The bullets went right over my head," he said. Before the marine could improve his aim, Hermann, who had seen Daniels's plane land, came to his aid. "He hit the marine over the head [with a rifle]," Daniels said.

That wasn't the last time Daniels's life was threatened that night. As he bunked down in quarters near Battleship Row, he listened to the explosions aboard the *Arizona* and *West Virginia* one hundred yards away. Sometime during the night, a round cooked off and a piece of shrapnel the size of a softball ripped through the wall and headboard and landed at the foot of his bed. "That was three times they tried to get me that day," he said.

Daniels holds no grudges for what happened that night. It was war, and the gunners were simply following orders. "I don't blame the guys that shot us," he said, but added, "it was a hell of an experience to be shot down by your own people."

The next morning he checked his plane's condition. He found one thirty-caliber bullet hole in the right wing. Mechanics fixed the hole with two rivet patches, and Daniels flew his Wildcat back to the *Enterprise* after breakfast.

What happened to the survivors of his air group? Lt. Gayle Hermann was lost at sea on May 25, 1942. Ens. Davey Flynn apparently decided he'd tempted fate enough. "He turned in his wings," Daniels said. "He never flew again." Daniels continued flying combat missions in his Wildcat.

On February 1, 1942, the *Enterprise* took part in what became the first U.S. offensive action of the Pacific War. Daniels's Wildcat was one of six fighters that attacked Wotje Island in the Marshalls, damaging several enemy planes on the ground. Later that day, three Bettys—Japanese twin-engine bombers—were spotted heading toward the *Enterprise*. Daniels and his commander, Wade McClusky, went to intercept them. The bombers dropped their payloads, but they missed the *Enterprise*. "We prevented the Bettys from getting to the carrier," Daniels said. "We shot down all three of them. Wade got one and a half and I got one and a half. We were so happy to be in on the first offensive, that we could strike back."

On October 26, 1942, Daniels shot down another enemy plane during the Battle of Santa Cruz off Guadalcanal. By the end of the war, he was flying Corsairs and commanding a fighter bomber squadron (VBF-2). In Korea, he flew the F9F-2 Panther, the first Grumman jet, and commanded an eighty-plane air wing. Later he commanded a fleet oiler and the attack carrier *Ticonderoga,* which operated in the Tonkin Gulf at the beginning of the Vietnam War. He retired as a captain in 1970.

Making his home in Hawaii, Daniels, who was eighty-two in 1997, still speaks to groups wanting to hear about his experiences during the war and especially on that fateful December evening with the Fighting Six. He usually ends his speeches with a reference to his Heartland roots. All in all, he'll say, it's been a pretty exciting life for "a little boy from Lee's Summit. . . . I always get a chuckle out of that."

Scapegoats

PEARL HARBOR, DECEMBER 7, 1941—It was supposed to be a relaxing day for Capt. Louis Truman. The aide-de-camp to Lt. Gen. Walter Short, commander of army forces on Hawaii, got up early that Sunday morning. He and General Short had a 9 A.M. golf game planned with Adm. Husband Kimmel, commander in chief of the Pacific Fleet.

Truman was dressing when he heard the sound of explosions coming from the direction of the harbor. "My gosh, those are bombs!" he shouted to his wife. He'd seen the training schedule and knew there weren't any bombing maneuvers planned. He gave his wife a stricken look and blurted, "That must be a Japanese attack!" Washington had been expecting a Japanese strike for weeks, he said, but most insiders believed it would be against the Philippines, not American soil. But when Truman heard the explosions, he thought immediately of the Japanese. "It wouldn't be anybody else," he said. "They were the only ones it could be."

Truman ran outside and saw a plane roar by about one hundred feet off the ground. The Japanese red sun emblem was unmistakable. "I could see the pilot's face as he was banking around," Truman said. He went inside and finished dressing and told his wife to go wait with Mrs. Short. He started for General Short's quarters and met the general on the way. Short told him to get over to Aliamanu Crater where the army had an advance command post in a space beneath a fifteen-foot rock shelf.

Truman was at the command post at 2:00 A.M. when he was awakened and told of reports of enemy paratroopers landing on the island's north beaches. He contacted General Short, who was dubious but told Truman to alert ground forces in the area. It turned out to be the first of many false sightings reported during that long and fearful night. "There were clouds going over the moon," Truman said, "and they mistook them for paratroopers."

Both Short and Kimmel were relieved of their commands after the attack. At the time, investigators accused the commanders of being unprepared and lax, but Truman believes they were made the scapegoats for a series of tragic miscommunications and a government that was arrogantly complacent. "I do, I absolutely do," Truman said during a phone interview in 1991 from his home in Atlanta. "I don't believe that the president or anyone else tried to keep anything away from Short or Kimmel." But, he said, they weren't allowed to see the intercepted Japanese ciphers—code-named Magic—for fear the Japanese would discover that their top-secret code had been broken. Truman feels if the commanders had been privy to the information the State Department had, "I think [the outcome] would have been a whole lot different."

Truman said Short and Kimmel also received numerous ambiguous communiqués from Washington. They were warned that Japan was planning something but were told not to alarm the civilian population with unnecessary alerts. And Pearl Harbor was never specifically mentioned. "There was certainly no indication from Washington that a surprise attack would be made on Hawaii," Truman said. In fact, what they were specifically warned about were civilian saboteurs—not surprising since nearly 40 percent of the island's population were of Japanese origin. "The biggest thing was, watch out for sabotage. [It] was our most serious consideration," Truman said. That's why, after Short's request to erect fences around the army airfields was denied, he ordered the planes parked wingtip to wingtip in the middle of the runways. That way they were easier to protect from sabotage. But they also were sitting ducks for the Japanese pilots.

Truman, who served under Short when he commanded the Sixth Infantry, was a first lieutenant in the Second Armored Division—George S. Patton was their brigade commander—when Short made him his chief aide. Short had taken command of the army forces in the Pacific in February of '41, and Truman, promoted to captain, arrived in March. As aide-de-camp, he accompanied the general wherever he went. "Whatever Short wanted me to do, I did," Truman said. When Short met with Kimmel on official business, Truman usually sat outside their office with Admiral Kimmel's aide. Afterward, Short would summarize the meeting for him, asking his opinion on various topics.

Truman knew Short as well as anyone and feels the general shouldn't be blamed for what happened at Pearl Harbor. "He certainly was not asleep at the switch as far as I'm concerned," Truman said. On that point he differed radically from his soon-to-be-famous cousin, Harry Truman, then a senator from Missouri. Harry, who was a first cousin of Louis Truman's father, lambasted Short and Kimmel on the Senate floor following the attack. "I disagreed with the president when he was a senator because he was quite adamant that everyone was asleep out there," Truman said.

Later in the war, Louis Truman was promoted to colonel and sent to Europe in September of 1944 as a division chief of staff. He retired as a three-star general. He decided against going to Hawaii to attend the fiftieth anniversary commemoration of the attack on Pearl Harbor in 1991. "It's going to be a mob scene out there," the eight-three-year-old said at the time. "I think I'd be lost in the crowd." Besides, he'd been back to Hawaii two or three times since the war and would rather go when he could relax and enjoy a few rounds of golf, which he still played regularly.

Noting the large Japanese presence in Hawaii both during and after the war, Truman was asked whether Japanese officials should have been invited to the Pearl Harbor ceremonies. "I don't think they should have been invited," he said, his voice growing momentarily harsh. "They don't want to apologize and I don't think we should apologize either."

Abandon Ship

Pearl Harbor, December 7, 1941—Apprentice Seaman Ronald D. Hollingsworth was scraping dried food into "honey dew" barrels aboard the battleship USS *West Virginia.* He had mess duty, and breakfast had just ended when he suddenly heard distant explosions. Turning, he saw smoke and dust rising from the direction of Hickam Field. He couldn't figure out what it could be. There was a radio on, and an announcer cut into the program to report airplanes attacking the island. As Hollingsworth heard the news, he looked up the harbor channel and saw two torpedo bombers diving directly toward his ship. The red sun emblem was clearly visible. Paralyzed, he watched as both planes released torpedoes. Seconds later, the deck of the *West Virginia* jolted as the two torpedoes struck it broadside.

On that Sunday morning, the *West Virginia* was moored on Battleship Row. Tied up next to her was the USS *Tennessee.* Directly behind was the *Arizona.* Ironically, it was the first weekend in six months that all of the Pacific Fleet battleships had been in port at the same time.

With the general quarters alarm clanging in his ears, Hollingsworth sprinted to his battle station, the lower powder room, which was deep in the bowels of the ship. As he descended, he could feel the hull vibrate from the explosions overhead.

One of those explosions killed the *West Virginia*'s skipper, Capt. Mervyn Bennion, as he directed the ship's defense. Another was undoubtedly the massive detonation aboard the *Arizona,* which sent a ball of fire and a mushroom cloud of smoke five hundred feet into the air.

Down below, in the *West Virginia*'s powder room, the sailors waited nervously. The ship's communications were out and the airtight hatches closed. The men were completely cut off from the outside. One of those in the powder room with Hollingsworth was his close friend Gerald Smith. The teenagers had known each other in Kansas City before the war and had gone through boot camp together. Smith wanted to be a radioman and spent much of his free time hanging around the communications shack, trying to get a head start on radio school.

After about an hour, the ship shuddered, and the powder room began filling with seawater. When the men tried the hatch, it wouldn't open. The water rose past their ankles to their knees. When it reached waist level, "we started worrying," Hollingsworth recalled forty-four years later. Finally, they got the hatch open and went up to the next level. The water continued to rise. There was no doubt about it. The ship was sinking. The seamen decided to go topside. When they reached the gun room on the top deck, they found some bodies. An armor-piercing shell had punched through the top of the gun turret, killing several men.

One of the sailors stuck his head out of the hatch and saw someone on deck. "Where is everybody?" he asked.

"They abandoned ship an hour ago," the sailor replied.

Japanese planes were still circling overhead when Hollingsworth ran out on deck. The first thing he saw was the *Arizona,* engulfed in black smoke and flames. There were men clinging to the ship's mast who tried to jump past the slick of burning oil surrounding the ship. "Some of them just didn't jump far enough," Hollingsworth said.

The USS *California,* moored at the head of Battleship Row, was burning. The *Oklahoma* had capsized. The *Nevada,* docked behind the *Arizona,* had managed to get under way and had been immediately attacked. The Japanese had tried to sink her in the channel and block the harbor entrance, but her captain managed to run her aground at Hospital Point.

On the other side of, and screened by, the *West Virginia* was the *Tennessee,* which had escaped serious damage. Hollingsworth and Smith made a run for her. Hollingsworth would lose three close friends on the *West Virginia.* One of them was Gerald Smith. As they ran, a bomb exploded on the deck of the *West*

Virginia. Smith, dark-haired and gregarious, went down. "A piece of shrapnel . . . went across his neck," Hollingsworth said quietly. "Just laid him wide open. . . . I never thought about dying. I don't know why. I always said I'd be back. I always thought if I thought something like that, I'd do something foolish and not get back. But scared, yes. I was very scared. And I've always said, anybody who said they wasn't scared, wasn't in their right mind."

Hollingsworth enlisted in the navy on April Fools' Day, 1941, at the age of eighteen. Two months away from graduating from Garnett (Kansas) High School, he and a friend had been expelled for two weeks for shooting craps during a school assembly. "During those two weeks, we decided to go to Kansas City and join the navy," he said. "It sounded real good. It sounded better than the army and the marines. Also, we thought we'd see more of the world that way."

After boot camp, Hollingsworth was assigned to the USS *Colorado,* based in Pearl Harbor, and was put on a tanker bound for Hawaii. While at sea, the tanker passed the *Colorado,* which was heading back to the states for refitting. When Hollingsworth reached Hawaii, he was reassigned to the *West Virginia.*

He started out as a member of the deck force, whose main job was equipment maintenance. He remembers a lot of hours spent scrubbing the deck. His battle station was the lower powder room, which was "just as far down as you can go" in the ship. He also was trained as a primer man in the gunroom. The primer man's battle station was at one of the ship's eight sixteen-inch guns. When the breech was thrown open to load a shell, the primer man inserted the primer shell used to ignite the ninety-pound powder bags that fired the guns. It took five bags of powder to launch one of the two thousand-pound projectiles.

Of the ninety-six ships that were in Pearl Harbor on December 7, eighteen were either sunk or seriously damaged, among them the battleships *Arizona, Oklahoma, West Virginia, California,* and *Nevada.* The *West Virginia, California,* and *Nevada* were salvaged and saw duty later in the war.

One ship that escaped the Japanese attack was the USS *Minneapolis.* At the time of the raid, she was out to sea with a Hollywood film crew on board. The "*Minnie*" was a 10,000-ton cruiser 580 feet long and 60 feet wide. During peacetime, she was designed to accommodate 700 enlisted men and 60 officers. After Pearl Harbor, she was refitted for 1,160 crewmen and 90 officers.

In early 1942, Hollingsworth was transferred to the *Minnie,* which was heading to the South Pacific to join the carrier war. For Hollingsworth and the rest of America, World War II had begun.

First Strikes

The Doolittle Raid

On April 18, 1942, America launched the most daring and expensive mission of its size in the annals of air warfare. Four months after Pearl Harbor, sixteen pilots in B-25B Mitchell medium bombers, led by Lt. Col. James H. Doolittle, took off from the aircraft carrier *Hornet* and bombed targets in the Japanese cities of Tokyo, Kobe, Nagoya, and Yokohama. None of the planes returned, although most of the crew members survived. Eight men were captured, and the Japanese executed three officers. Despite those losses, the mission was considered a resounding success. It marked the first time during World War II that enemy bombs fell on the Japanese home islands.

"The Doolittle Raid was a strike of psychological warfare," said retired Col. Travis Hoover, the pilot of bomber number two, who followed Doolittle off the *Hornet*'s pitching flight deck. Although the raid accomplished little of strategic value, it struck a stunning psychological blow to the Japanese people's sense of invulnerability. It also provided a tremendous boost to American morale during the dark days of early 1942. "Ours started the air war with Japan after they started everything at Pearl Harbor," Hoover said.

For Hoover, the memories are still vivid. "Fifty-two years ago today," he said during a speech at the Harry S. Truman Library in Independence in 1994, "I was in the middle of the Pacific Ocean getting ready for my mission to bomb downtown Tokyo."

Following the sneak attack on Pearl Harbor and the subsequent fall of Malaya, Singapore, Guam, and the Philippines, the U.S. Navy conceived a plan to strike back at Japan. The plan would utilize specially modified long-range army air corps bombers launched from a carrier task force, which would get as close as possible to Japan. The twin-engine B-25 was chosen because it was the only bomber that could take off from the aircraft carrier's 460-foot flight deck; however, the plane was too big to land on the carrier after the mission was completed. It would be a one-way trip for the sixteen five-man crews. The mission planners decided that after the bombing missions, the planes would proceed to China where hopefully they would be able to land and the crews smuggled out of the country by Chinese partisans.

The plan was for the task force to get within 400 miles of Japan, which would give the planes enough fuel to bomb their targets and get deep enough into China to avoid the Japanese troops, which occupied much of the Chinese coast. But with 50 percent of the Pacific Fleet still lying at the bottom of Pearl Harbor, Admiral Halsey, commander of Task Force Sixteen, was told not to take chances with his ships, which included the carriers *Hornet* and *Enterprise.*

Hoover first saw the *Hornet* when he landed his B-25 at the Alameda naval air base. Cranes immediately loaded the planes onto the carrier deck. Hoover had never seen a ship that large. "I was awestruck by it," he said. "I proceeded to take a look at my new airport." When he saw how short the runway was, "my awe turned to goosebumps."

Because of the top-secret nature of the mission, none of the pilots had ever taken off from a carrier deck. They had practiced taking off from a shortened runway, but whether they would be able to do it from a carrier deck in mid-ocean remained to be seen.

The B-25s had been significantly modified for the long-distance mission. Extra fuel tanks were installed in the bomb bay and fuselage, and the tail gunner was eliminated so the crawl space could be used to store ten five-gallon gas cans for in-flight refueling. The tail gun was replaced with two black broomsticks.

The crewmen aboard the *Hornet* were initially told they were taking the planes to bases in Hawaii. The carrier was newly commissioned, and Hoover said the sailors weren't happy that their first mission was to serve as a ferryboat for the army. Their real mission was revealed once they were out to sea, and attitudes changed, but Hoover noted that the sailors still "wouldn't give back the money they won at poker."

The task force was 650 miles from the coast of Japan when it sighted a Japanese trawler being used in the picket screen of the home islands. Destroyers sank the ship but not before she had transmitted a warning that enemy ships were in the area. Halsey, knowing the U.S. could ill afford to lose any of its remaining fleet, made a difficult decision. From his command post on the *Enterprise,* he gave the order to launch the planes. With the klaxon blaring, the B-25 crews scrambled to their planes. Hoover remembers it was a gray day of heavy seas and shrieking wind. "It was the stormiest day we had at sea," he said. Hoover was given the honor of following Colonel Doolittle off the pitching flight deck. "The prop wash he was giving me was unbelievable," he recalled.

At the signal, Doolittle's plane roared down the runway and lifted off with yards to spare. Five minutes later it was Hoover's turn. "Thank God I had my gloves on so my crew wouldn't see my white knuckles," he said. For one hair-raising moment after lifting off, the plane's nose shot up in the air, threatening to stall the engines. But Hoover was able to level out, and he headed for the Japanese coast. He learned later that there had been a casualty just before bomber number sixteen took off. The wind was so fierce that the sailors on the flight deck had had to hold onto to something to keep from being blown overboard. "One sailor lost his grip and was blown into one of the propellers of a plane in the back of the formation. Unbelievably he only lost his arm. I don't know how he wasn't ground into hamburger."

Fuel limitations forced the bombers to abandon formation, and each plane headed for the coast individually, at times barely skimming over the water. Hoover said they were flying at altitudes of between fifty and one hundred feet when they crossed the peninsula onto the Japanese mainland. They were so low that Japanese bicyclists, thinking they were friendly planes, waved to them from the streets. It was a beautiful sunny day in Tokyo, a Saturday, about noon. As luck would have it, an air-raid drill had just ended, and people were returning to their normal activities. The barrage balloons had been lowered, and most of the Zero fighters, which had been scrambled for the drill, had returned to their airfields. Many on the ground thought the bombers were part of the drill.

Hoover reached his checkpoint and began gaining altitude for the bombing run. Generally, bomber pilots were instructed to stay above fifteen hundred feet to avoid debris and shrapnel from their own bombs. But Hoover's plane was only at nine hundred feet when the bombardier informed him that it was over the target area. Concerned about wasting fuel, Hoover leveled off and gave the go-ahead to his bombardier.

"Bombs away!" the bombardier shouted over the radio. The announcement was unnecessary.

"It doesn't take five hundred-pound bombs very long to fall nine hundred feet," Hoover said. "It was the worst [turbulence] I'd ever flown in."

His mission accomplished, he took the plane back to a low altitude and headed west. By now, antiaircraft guns were firing at it. Some of the guns, mounted on the city's tallest buildings, were actually firing down at the plane, and the Americans could see the shells exploding on the street below. Soon Hoover and his crew were out over the ocean again. As the day wore on, the weather deteriorated. Although aided by a twenty to thirty mile-per-hour tailwind, the plane was using up its fuel. The crew had hoped to follow a signal to a friendly airfield, but the plane carrying the homing device had crashed, killing all aboard. They were on their own.

By twilight, it was time to make a decision. "I knew I had to put the airplane in the sea before it got dark and the engines quit," he said. As he searched for a place to ditch, the crew suddenly spotted breakers, which meant they had reached the Chinese coast. With engines sputtering, Hoover managed to get the plane up to six hundred feet and gave the order to bail out. Then someone pointed out a tidal flat. Hoover sighted on a long, straight rice paddy, circled, and brought the plane down. "It was the smoothest, slickest, nicest landing I ever made," he said. When he popped the hatch and jumped out into knee-deep muck, he discovered that the rice paddy had been freshly fertilized. "I could even smell why the landing was so good," he said ruefully.

Hoover and his crew evaded Japanese troops in the area by sleeping during the day and traveling at night. After several days without food, they finally sought help at a small village. A Chinese engineering student, who knew some English, helped smuggle them into friendly territory. "I think I owe that young man my life," Hoover said.

Not all the crews were so lucky. One plane went down off the coast of China, and two crewmen drowned. Another plane crashed on land, killing a member of its crew. Of the eight airmen captured, three were executed as war criminals, and one died in captivity from malnutrition. The other four spent three and a half brutal years in Japanese prison camps and were freed when the war ended. One plane, unable to reach China, landed at an airfield in Vladivostok. The Russians, wishing to remain neutral in relations with Japan while they fought the Nazis on their western front, interned the crew for fourteen months.

Most of the original eighty crewmen are gone now. At the Air Force Academy in Colorado, there is a large display case with eighty silver goblets arranged in sixteen rows of five goblets each. On each goblet is printed a name—upside down. When one of the Doolittle raiders dies, his goblet is turned over so his name can be read. In the center of the display case is a bottle of 1896 brandy. The Doolittle raiders have promised that the last two surviving members will share the brandy, bottled the year Jimmy Doolittle was born, and toast their fallen comrades.

Hoover, who in 1994 was the sole survivor of crew number two, said he knows at least one of the men who will be at that final reunion. What he doesn't know is which "son of a gun will be spitting into the bottle with me."

The Flying Tigers

On May 7, 1942, a group of undisciplined, renegade fighter pilots began an attack on the imperial forces of Japan that was to become the turning point of the war in the China-Burma-India (CBI) theater.

The U.S. attack was focused on the point where the Burma Road crossed the Salween River gorge and caused horrendous loss of life among thousands of Chinese civilians and soldiers who were fleeing an invading Japanese armored column. But the Japanese fared much worse. When the Chinese Army destroyed the mile-high bridge spanning the gorge, Japanese tanks and armored vehicles were trapped in a bumper-to-bumper traffic jam twenty miles long. There was no escape.

Oddly, the attack is little more than a footnote in most history books—at least in this country. The Chinese view the incident differently. Despite decades of Cold War hostility and distrust, the Chinese people still feel a profound gratitude toward the American flyers who participated in the attack, which may have saved their country from Japanese domination. Back then, those U.S. pilots were known as the American Volunteer Group. But the Chinese had another name for them: *Fei Weing*—the Flying Tigers.

Back in 1994, Bob Layher was the last surviving Flying Tiger in Kansas; only twenty-five of the one hundred-odd pilots recruited into the program in mid-1941 were still alive. Layher had been flying multiengine patrol planes for the navy when he learned the government was looking for pilots to serve in a new experimental air wing in China. Their mission was to defend the Burma Road—a critical Allied supply line in the CBI theater—from the invading Japanese. The pay was excellent—a minimum of six hundred dollars a month, plus a five hundred dollar bonus from the Chinese government for every Japanese plane shot down. There was another bonus as well: They would have to resign their commissions and become civilians serving with the Chinese Air Force—essentially mercenaries—since the U.S. was not yet at war with Japan. That meant they would be freed from the constraints of military regimentation and discipline.

The American Volunteer Group was the brainchild of Claire Chennault, a maverick aviator who had resigned from the U.S. Army Air Corps to become a paid consultant to the Chinese government in 1937. China and Japan were already at war, and Chiang Kai-shek desperately needed to improve his air force, with its obsolete planes and poorly trained crews. In October of 1940, Chennault returned to the U.S. with a brash plan: the U.S. would launch a preemptive bombing attack on Japan. Like many military men of the time, he was convinced the U.S. and Japan would eventually be at war, and he wanted to strike the first blow. According to his plan, American pilots would be released from the army, navy, and marines to carry out the bombing missions. They would fly U.S. airplanes with Chinese insignia and would be paid by the U.S. through dummy corporations.

President Roosevelt authorized the attack on July 23, 1941—five months before the attack on Pearl Harbor. The strikes were to take place in November. However, opposition by the U.S. military, in particular Army Chief of Staff Gen. George C. Marshall, eventually scrapped the plan. As consolation, the government gave Chennault one hundred Curtiss P-40B Warhawk fighters and authorized the pilots and ground crews necessary to fly them. But few military officials gave the idea of a civilian air force any hope of success.

Layher said he joined the AVG for the "adventure and romance" and the money—about $675 a month. That summer, he and the other pilots signed one-year contracts; they were given fake identities and sent overseas. Layher's passport said he was a salesman. They arrived at the Royal Air Force base at Rangoon, where they met Chennault. The pilots spent the summer and fall learning to fly the P-40s and learning the capabilities of the Japanese Nakajima Type 97 fighter and the infamous Zero. Chennault had forwarded advance information on both planes to the army air corps prior to the war, but the U.S. military, in its infinite wisdom, had refused to put the information to use. "His [Chennault's] training proved to be very accurate," Layher said.

The popular image of the Flying Tigers, promoted by journalists at the time, was that of a group of fun-loving All-American boys fighting for God and country. The reality was a little different. They ranged in age from twenty-one to forty-three. While some joined out of idealism, others were there to make a quick buck or to escape personal problems. Greg "Pappy" Boyington, for example, was divorced and deep in debt when he signed up. He was also a self-described "whiz at a cocktail party" and like many of his fellow Tigers, usually spent his off-duty hours drinking and raising hell. Sometimes he was so hung over the next day he couldn't report for duty. Layher, who flew with the Panda Bears of the Second Pursuit Squadron, offered a diplomatic assessment of Boyington: "I would never take anything away from Boyington's flying," he said, but admitted he "was a renegade. . . . He was not a team player. Boyington always did things his way."

After the AVG was disbanded and the pilots were reintegrated into the U.S. military, Boyington joined the marines and commanded the famous "Black Sheep" Squadron in the Pacific, eventually shooting down twenty-two enemy planes. Later he was shot down himself and spent twenty months as a Japanese

POW. After the war he was awarded the Congressional Medal of Honor and returned to the States a war hero; he rode in the same ticker tape parade as Admiral Halsey.

The AVG had a uniform, which was usually reserved for funerals and formal occasions. Cowboy hats and shorts were more common apparel. Many of the pilots had beards and mustaches. None of them saluted. They were unkempt, unconventional, and undisciplined. And they were China's last hope.

Although the Japanese Zero was superior to the Warhawk, Chennault taught the pilots they could win in aerial combat. The Zero could climb faster, turn more quickly with its smaller turning radius, and operate at higher altitudes. The heavier, single-engine, single-seat P-40, however, had a higher top speed, a faster dive, and superior firepower—four thirty-caliber wing guns and two fifty-caliber guns in the nose. The American pilots were warned not to engage in individual dogfights with the Japanese; the trick was to attack the agile Zeros quickly and then escape. "It [the P-40] was a rugged airplane," Layher said. "We could take an awful lot of abuse and still get home." Later in the war, Layher got a chance to fly the navy's new Corsair fighter. He was impressed. "We couldn't help but think, 'If we only had that type of aircraft over there,' " he said.

The AVG was still training when the Japanese attacked Pearl Harbor on December 7. Two weeks later, they were ready for revenge. On December 20, spotters reported a flight of Japanese bombers crossing the border of Yunnan Province, apparently heading for Kunming. Chennault scrambled twenty-four fighters at Kunming's AVG base and sent them into battle. "We decimated that group of [bombers]," Layher said. "I think there were [ten] bombers and we got nine of them."

Three days later, fifteen P-40s took off from Rangoon to intercept fifty-four Japanese bombers and twenty fighters headed for the Mingadalon Airdrome. They ended up shooting down twenty-five enemy planes, but they also suffered their first two combat casualties. Neil Martin, a former army air corps pilot from Arkansas, was killed when his plane was hit by cannon fire from one of the bombers. Also, Nakajima fighters shot down twenty-one-year-old Henry Gilbert, the AVG's youngest pilot. On Christmas Day, the AVG shot down another nineteen planes, and all the AVG pilots returned safely. "It was a very lively time," Layher said. "Our successes continued very much in our favor."

The AVG provided a much-needed morale boost for the Chinese, who had suffered devastating losses during their four-year war with Japan. Not long after that, the Chinese newspapers coined the name Flying Tigers. The Allied newsmen soon picked up the name and were trumpeting their exploits all over the world.

By the spring of 1942, the Flying Tigers had virtual air superiority over southern China. They had proven their value to the war effort, and the U.S. military decided it was time to step in and take over. Chennault was returned to active duty in April as a colonel and was later promoted to brigadier general. Plans were initiated to dissolve the AVG and induct the Flying Tigers into the army air corps. But the AVG was in the midst of a morale crisis. With fewer enemy targets to hit, they were frequently called on to serve as escorts for British bombers on low-altitude bombing missions, which put them in range of Japanese flak guns.

In the meantime, the Japanese continued their ground offensive into China and Burma. The Flying Tigers already had been forced to evacuate their base at Rangoon, and by the end of April they had retreated from Loiwing. The Burma Road was now China's last link to the west, and its defense became the Tigers' first priority.

By May 5, a Japanese armored column was on the Burma Road seventy-five miles inside China. They were headed to Kunming, and there was no organized army to stop them. If Kunming fell, there would be no central distribution point available to planes flying over "the Hump" (the treacherous route over the Himalayas) from India; supplies for China's army would not get through. Without Allied aid, China was lost. On the road ahead of the Japanese were thousands of fleeing Chinese civilians and soldiers. To get to Kunming, the Japanese had to cross the mile-deep Salween River gorge. Just before the Japanese arrived, the Chinese blew up the suspension bridge spanning the gorge, sealing the fate of thousands of Chinese refugees trapped on the other side. The Japanese armored vehicles stopped at the edge of the gorge; the road was too jammed for them to turn around, and so they waited while a construction team began building a pontoon bridge at the bottom of the gorge.

When Chennault found out what had happened, he had a grim decision to make. If he attacked, thousands of trapped refugees would die with the Japanese. But there were no ground forces to contest the river crossing. It was the AVG or nothing. Rather than take sole responsibility for the decision, he sent a radiogram to Chiang Kai-shek describing the situation and outlining the options. Chiang replied the same day: Destroy the Japanese.

The attacks began May 7 and lasted four days. The Flying Tigers had just received a shipment of the new P-40Es equipped with bomb racks under the wings and belly. The first attack wave carried 35-pound fragmentation bombs and Russian-made 570-pound bombs that were dropped with deadly accuracy on the closely packed column. Vehicles and people disintegrated in fiery explosions. Portions of the cliff face broke off, blocking whole sections of the road and ending any hope of escape. After their bombs were gone, the Tigers strafed the blazing column until they ran out of ammunition. In later waves the planes dropped incendiary bombs that set off chain reactions of exploding ammunition and fuel.

Layher, who participated in the massacre, said the pilots called it the Salween Turkey Shoot. "That was a very vital time and was probably one of the greatest contributions we made," he said. "Had we not done it, I hesitate to think how much longer the war would have gone on. You never know how many refugees were killed, but there were thousands," he said. "War is war."

AVG attacks along the road continued until the onset of the monsoon season in early June. The Japanese, under constant threat of air attack, were never able to attempt a crossing of the Salween River. Kunming was safe and with it China's lifeline to the west. Salween was the Flying Tigers' finest hour and the Chinese people have never forgotten.

Most of the AVG pilots ended their service with the Flying Tigers on a bitter note. Most refused to sign up with the new air group, which would become part of the Tenth Army Air Force, because of an intense dislike for Gen. Clayton Bissell, who would be one of their commanding officers. Bissell tried to bully the pilots into joining the air force by telling them if they didn't, they would be drafted as soon as they returned to the States. He also told them they wouldn't be able to use military transportation to return home. If they weren't going to rejoin, they were on their own. Of the 250 pilots and ground crews of the AVG, only 5 pilots and 22 crewmen accepted induction into the air force.

On July 4, 1942, the American Volunteer Group officially disbanded. True to Bissell's word, the pilots who didn't reenlist had to return home any way they could. A few were able to get rides on army planes from Karachi, but by mid-July, nearly all air transportation, including Pan Am, which was under contract to the army, was closed to them. The only way out was by ship, and few ships were going to the U.S. Most of the pilots paid their way home on passenger ships or freighters and didn't arrive home until mid-September. Most of those who returned to the U.S. reenlisted. Layher went back into the navy and flew transport planes for the remainder of the war.

Chennault remained in China another three years, commanding first the newly organized China Air Task Force and later the Fourteenth Air Force.

Although he reached the rank of major general, his longtime detractors eventually forced his premature retirement in July 1945, a month before the Japanese surrender. He left the service angry and embittered, and the men he commanded haven't forgotten. "I think he was not treated fairly at the end," Layher said. "He certainly deserved to be on the [battleship] Missouri for the surrender."

Because of the AVG's covert nature and the fact that its members were officially civilians during their service, it wasn't until 1991—fifty years later—that the U.S. government finally extended the Flying Tigers' veterans' benefits to cover the year they spent in China.

The AVG is credited with destroying 297 Japanese planes, with another 150 listed as probables. They destroyed vast quantities of enemy supplies and killed thousands of Japanese soldiers and airmen. Layher, who had two confirmed kills and three probables as a Flying Tiger, credits Chennault's training for the AVG's success. "We happened to be a well-trained group in the right place," he said. "We were one little bright spot at that time."

War in the Pacific, Part 1

Worth Fighting For

OFF THE COAST OF SAVO ISLAND, THE SOLOMONS, DECEMBER 1942—Radar operator Ronald D. Hollingsworth was standing on the darkened bridge of the USS *Minneapolis* when the torpedoes hit. One struck the heavy cruiser broadside. The other smashed through the bow. "When it hit, it just knocked me clear away from the radar set," Hollingsworth recalled in 1985. The second torpedo ignited two thousand gallons of aviation fuel stored in the bow. Within seconds, seventy men in the forward firerooms were enveloped in flames. Eyewitnesses to the destruction said a ball of fire erupted from the bow and arched over the entire length of the 580-foot vessel. The bow, reacting to the explosion, plunged deep into the ocean, and a towering wall of water washed over the front of the ship, extinguishing the fire. The *Minneapolis* resurfaced but was without power and lay helpless in the water. The captain ordered all hands to prepare to abandon ship. They waited through the fearful, seemingly endless night, but inexplicably, no more torpedoes came. At sunrise, the *Minnie* was still afloat, despite having lost eighty-eight feet of her bow. There were only five survivors in the three forward firerooms. "It was really a miracle not to lose any more men than that," Hollingsworth said.

After Hollingsworth's former ship, the USS *West Virginia*, was sunk at Pearl Harbor, he was transferred to the *Minneapolis* and assigned to radar duties. The *Minnie*, a heavy cruiser commissioned in 1934, had nine eight-inch guns, eight five-inch antiaircraft guns, and two three-inch guns on the stern. She also carried depth charges for use against submarines.

"When I was in radar, I was in fire control some of the time," he said. "Your radar was connected from your fire control station down to the [antiaircraft] guns. When the radar would get on track and lock in with your guns, it would automatically follow and then you could fire your guns from up there in the fire control station." Every fourth round was a tracer shell, so the antiaircraft gunners could often tell which gun shot down which plane. "I can 'count for about four or five [downed planes]," Hollingsworth said.

In early 1942, the *Minnie* was assigned to screen the aircraft carrier *Lexington* from enemy warships and planes. "We were to take 'em [enemy strikes] if at all possible instead of letting them get to her," Hollingsworth said. On February 20, the *Lexington* was part of a task force enroute to attack Rabaul on the northeastern tip of New Britain when Japanese bombers attacked. During the ensuing battle, Lt. Edward "Butch" O'Hare, flying a navy Wildcat, shot down five enemy planes in four minutes to become the navy's first ace of World War II. He later received the Congressional Medal of Honor.

In the Battle of the Coral Sea, which began May 7, planes from the *Lexington* and the *Yorktown* attacked the light carrier *Shoho,* which was sent to shell New Guinea. During the 30-minute battle, the *Shoho* was hit by 13 bombs and 7 torpedoes, and she went down with a crew of 545. Only 3 U.S. planes were lost in the attack. The next day, the *Lexington* was attacked by 69 planes and suffered 3 torpedo and 2 dive bomb hits; 216 crewmen died in the attack, and the remaining 2,735 abandoned ship. The *Minneapolis* picked up 624 survivors and later helped the destroyer *Phelps* scuttle the *Lex* with torpedoes.

The *Minnie* escorted the carrier *Hornet* in the Battle of Midway on June 4. During the battle, which is considered the turning point of the Pacific War, the Japanese lost 4 aircraft carriers, a heavy cruiser, 234 planes, and 2,500 men, including many of their most experienced pilots. U.S. losses included the carrier *Yorktown,* 1 destroyer, 147 planes, and 307 men. The defeat forced the Japanese to abandon plans to invade Midway.

On August 9, the *Minnie* was escorting the USS *Saratoga;* the *Saratoga*'s planes were providing air support for the landings on Guadalcanal in the Solomon Islands. The cruiser was originally supposed to have been detached from screening duties to join three other cruisers ordered in to protect the troop transports anchored off Lunga Point, but another ship got the assignment at the last minute. That may have saved Hollingsworth's life. Early that morning, the Japanese sank all four cruisers in what became known as the Battle of Savo Island. The U.S. lost more than a thousand sailors.

Relieved from screening duties, the *Minneapolis* remained in the Solomon Islands to disrupt the Japanese supply line, nicknamed the "Tokyo Express." It was during one of those search-and-destroy missions that the *Minnie* lost her bow. The crew knew there were enemy ships in the area on that December night in 1942. "We were goin' in huntin' for 'em," Hollingsworth said. "That's what we was sent in there for." Sometime around midnight, the *Minnie* was south of Savo Island, which is northwest of Guadalcanal. Up ahead in the darkness was a Japanese convoy carrying troops and supplies. Also up ahead was a Japanese destroyer, which wasn't on the *Minnie*'s radar screens.

"Truthfully, he did slip in on us," Hollingsworth said. "We were concentrating on the ones up there ahead of us. Where he come from, we don't know." The destroyer fired off two torpedoes. Hollingsworth remembers that the noise from the explosions was deceptively mild.

"It was more of a thud since it was so large," he said. "It's just like firing a gun. The smaller the barrel of the rifle, you get a cracking noise. Your sixteen-inch guns, your fourteens, it's just a whoom. . . . Well, that's just the way this explosion was. 'Cause you take two thousand gallons of aviation gasoline exploding, it's just gonna be a whoom.

"I didn't know it till a couple hours later, because the ship did, boy, she came doggone near to a dead halt in the water. Then the damage unit started callin' in on the phones and sayin' that the bow was pullin' us down, and we couldn't figure out why. We couldn't see really because it was so dark. Then they come around and said the bow was going down. It was broke off, blown off, mostly.

"The captain told everybody to get ready to abandon ship. But he didn't want us to abandon ship 'cause we were so close to [Tassafaronga] beach that we were really in Japanese waters. He wanted to try to get us over to Tulagi [a U.S.–held island north of Guadalcanal]."

To nearly everyone's surprise, the *Minneapolis* was not attacked again and stayed afloat until she could be towed to Tulagi. There repair crews used welding torches to cut off the remainder of the bow, and then they built a false bow out of coconut logs, which enabled the ship to return to port under her own power for major repairs.

Hollingsworth developed severe bleeding ulcers and received a medical discharge on September 15, 1944. He believes the ulcers were combat-related. After his discharge, he returned to Kansas City and worked for a variety of companies before settling at a local furniture store. He retired in 1984 at age sixty-two.

Like many World War II veterans, Hollingsworth has mixed feelings about the war. "It was good and it was bad," he said. "I can say that I was glad I went in when I did and had the training I had before the war started. Because I saw too [many] men injured and a lot of them lost their lives just because they didn't. . . .

"This thirty days they run 'em through and then send 'em on out . . . it was no good. A lot of 'em . . . didn't even know which end of a gun to grab a hold of. It was really heart sickening to see it. . . . I've always said I'm glad I had the training that I had 'cause I think it saved my life."

But Hollingsworth doesn't regret the part he played in the war. "It was something that had to be done," he said. "I always felt, myself, that this country had treated me right. It was worth fighting for."

Marine Love Story

When Betty Smith heard the slogan "Free a Man to Fight," she took it literally. She joined the marines. In fact, she was one of the first women allowed to join the U.S. Marine Corps during World War II. She had been a secretary for a finance company and thought the corps would utilize her clerical skills, but on her aptitude test, she scored high in radio communications. She was surprised. "The only thing I knew about radios was how to turn one on and off," she said, laughing. After she left boot camp, she went to school to learn radio operation and radio/telephone maintenance. "I thought the war was going to be over before I got out of school," she said. Eventually she ended up in San Francisco and was put to work testing radio equipment to be shipped to the troops overseas.

Mike Norris was also a marine. He was a combat radioman with the Third Marine Raider Battalion in the South Pacific. While the division was preparing for the invasion of Bougainville, he came down with a tropical disease and was shipped back to the States. After several months convalescing in naval hospitals, he was assigned to the supply depot in San Francisco. Mike and Betty met, fell in love, and married.

Like many who came of age during the war years, the Norrises have their stories to tell—tales of combat, brushes with death, enduring friendships, and a brief but magical liberty one scorching afternoon in New York City. Here are a few of those stories.

Mike was one of five brothers to serve his country during World War II. He enlisted with his brother Joe, who had just received his draft notice. "He [Joe] said, 'Why don't we join the marines together?' He didn't want to go into the army," Mike said. Their brother Arlie was already in the marines, and another brother, Millard, was a sailor aboard the USS *Ramsey,* a World War I–era destroyer. Mike's twin, Pat, would enlist in the navy a few months later and join Millard on the *Ramsey.* "We were all pretty patriotic in those days," said Mike. Mike and Joe signed up on February 20, 1941. Mike was nineteen. "We got our pictures in the paper, in the *Kansas City Post,*" Mike said. "They thought it was pretty interesting that we joined together."

Mike became a radio operator/forward observer. His job was to relay fire directions for 105mm howitzers. When the Japanese attacked Pearl Harbor, he volunteered for combat duty. (Brothers Pat and Millard didn't have to volunteer—they were at Pearl Harbor when the bombing started. Both the men, as well as the *Ramsey,* survived the attack.)

Early 1942 found Mike on a troop transport with four thousand other marines headed to British Samoa in the Pacific. "We lost one man going over. They figured he fell overboard," he said. Mike was attached to the Third Marine Raider Battalion. When he arrived in British Samoa, he began jungle warfare training. Armed with mortars, BARs, Thompson machine guns, and Springfield rifles, the raiders were trained to fight behind enemy lines, where they would terrorize the Japanese, disrupt supply lines and communications, and generally cause as much chaos as possible.

Later that year, the raiders were shipped to New Hebrides. Shortly before they arrived, a Japanese submarine torpedoed the USS *Coolidge,* a troop transport, in the harbor. When the marines arrived on the USS *Adams* a couple of days later, the sub was still lurking in the area. "They tried to get us too, but the Jap sub was sunk by our destroyers. At least that's what they told us. They sure dropped a lot of depth charges." Mike said the USS *Enterprise* also was in the harbor to repair an enormous hole in her hull from a torpedo hit.

Although the island was under Allied control, the Japanese were never far away, he said. "We had a bombing raid at two o'clock every morning." They got so accustomed to the night attacks that they sometimes slept through them; once Mike was sleeping so deeply he did not hear the air raid sirens. He remembers waking briefly when someone shook his bunk, but he dropped back off to sleep and didn't wake again until the other marines returned after the all clear was sounded. They told him no one had shaken his bunk—the bombing, which had been closer than usual, must have jarred it. Then a nearby bunkmate showed him just how close the bombing had been. "The guy's bunk next to me had a piece of shrapnel [embedded] where his head would have been," Mike said.

When Betty enlisted, many of her male counterparts felt women didn't belong in the marines. But she believed she was just doing her part for the war effort. She was sent to New York for basic training. Since there were no facilities to train female marines, the women went to navy boot camp alongside the Waves and were housed with them in the dormitories at Hunter College. But that didn't mean the training was easy.

"They gave us some drill sergeants that weren't too happy about having women in the service," Betty said. "They gave us some pretty [rigorous] drilling."

The first women marines graduated in the summer of 1943. Unfortunately, it was a sweltering day, their summer uniforms weren't ready, and they had to go through the ceremony wearing heavy woolen skirts and woolen caps. But they were allowed to doff their wool dress coats. They performed their regimental review for First Lady Eleanor Roosevelt and Madame Chiang Kai-shek. Afterward, Betty was allowed only an afternoon of liberty before she had to report to radio operations school in Wisconsin. So she joined a group of fellow women marines on a whirlwind tour of New York City.

Their itinerary included a stop at the Waldorf Astoria for ice cream, as well as tours of the Statue of Liberty and Rockefeller Center. Eventually, they wound up at a USO-run club for servicewomen. There they met dance instructor Arthur Murray and his wife, Catherine. "We were the first ones [female marines] they had ever met," Betty said. "They seemed to be just as excited about meeting 'the Marine girls' as we were excited about meeting them." Some of them even cut the rug with Arthur. But not Betty. "No, I was too shy," she said.

When it was time for the women to leave, the Murrays insisted on walking them to the subway to ensure that they didn't get lost. Betty has a picture of all of them gathered outside the women's service club. "They were such charming people," she said.

The Third Marine Raider Battalion landed on Guadalcanal five months after the initial invasion by the First Marine Division in August of 1942. Guadalcanal had the distinction of being the first American land offensive of the war. The August 7 invasion came two months after the U.S. crippled the Japanese fleet during the battle of Midway. For the first time since Pearl Harbor, the U.S. had the Japanese on the defensive and needed to maintain that advantage.

Invading Guadalcanal turned out to be easy, but the Japanese high command had no intention of giving it up without a fight. It poured thousands of reinforcements down the Slot—the corridor of waters between the islands in the Solomons chain—to retake the tiny malaria-ridden island, which, except for an airfield, had little strategic value. The bloody fighting went on for six months. The marines were in the mop-up stage when the raiders arrived in early 1943. Mike remembers walking into a field hospital and recognizing a friend of his: "He had been hit by a flamethrower and begged me to kill him," Mike said.

The raiders quickly distinguished themselves in combat. One member of their battalion was only fifteen, Mike said. He had lost a finger at the knuckle and everyone called him "Stub." When the marines found out he'd lied about his age, there was talk of discharging him, but he had performed so well in combat that they let him stay. Mike shrugged. "Those things happened," he said.

After Guadalcanal, the raiders were sent to the Russell Islands to hunt enemy troops. "We came in on one side, hoping to catch the Japs, but they went off the other side," Mike said. The troops were evacuated by a Japanese sub, but hours later it was sunk, "so they didn't get away." Throughout 1943, the raiders continued to play cat and mouse with the Japanese. They spent four months on a destroyer, following leads and rumors of enemy troop concentrations in the Pacific. "We were landing everywhere they thought there were enemy forces," Mike said. Sometimes they found the enemy; other times they didn't. Often they were cut off from reinforcements and supplies for long periods. On one landing they carried rations for a three-day mission. They ended up staying thirty-three days. "We lived on powdered eggs twice a day," Mike said. "And those powdered eggs weren't delicious."

During a brief rest period, Mike was manning the base radio when a plane zoomed in under the radar and buzzed a group of bathing marines. It was a marine fighter, and Mike told the pilot to identify himself. However, the pilot was laughing so hard he couldn't talk. When he finally got his breath, he said, "I never seen so many marines run so fast." The pilot turned out to be future Medal of Honor winner Joe Foss, the marines' number one ace, who eventually shot down twenty-six enemy planes and survived four crashes.

In the fall of 1943, preparations began for the invasion of Bougainville. The raiders were sent to New Caledonia for training in amphibious landings. But Mike wouldn't be accompanying his battalion on the invasion. He woke up one day, and his joints were so swollen he couldn't walk. It wasn't long before he was headed back to the States. The assault on Bougainville began on November 1. "I guess somebody was watching over me," he said, "because that's where they cut my company up good."

Mike and Betty began dating after he was released from the hospital. At around the same time Mike met Leon Uris, who was then a radio operator with the Sixth Regiment, Second Battalion of the Second Marine Division. Uris had served in combat on Guadalcanal and Tarawa before being rotated home. Mike and Leon worked together in the machine shop, and since both were dating marines, they would often double date. "Me and Leon, we got along real well," Mike said. After the war, Uris went on to write *Battle Cry,* a semiautobiographical novel about his wartime experiences with the Sixth Marines, which was later made into a movie. Uris also wrote an epic about the Jews, *Exodus.* "We still hear from him," Betty said. Although Uris is Jewish, he always sends them a greeting card at Christmas.

The last time Mike and Betty saw Uris was in 1960, when he presented Harry Truman with the original manuscript of *Exodus,* which is now in the Truman Library. "We were there for the presentation," Betty said. Afterward, Uris introduced the couple to Truman, who shook their hands and then took them on a private tour of the library. "He made us feel like VIPs," Mike said.

Island Hopping

When the Japanese bombed Pearl Harbor in December 1941, Elmer Kreeger and Rusty Fetters did what thousands of other young men did: They joined the service. "We were the first ones to volunteer from Lee's Summit High School," Kreeger said. Both teenagers quit school midway through their junior year, a move Kreeger said he never regretted. "I learned more in the service than I ever did in . . . school," he said.

Kreeger joined the navy in December of 1942 and ended up on the newly commissioned battleship USS *Iowa,* which would soon be fighting her way across the Pacific. Nate Fetters, nicknamed "Rusty" for his red hair, ended up in the Pacific as a Seabee. "We wanted to stay together," Kreeger said, "but they separated us right off the bat."

Kreeger spent the war as a "fresh water and oil king," maintaining the *Iowa*'s fresh-water evaporators and pumps and helping to fuel destroyers. As his battle station, he was assigned first to the ship's massive sixteen-inch guns and later to the forty-millimeter and twenty-millimeter antiaircraft batteries. He spent eighteen months in the Pacific, survived numerous kamikaze attacks, and was in Tokyo Bay, his ship anchored next to the USS *Missouri,* when the surrender documents were signed, ending World War II on September 2, 1945.

Many of Kreeger's schoolmates weren't so lucky. "I lost a lot of [friends] that I went to school with. A lot of 'em," he said. Rusty Fetters survived the war. Ironically, after the war he transferred to the air force and was killed in a plane crash during a training mission.

Kreeger helped put the *Iowa* into commission at the Brooklyn Naval Yard on February 22, 1943. In November, she was given her first important task:

transporting President Franklin Roosevelt to Oran, North Africa, for a three-day conference with British Prime Minister Winston Churchill to discuss war strategy. (Later the two leaders flew to Tehran to meet with Joseph Stalin; that was the first combined meeting of the Big Three powers.)

Kreeger said, "I was one of the guys that helped Roosevelt aboard. I was kind of proud of that." Four men carried the wheelchair-bound FDR onto the ship as a phalanx of marine sharpshooters watched their every move. The *Iowa*'s captain, John L. McCrea, was with them. "The first thing he [Roosevelt] said was, 'Hi John,' to our captain. That was the only thing I heard him say." They carried FDR to an elevator, specially installed for the trip, which took him to the upper decks. "They had a special place for him in the admiral's quarters," Kreeger said.

After returning the president to the States, the *Iowa* sailed south with the USS *New Jersey*, traversed the Panama Canal, and entered the Pacific. The battleship's first combat duty came near the end of January 1944, when she joined Task Force Fifty-eight and was assigned to support carrier air strikes against Kwajalein and Eniwetok atolls and nearby Roi-Namur as part of Operation Flintlock, the invasion of the Marshall Islands. On February 16, the *Iowa* shelled the Japanese naval base at Truk in the Carolinas. In a naval battle off Truk, the *Iowa* sank the light cruiser *Katori*.

The ship's sixteen-inch guns were generally used to batter enemy fortifications and airfields. Kreeger said sometimes they used phosphorus shells to burn cane fields and jungles where the enemy was hiding. The five-inch guns were used for more close-in fighting, such as knocking out coastal gun emplacements.

Truk was the first in a series of island-hopping battles for the *Iowa*. In mid-March, while bombarding Mili Atoll in the Marshalls, she sustained minor damage when a shore battery opened up with 4.7-inch shells. Two hit the ship. "They hit us with a . . . projectile and it tore a hole in us big enough to drive a jeep through," he said. "But we got the guns."

Crew members received some minor shrapnel wounds but no Purple Hearts. Kreeger said Captain McCrea told his men "there'll be no Purple Hearts on this ship." His philosophy was that you might get killed in the line of duty, but no one on the *Iowa* was going to be honored for getting wounded.

In June of 1944, while the Allies were opening the long-awaited second front at Normandy, the *Iowa* was supporting the landings on Saipan in the Marianas. On June 13, while shelling Saipan and Tinian, the *Iowa* blew up a huge munitions dump. Six days later, during the Battle of the Philippine Sea, the ship's antiaircraft gunners downed three enemy planes. "Them kamikazes kept us awake all the time," said Kreeger, who often slept near his antiaircraft gun, using his helmet as a pillow. "I remember one day we shot down forty-four kamikaze planes and sank two sampans and one cruiser, all in the same day." He doesn't know which gunners were responsible for shooting down planes. "I don't know, we were all shooting at 'em. You didn't know things like that," he said.

His closest call came during one attack. He doesn't remember much about it except that there was an enemy plane coming straight at them. "One of the damn things was about to come down on us," he said. Things get hazy after that. The only thing he knows for sure is that the plane didn't hit the ship. "I woke up with six stitches in my head. I don't know what happened." And he didn't get a Purple Heart. The scar on his scalp is recognition enough.

The island-hopping continued through the rest of 1944 (Palau, Guam, Peleliu) and into 1945 (Luzon, Okinawa, and Formosa). "I've got eleven major battles to my credit," Kreeger said. "I didn't think any of us would get back alive. We were out there too long." It's been more than fifty years, but he still remembers the blistering heat, the lousy navy chow ("They always served you baked beans for breakfast"), and the lost friends.

Once, during a typhoon off Okinawa, he said, they were unable to refuel three destroyers, which foundered in the storm; all hands were lost. "We lost a lot of men that day," he said.

Like many who served on the *Iowa,* Kreeger believes the wrong ship was chosen to host the surrender ceremony in Tokyo Bay. "The peace treaty should have been signed on the *Iowa* instead of the *Missouri,*" he said. "We were the ones that fought our way across the Pacific. The *Missouri* didn't."

After the surrender, Kreeger was assigned to a naval landing force as part of the Japanese occupation. "We were all packed and ready to go. Then at the last minute they decided to let the army and marines do it." The sailors were given shore leave the next day but with strict instructions to always travel by threes for safety. But Kreeger said whenever they met a Japanese on the street, the Japanese bowed and got off the sidewalk to let them pass. "Ain't that something? I was expecting them to be hostile. I guess they knew better."

Choisuel

Choisuel, the Solomon Islands, October 1943—Pvt. James Raleigh Bennett walked slowly through the jungle clearing. His eight-man squad had fanned out, and the nineteen-year-old was on the wing, his finger on the trigger of his M-1 rifle.

Up ahead there was sudden movement in the tropical undergrowth. A soldier in the uniform of the Japanese Imperial Marines materialized about ten yards away. The marine next to Bennett fired a burst from his Thompson machine gun. The Japanese crumpled. The incident on the enemy-held island was one of several recalled by Bennett, who served most of his four-year tour with the Fifth Marine Division in the Pacific.

The lifelong Kansas City North resident was working for the railroad before the war. After the Japanese attack on Pearl Harbor, he enlisted in the Marine Corps and was sent first to San Diego for boot camp and later to parachute school. He shipped out a few months later and ended up on Vella LaVella, in the Solomons. "Vella LaVella was still under Japanese bombardment," he said. "They was bombing it nights. It was still in the war zone. . . . I joined the parachute outfit [Second Battalion] there at Vella LaVella. We took jungle training while we was waiting to make the invasion on Choisuel.

"We was used as raiders because we couldn't parachute in those jungles, see. That's why they broke up the parachute outfit. In the Solomons and those jungles, there wasn't anyplace to jump."

The operation on Choisuel was designed as a diversion for the invasion of Bougainville, scheduled for November 1, 1943. The Second Parachute Battalion landed at Voza Village, behind enemy lines, on October 27 and spent the next seven days making as much mischief as possible. Members raided enemy positions and supply depots, hoping to convince Japanese intelligence that a large attack force had landed and that some of the Japanese forces should be rushed from Bougainville to Choisuel.

"That's where I run into this Imperial Marine. [He] jumped up and this fella next to me had a Thompson machine gun and shot him," Bennett said. "I think this Japanese was getting ready to throw a grenade. . . . But I thought that was the biggest man I ever saw for a Japanese. I thought they were all small, but this Imperial Marine was big."

Running low on ammunition and supplies, the Second Parachute Battalion was picked up by a landing craft on November 4. The operation was considered a success. "After we got off the island, they [the Japanese] bombed where we was at. They thought we was still there and we'd already got out."

Bennett returned to the States and his outfit was merged with the Fifth Marine Division. He was assigned to the Third Battalion of the Twenty-seventh Marines, an eighty-one-millimeter–mortar platoon. Soon the Fifth Marines would be headed back overseas. Their destination: Iwo Jima.

Ocean War

Coast Guard

AMCHITKA, THE ALEUTIAN ISLANDS, NOVEMBER 1942—Seaman James Pendleton Farmer was roused from his rack in the dead of morning. Within an hour, he and his three-man crew were maneuvering the thirty-six-man Higgins boat through the choppy North Pacific. Usually invasions took place at dawn, but in the Aleutians, the sun didn't rise until late in the morning, and it was dark again by early afternoon. The Americans would have to invade Amchitka in the dark. But the landing was still hours away. In the meantime, Farmer's men and the other landing craft crews circled in the cold, dark water in ten-boat spirals. Finally, they received orders to return to their ship, the assault transport USS *Arthur Middleton,* to load up. The soldiers crawled down the debarkation nets like slow-moving spiders and took their places in the Higgins boat. Hardly anyone said a word. During other invasions, the boats would sometimes resume their seemingly endless circling before receiving orders to head toward land; however, this time, they were done circling. The boats lined up quickly and drove toward the island, ten abreast.

By 1984, many of the memories had dimmed for Farmer, seventy-five, but some were still crystal clear: the biting cold, the 125-mph winds howling in from the sea, the endless miles of barren tundra, and the fear of what was waiting for them on shore.

Bill McMullen was also on the *Middleton,* an engineer assigned to a landing craft. Now seventy-four (in 1992), he was working for an oil tool manufacturer in 1942 when he learned his draft deferment was about to end. U.S. casualties were mounting in the Pacific, and warm bodies were needed for Operation Torch, the Allied invasion of North Africa, planned for November. McMullen, then living in California, went to Long Beach to enlist in the navy. When he was told at the recruiting station that they weren't accepting volunteers, he headed to Los Angeles to try the Coast Guard. Like most people, he didn't know much about that branch of service, which had been absorbed into the navy after Pearl Harbor. Although the name suggests the service operated only near the U.S., Coast Guard sailors were used extensively in both the Atlantic and Pacific theaters, serving as seamen on convoy escorts and as landing craft drivers during amphibious invasions.

The Coast Guard was taking volunteers, and McMullen's industrial experience allowed him to enlist at a fireman's rating. He soon found out what he would be doing. "They wanted me as an engineer in a landing craft," he said. He was pleased, considering his knowledge of the ocean didn't go much farther than Southern California's beaches. "All I knew was there was waves on the ocean," he said. "That was about the extent of it." Whatever the future had in store for him, he figured it was bound to be better than being in the army. "I didn't particularly care about sleeping on the ground," he said.

Farmer was thirty-two and working for a company that manufactured waterproofing materials when he enlisted in the spring of 1942. "All my friends were getting drafted," he said. "I was single and knew they'd be gettin' me." He went to the recruiting station in downtown Kansas City and got in a line marked navy. He ended up in the Coast Guard.

After three weeks of wartime-shortened boot camp, he was assigned to the *Arthur Middleton* and soon was heading to the Aleutian Islands. The Japanese had landed there in June of 1942, and now the U.S. was ready to clear them out. On board the *Middleton* was a contingent of army engineers who would go to work, after the island was secured, building an airstrip and a pier to accommodate U.S. warplanes and ships.

Farmer's job was to ferry the invasion troops from the transport ship to the shore in an LCVP (landing craft, vehicle and personnel), also called a Higgins boat for its designer, New Orleans shipbuilder Andrew J. Higgins. The Higgins boat was thirty-six feet long and could carry up to thirty-six men or a two-and-a-half-ton truck.

During the invasion of Amchitka, Cpl. Larry Kellar was aboard a Liberty ship with other members of the Tenth Ordnance Service Company, anxiously awaiting word from the first wave of men to reach the island. Would the Japanese put up a strong defense at the shoreline or pull back to fortified positions inland? The reports that came back weren't what they expected. "It was routine. There were no Japanese on the island. They were all gone," said Kellar, eighty-one (in 2002). "The only thing they could figure out was that they got off on a submarine."

Kellar, who grew up on a farm in Pennsylvania, was living in Chicago when he joined the army on August 8, 1940. Originally assigned to the Tenth Quartermaster Corps, he was sent to Alaska as part of the army forces assigned to pry the Aleutians away from the Japanese. The only real excitement they experienced occurred on the way to Amchitka. "We went though an earthquake aboard ship . . . somewhere, I believe, between Dutch Harbor and Adak," he said. "[It was] like someone was rubbing their knuckles down the bottom of the ship."

After it was determined that the Japanese had evacuated the island, Farmer spent his time hauling supplies and equipment to the beach. While the ships were being unloaded, an arctic storm hit the island. One of the task force's escorts, the destroyer USS *Worden*, was wrecked on December 1. "It was blown up on the rocks and broke in two," McMullen said. Landing barges were dispatched from the *Middleton* to pick up survivors. McMullen said they had to work quickly because a few minutes in the twenty-eight-degree water and "you didn't give a damn whether you got out or not."

While the Higgins boats were busy picking up survivors, the storm continued to batter the ships. The *Middleton* became another casualty as the gale-force winds blew the transport, anchor dragging, onto the rocks, puncturing the hull and flooding the engine room. Suddenly the ship was without engine power, light, and heat.

The *Middleton* stayed aground for three months. Only the gun and boat crews were kept on the ship, McMullen said. Everyone else was moved ashore or reassigned to other ships. Life aboard the *Middleton* was anything but comfortable. The ship's fresh water supply was contaminated, so only frigid seawater showers were available. Most of the sailors limited themselves to sponge baths from buckets, McMullen said, "and not very often." Although the crew tied up to the buoy tender *Buckeye* to patch in lights, the transport remained without heat through the long, dark winter. The never-ending, bone-chilling cold made everything difficult. "We just tried to wear enough clothes to stay warm," he said, "to keep moving. The worst part was trying to stay warm in that cold, iron ship."

Meanwhile, Kellar stayed busy hauling medium ordnance. "I mainly took care of the forty millimeters," he said. Later he volunteered to operate a caterpillar tractor to help build a fighter airstrip. The work continued around the clock. "I would sleep in the CAT while they were loading me and I would sleep in the CAT while they were unloading me," he said. During one marathon period he was on duty for fifty-two hours straight.

The construction of the airstrip and pier attracted the attention of the Japanese, who paid regular visits to the island. "They strafed a little and dropped some thirty pounders from Zeros," McMullen said. The enemy planes sometimes were challenged by U.S. P-38s and P-40s, which provided air support for the base.

Among the first planes to land at the partially completed airfield were a group of Flying Tigers, newly reassigned to the army air corps. McMullen said one day they heard one of the planes had crashed, and out of curiosity, he and a group of sailors went ashore to see the crash site. "It was just one glob of iron," he said of the P-40 fighter. The rumor was that the pilot had bet another pilot that he could do more barrel rolls over the airfield and had gotten too close to the ground. "He caught the ground with one wingtip and that was it," McMullen said.

When the airstrip was finally completed, a squadron of P-38s flew in. The next time the Japanese showed up for a strafing attack, the P-38s scrambled. They made short work of the Zeros. "They got the last one at the far end of the island," Kellar said. "They got 'em all." After that, the enemy attacks were limited to high-altitude bombing. "They never got close enough where we could engage them with twenty millimeter or antiaircraft," McMullen said. The sailors' main concern was that a Japanese task force would suddenly show up to take back the island. There, beached on the rocks, he said, "we'd [have] been like ducks on a pond."

In February 1943, Kellar fell from a tractor, which seriously injured his back. After months in a field hospital, he was finally diagnosed with a crushed disk and a compressed spine. When he eventually left the service, he was considered 40 percent disabled. The same month Kellar was injured, some tugs carrying navy salvagers arrived at Amchitka. They patched the hole in the *Middleton*'s hull, pumped out the seawater, and towed the ship to Bremerton for refitting.

The next spring, the newly shipshape *Middleton* stopped in San Francisco to pick up twelve hundred army troops. She transported them to the Fiji Islands, where she picked up Australian and New Zealander troops, who had participated in the Guadalcanal campaign, and took them to Wellington, New Zealand. In New Zealand, the *Middleton* picked up U.S. Marines and joined a task force headed for Tarawa atoll.

Operation Galvanic would send the Second Marines against tiny Betio Island, which was heavily fortified and protected by a barrier reef and would make the amphibious landing difficult. McMullen remembers getting up at 3:00 A.M. and listening to the artillery from the escorting warships hammering the island. "Everything that fires is firing on the beach," he said. "You figure there won't be anything alive there. Guess what? It didn't even scratch the surface." The invasion began just after 5 A.M., and the landing craft had to fight their way to shore past treacherous reefs and mines and through withering enemy fire coming from entrenched positions. Farmer remembers struggling with his Higgins boat, and it isn't a pleasant memory. The LCVPs couldn't land on the beach because the propellers kept getting caught on the coral reefs ringing the islets. That forced some of the Higgins drivers to drop their ramps a half mile from shore. The water was waist deep, but the marines had to wade, rather than swim in, to keep their weapons dry. Everything from machine-gun fire and mortars to heavy artillery shells were coming from the beach. Once, after dropping off a load of troops, Farmer turned his boat around and glanced back at the marines who had just gotten out of his landing craft. Most of them were already dead, and more died as he watched. "They just got mowed down," he said. "It was terrible."

McMullen was assigned to a landing barge armed with torpedoes to detonate antiship obstacles. He spent five days on the barge, mainly helping other landing craft with engine problems. He slipped ashore only once to look for souvenirs. By the third day, he and his fellow crew members still hadn't found any obstacles, so they took their torpedoes a mile offshore and dropped them over the side to prevent the barge from being blown up by a stray bullet. Once the barge picked up a wounded marine and transported him to a destroyer. While they were tied up alongside, the destroyer opened up with her five-inch guns, sending the projectiles directly over their heads. McMullen felt the buttons pop off his shirt. One of his crewmen wasn't so lucky. The concussion burst his eardrums. McMullen said the barge was never hit, but not for lack of trying. "That stuff was going over our heads all the time," he said.

After Tarawa, the *Middleton* transported troops to Kwajalein (January 31), Eniwetok (February 17), and Saipan (June 15). On October 20, she landed the first wave of marines on Leyte in the Philippines. The next day, ships in the task force saw a gruesome sight—more than fifteen hundred bodies floated by, Japanese victims of the sea battle in progress in Leyte Gulf.

Later, McMullen went ashore and got to know some of the residents, who had suffered nearly three years of atrocities and deprivations under Japanese occupation. "Those poor Filipinos," he said, "the Japs really beat 'em up."

In February of 1944, Farmer transferred to the USS *Calvert* and participated in the invasions of Saipan and Tinian. At Tinian, he and other Higgins boat crews were used to draw fire from hidden Japanese artillery emplacements so the navy warships and bombers could locate and destroy them. While the marines were invading the other side of the island, the LCVPs would come within one hundred yards of shore, hoping the enemy gunners would find the landing craft too enticing a target to hold back. During the dangerous maneuvers, the boats held only the four-man crews.

After Tinian, Farmer got thirty days leave and returned to the States, where he was reassigned to land duty at Charleston, West Virginia. There he met Lucille, a department store clerk, and the two were married May 15, 1945. Farmer admits he was one of the lucky ones. In three years of combat duty, he was never wounded, and he never fired a shot at the enemy. Although there were machine guns aboard the Higgins boats, he was too busy darting to and from shore to worry about firing one.

But the years haven't healed the emotional wounds. Like many World War II veterans, Farmer still looks upon the Japanese with a mixture of distrust and hostility. "I remember too much." During the war, when American ships would transport Japanese prisoners, he said it wasn't uncommon for a seaman, sweeping below decks, to suddenly jab a broom handle through the bars into a prisoner's ribs when the officers weren't looking. But he said that kind of treatment was mild compared to what Allied POWs endured under the Japanese.

Farmer remains intensely patriotic. His coworkers used to kid him that if there was another war he'd probably head to the nearest recruiting station to reenlist. "If something happened, you'd be right back down there tomorrow," they'd tell him. "And you're damn right," he said. "I would be."

After the war, Kellar worked as a mechanic and drove trucks for a living. He retired in 1993, after suffering a heart attack, and moved to Missouri. He now makes his home in Las Vegas, Nevada.

After he left the service, McMullen moved back to the Kansas City area and spent thirty years at the Bendix plant before retiring in 1982. He said one of the things his years in the Coast Guard taught him was an appreciation and respect for the ocean. "The sea can be one of the most beautiful places on the face of the earth," he said. "Of course, the sea can also be very angry and unforgiving."

R-e-s-p-e-c-t

The aging seamen get together every month to reminisce about the war. But they aren't navy veterans. They're World War II–era merchant marines and damn proud of it. "If it wasn't for the merchant marines," said George Kolb, "the war would have lasted much longer."

The merchant marine, officially a branch of the U.S. Coast Guard, had the task of transporting all the material needed to keep the Allied war machine running. Many of the long, dangerous voyages across the Atlantic and the Pacific were made in old tankers and cargo ships, some built before World

War I, in waters infested with enemy submarines and warships. By the end of the war, more than seven hundred merchant ships had been sunk and more than eleven thousand merchant seamen had lost their lives.

Ironically, merchant marines have only recently been considered war veterans. For more than four decades, they were not eligible for veterans' benefits, despite having the second highest casualty rate of all services during the war. One reason for the lack of acknowledgement was the government's wartime policy of keeping the merchant marine's high casualty rate a secret for morale and security reasons. It was a long time before the true extent of the service's contributions to the war became widely known, and it wasn't until 1988, after decades of lobbying and legal battles, that merchant marines finally were given veterans' status. However, discrimination against the merchant seamen still exists. Often they still aren't allowed to join groups like the Veterans of Foreign Wars because they don't have the required military overseas campaign ribbons.

J. B. Shackleford thinks it's about time the merchant marines got some respect. Like many merchant seaman who "retired" after the war, he was drafted into the army for the Korean War, so he received veterans' benefits. But it always rankled him that the government refused to recognize his merchant service during World War II.

Others, like Edward O'Connell, aren't bothered by the lack of recognition. In fact, he joined the merchant marine to avoid military duty. "I wanted to be a civilian," he said. But O'Connell, who served as an oiler on a Liberty ship—he kept the vessel's steam engines lubricated—saw his share of combat. On July 14, 1943, the German submarine U-178 torpedoed his ship in the Mozambique Channel between Madagascar and the African mainland. "They waited for the moon to set because it was very dark—couldn't see anything," he said.

The first torpedo hit the ship, which was empty of cargo and returning to the States, at 2:30 A.M. Like most of the crew, O'Connell was asleep. "The first thing we heard was the explosion," he said. The captain gave orders to abandon ship. O'Connell and six others ended up on a wooden raft. Although crippled, the old Liberty ship refused to sink; the submarine fired two more torpedoes into her, and she finally went down. All things considered, O'Connell said, things didn't look too bad. They had plenty of provisions stored in the raft—water, K-rations, vitamin pills—and since it was winter in Africa, they didn't have to worry about searing daytime heat.

The main thing that worried them was where the ocean currents would take them. Although they rigged up a makeshift sail, they found they couldn't steer the rectangular raft. "We didn't want to drift south into the Indian Ocean because we figured they'd never find us out there," O'Connell said. A week after the sinking, they spotted a Swedish ship and signaled her with a mirror. O'Connell is sure the ship's crew saw them but didn't pick them up. "They changed course and left us. We don't know why," he said. "We lost a little heart there." They were finally rescued on the thirteenth day.

Kolb also is a survivor of a merchant ship sinking. His ammunition ship was hit by a kamikaze off Okinawa in April 1945. Assigned to deck duties, Kolb was topside during the attack. He said the ship's gun crew hit the plane as it came in: "I think the pilot was dead when he hit the ship." Kolb, on the starboard side of the ship, just had time to duck as the plane, filled with high explosives, crashed into the port side. Oddly, he doesn't remember hearing anything. But when he got up, he noticed a half-inch-thick steel door had taken the brunt of the blast. "The corner had curled back from the explosion," he said.

The Japanese pilot had done his job. Thirteen crewmen were dead, and the ship was aflame. Kolb said he and the other survivors were only in the water about twenty minutes before a minesweeper picked them up. Although shark attacks were a concern in the Pacific, Kolb said that wasn't on their minds. "Nobody thought about sharks. We were thinking about Jap planes."

The merchant marine differed from the regular navy in several ways. For instance, most merchant seamen weren't required to take military oaths, wear military uniforms, or salute officers. They also were paid per delivery, which often meant larger paychecks—another sore point for their military counterparts. Some seamen, like those who worked in the engine room, had little contact with the military; however, the deckhands assisted the armed guards, regular navy sailors who manned the antiaircraft guns installed on many of the ships.

Mat Oglesby joined the merchant marine when he was seventeen and became a "hot shell man" on his ship's three-and-a-half-inch bow gun. Wearing asbestos gloves, he caught the spent shell as it was ejected and threw it over the side.

Oglesby, who was later drafted as a combat infantryman in the Korean War, said the navy gunners never told him he was supposed to wear earplugs. "The noise [those guns] made was about as bad as any artillery piece I ever heard fired," he said. "It hurt my ears so bad for weeks that I couldn't hardly stand it."

Oglesby started out as an apprentice seaman on an old cargo ship hauling coal from Boston to Norfolk and later signed onto a tanker bringing oil to the East Coast from Venezuela. After D-Day, he sailed on Liberty ships hauling men and supplies to Europe. One evening in late 1944, a German fighter strafed his ship while she was tied up in the harbor at Marseille. The attack was brief and did little damage, but it underscored the ever-present danger of merchant duty.

Although the merchant ships often sailed in vast convoys protected by a fleet of destroyers and destroyer escorts, there was little safety in numbers. Oglesby remembers being in the center of a huge convoy—hundreds of ships stretching as far as he could see—and every so often a destroyer would appear and drop depth charges between the merchant ships, close enough to rattle their hulls. That usually meant a U-boat had been detected. "It was no sure thing that they [submarines] wouldn't get into the middle of a convoy," he said.

For the merchant seamen, like other veterans, World War II was a time of high adventure—of sailing to exotic ports and doing an important, dangerous, and, at times, thankless job to help the Allied war effort. Some men saw their share of death and destruction, while others emerged from the war largely unscathed. Most of their memories are good.

Dale VanLerberg's most vivid recollection was of standing on the deck of a Liberty ship in the middle of a huge convoy anchored off Okinawa. It was a simmering day in August 1945, and the Allies were preparing for what was expected to be a bloody invasion of the Japanese home islands. "As far as you could look in any direction—east, west, north, south—all you could see was ships at sea," VanLerberg said. "I've never seen that many ships in one place in my life." Then came word that the invasion was off. The U.S. had dropped some kind of "super bomb," and Japan had surrendered. Suddenly everyone was shouting at the top of their lungs. "I'll never forget that day," VanLerberg said. "Those boys aboard ship were real, real happy." While some have second-guessed Truman's decision to drop the atomic bomb on Japan, VanLerberg isn't one of them. "I was glad when he dropped it," he said. "If you'd have been where I was, you'd have been darn happy too."

Murmansk Run

Leonard Jordan was drafted in 1942, took a military oath, and served two years on a U.S. ship during World War II, including several months during which his ship was chased through the North Atlantic by Nazi U-boats while carrying war supplies to Russia along the treacherous Murmansk convoy route. But for decades the U.S. government didn't consider him a military veteran.

Jordan (seventy-two in 1991), was in the merchant marine, a part-civilian, part-military branch of the Coast Guard, which had the second highest casualty rate among U.S. military services during World War II. The Marine Corps had the highest rate, at 2.9 percent, followed by the merchant marine, at 2.7 percent. The army's casualty rate was 1.2 percent. The reason the casualty rate was so high among merchant seamen was brutally simple: You couldn't survive for long in the waters of the stormy North Atlantic. "Our casualties were easily measured," Jordan said. "There were almost no wounded."

Jordan was a twenty-four-year-old radio operator when he set sail for England in November of 1944 aboard the USS *Paul H. Harwood,* a 453-foot tanker built in 1918. She was his second tanker—his first had been the USS *Jamestown,* which was sent to the repair docks after an accidental ramming earlier that year. "I got my bloody fill of tankers," he said. The *Harwood* could carry 78,000 barrels—"Quite small by today's standards," he noted—and a crew of 65, including a U.S. Navy officer (usually a lieutenant) and a dozen armed guards to stand watch and man the two 50-caliber, two 30-caliber, and six 20-millimeter guns. The merchant seamen took care of the rest of the ship operations—the engines, maintenance, and communications—but were available to lend a hand if attacked. "I expect we could have been used as shell handlers if it came to that," Jordan said. When Jordan was drafted, his grades were good enough to qualify him for radio school. His first choice was the regular navy, but he was turned down due to an eye problem.

"Dad was an infantryman," he said, was promoted to captain on the battlefields of World War I, and later commanded stateside POW camps in World War II before retiring as a colonel. His father's axiom was that the infantry was the lowest form of military life and should be avoided at all costs. Jordan opted for the merchant marine. While the merchant marine differed from the regular navy in several ways, there were similarities as well. While there were no spit-and-polish dress uniforms, seamen wore the same seagoing dungarees and navy-issue shirts as most U.S. sailors.

Seamen weren't required to salute and were paid up to sixty dollars more a month because, unlike the regular navy, they were paid for their deliveries. But after each delivery, they had thirty days to sign on with another merchant ship. If they didn't, they were automatically assigned A-1 draft status.

The first leg of Jordan's trip aboard the *Harwood* was to England to deliver seventeen amphibious troop carriers—code-named DUKWs, but called ducks by the troops—and a PT-boat. Also onboard were 58,329 barrels of industrial alcohol needed by the Russians for munitions and hospital supplies. The alcohol was nondenatured, which meant it was safe to drink. It also meant the *Harwood* was very welcome among the ships of alcohol-deprived sailors. "It tasted more like iodine," Jordan said. He added, smiling, that he did his tasting "in the interests of science."

The *Harwood* spent Christmas 1944 off the coast of Scotland and in early 1945, she joined a convoy gathering north of the Shetland Islands. The thirty-three ships, mostly American and English and a few Norwegian vessels, included a heavy escort—two aircraft carriers, a cruiser and several destroyers, most of them British—to protect the convoy from air and sea attack. Because of her volatile cargo, the *Harwood* was placed on the outside of the convoy in an area the sailors called "coffin corner." "If we blew up," Jordan said, "we'd only take two or three ships with us. Alcohol is very explosive."

Their route would take them north, past the Arctic Circle into the Barents Sea, past Norway and Finland, and eventually to Murmansk on the Kola Peninsula. There the convoy would await a Russian convoy, which would include icebreakers, before continuing on to their delivery point at Arkhangelsk on the White Sea coast. The Murmansk convoy was a closely guarded secret, but Jordan managed to slip a letter through the military censors to his wife, Betty, at home in Chicago. He didn't tell her where he was going, but he mentioned that he'd been given a fur-lined vest. That was enough, she said. "I knew very well where he was headed."

The voyage to Murmansk was uneventful except for a brief attack by German dive-bombers off the coast of Norway. Jordan said the navy gunners must have been inexperienced because they fired at the planes while they were still out of range, and by the time they reached the convoy, "there wasn't a single shot fired. . . . They got better later on." The bombers strafed the convoy but released no bombs, and the *Harwood* escaped with only minor damage. The convey had a nine-day layover at Murmansk, waiting on the Russians, and on the way to Arkhangelsk became involved in their first pitched battle with German U-boats. The seamen found out later that two Russian destroyers were torpedoed in the attack.

They spent several weeks anchored at Arkhangelsk. The temperature stayed around thirty-four degrees below zero, and the ice was so thick the crews could walk from ship to ship. The ships' engines were run all the time to keep the propeller screws free. But Jordan said it didn't feel that cold. "The lack of wind had a lot to do with it," he said. And because they were so far north, they had about ninety minutes of sunlight a day.

On the way back to Murmansk, the ships had to form a single column to get through Kola Inlet. An acoustic torpedo, drawn by the sound of the ship's screw, hit the Norwegian *Nortfjil,* two ships ahead of the *Harwood.* The Nortfjil sank into the mud. Moments later, a Liberty ship behind the *Nortfjil* was torpedoed. The captain of the *Harwood* swung his ship hard to the right, expecting her to be hit as well, but nothing happened, and she proceeded to Murmansk. The U-boat was never found.

They left Murmansk in mid-February with two aircraft carriers, a cruiser, and several destroyers, all British, as escort. Jordan said they purposely chose the stormy winter months to run the convoys because the submarines usually didn't attack in bad weather. "Storms were very welcome," he said. "That's the one thing we all hoped for." Early in the war they had tried running convoys during the summer months. The ships sailed on beautiful, calm seas, and the U-boats took advantage of the excellent conditions. "It was just a fantastic slaughter of ships," Jordan said.

On February 17, he saw a sight he'll never forget. He was topside when he heard a huge explosion astern. Just moments before, the HMS *Blue Bell,* a British destroyer escort, had been sailing next to the *Harwood.* Judging from the size of the explosion, Jordan thought the torpedo must have hit the ship's ammunition magazine. "This plume went up and when the plume disappeared, there was no ship. There were one or two survivors. That was one of those calm days." Luckily, they ran into heavy gales after that, and when the seas calmed, they dropped depth charges constantly to keep the submarines at bay. Jordan said reverberations from the explosions were transmitted through the entire ship. "You felt like a mouse inside a steel drum being hit by a sledgehammer," he said. Finally the convoy arrived in England and made a grim accounting: eleven of thirty-three ships had been lost to German U-boats. The *Harwood* soon joined another convoy headed back to the States. She arrived in New York Harbor on March 25, 1945.

After the war, Jordan stayed in the merchant marine another five years, which he spent delivering railroad cars, engines, and rails to Iran. When he left the merchant service, he opened the first TV repair shop in Lee's Summit; he retired in 1981. Ten years later, he was among thousands of U.S. Merchant Marines to receive medals from the Russian government as thanks for their help in keeping Russia supplied with food and equipment during the war. The English and Australian seamen who had taken part in the Allied convoys had received their medals a couple of years before.

Jordan said the ceremony, held at the Russian Embassy in Washington, D.C., in 1991, was made possible by improving relations between the U.S. and Russia. "It's a glasnost thing," he said.

Better Late than Never

ABOARD THE USS *MATAGORDA*, THE SOUTH PACIFIC, 1944—Ens. Ed Henry had just gotten off morning watch and walked into his cabin when he heard the second mate yell for the captain. When the captain ran past his door, Henry, the ship's third mate, followed. "I knew something was wrong," he said. When he emerged topside, he found the other crewmen on deck looking at something off the port side. There, two thousand feet away, was a Japanese submarine. "That was really something, to look off the port side and see that big black submarine," Henry recalled nearly fifty years later.

The *Matagorda,* a merchant marine tug, had a complement of armed guards, but before the guards could reach their guns, the submarine slipped beneath the surface. Everyone waited for the torpedoes to hit, but after several hours, they began to relax. There was a Liberty ship on the horizon; they figured the sub was shadowing her since she was a bigger prize. "He didn't waste a torpedo on us because we were a seagoing tug," Henry said.

They wanted to warn the Liberty ship, but they were under strict orders to maintain radio silence. The submarines used radio signals to home in on their targets. During Henry's watch later that night, a coded message came over their radio: An enemy submarine had sunk a nearby Liberty ship. It wasn't hard to put two and two together. "Naturally we felt pretty bad about it," he said. "We felt like we could have at least warned them."

Henry was on his second tour of sea duty, but his first during wartime. He had joined the regular navy in 1934 and spent two years on the USS *Lexington,* an aircraft carrier that would be sunk eight years later during the Battle of the Coral Sea. He had spent the remaining two years of his enlistment as an aircraft mechanic on another flattop, the USS *Ranger.* He had also worked on the Grumann F4F, an obsolete fighter with linen-covered wings and fuselage.

Discharged as a seaman first class, Henry had gone back to civilian life—gotten married and had a daughter—and when war broke out, he had gone to work in the defense industry. But by 1943, at age thirty, he had been ready for a change from his job as a tool inspector at an aircraft plant in St. Louis.

He had decided to rejoin the service and had chosen the merchant marine because his previous navy experience qualified him for their officers' training program. He said his wife, Charlotte, took the news well. "It wasn't too difficult [to convince her]," he said. "She seemed to accept it."

"I went along with it," Charlotte agreed. "I guess patriotism was involved."

Henry's first assignment was on the *Matagorda.* The ship's mission was to tow a section of what would become the largest floating dry dock in the world. Because the dock was so large, it had to be towed in seven sections and assembled in the Philippines, which, at the time, was still under Japanese control. "We were taking one section of it out to the Philippines," he said. "It must have been a block long and three-quarters of a block wide."

The tug used a two-and-a-half-inch, two thousand-foot-long metal cable to pull the dock section. But there was one problem: One of the *Matagorda*'s two diesel engines kept breaking down, and when the ship lost speed, the weight of the cable pulled the tug and the dock section together with a crash.

The crew struggled with the problem for a month; finally, outside the Marshall Islands, the captain broke radio silence and requested to return to Pearl Harbor for repairs. On the way to Hawaii they saw the Japanese sub. The problem couldn't be repaired in Hawaii, so another ship took the section of dry dock, and the *Matagorda* headed back to the States on one engine.

Henry was discharged from the *Matagorda* in November of 1944. He signed onto another seagoing tug, the USS *Fire Island,* but his tour was cut short by an attack of appendicitis. In the spring of 1945, he signed onto the USS *William D. Bloxham,* a Liberty ship carrying wheat to Italy. Sailing from New Orleans, the *Bloxham* steamed around Florida into the Atlantic to join an escorted convoy, a first for Henry. "The other times we were alone. We had no protection of any kind." On the voyage to Italy, a German U-boat sank one of the ships ahead of Henry's. "They must have been carrying ammo or bombs because they blew up and sank right away," he said.

Henry was on duty on May 8, 1945, when the ship received a radiogram announcing Germany's surrender. Although it was welcome news, he said, there was no celebration onboard. "There was relief," he said, but the crewmen knew they were still under wartime conditions. "There were still submarines out there." When the *Bloxham* arrived in Italy, she was reloaded with five hundred-pound bombs and dispatched to the Philippines. But in mid-August, there was a radiogram announcing that Japan had surrendered. The war was over. A few days later, the crew received orders to head to California. "They didn't need the bombs anymore," he said.

For forty-three years, Henry wasn't considered a veteran of World War II. "We weren't ever considered for any veterans' benefits. We couldn't even join the American Legion," he said. "It was kind of a hard feeling because we were out there with the other services. . . . There were a lot of merchant marine vessels sunk. I was lucky." After Congress formally recognized the merchant marine as a branch of the military in the late 1980s, Henry received his honorable discharge certificate in the mail, and he was informed that he was eligible for full veterans' benefits. But for Henry, and many other merchant seamen, it was forty years too late. "I would have probably gone to school under the GI Bill," Henry said. Now the benefits are of little use to him. But then again, better late than never, he said. "It does make you feel a little better that you're finally recognized."

Das Boot

THE NORTH ATLANTIC, WEST OF AFRICA, OCTOBER 27, 1942—The U-boat wolf pack was heading south, eight abreast, when Lt. Hans Massmann spotted the stacks of a distant convoy, west of Morocco. Massmann, commander of U-409, immediately radioed headquarters that targets had been spotted. Soon he and other commanders of the *Streitaxt* wolf pack received orders to attack. In the three-day raid that followed, the German submarines sank nine Allied ships. One of the U-boats—U-659—was damaged by depth charges. U-409 sank two ships with a combined weight of nearly fourteen thousand tons. In an ironic twist, while the wolf pack was successfully attacking the Allied ships, another, much larger, convoy was passing unseen to the north. It was the convoy for Operation Torch, the Allied invasion of North Africa.

Actually it was two huge convoys—one steaming south from Britain with twenty-three thousand British troops, and the other sailing from the U.S. East Coast with eighty-four thousand American soldiers. With the submarines concentrating on the smaller convoy, the Allied Expeditionary Force, comprising five hundred warships and three hundred fifty transports, was able to reach North Africa unmolested. "Nobody had even detected it until they fired the shots on the Casablanca coast," Massmann said. He believes that if he hadn't seen the smaller convoy first, he or one of the other commanders undoubtedly would have discovered the Torch convoy, still twelve days from the African coast, and that advance warning might have doomed the landing, perhaps even changed the course of the war.

Massmann visited Missouri in 1992 to see a former shipmate, Karl Wagner, who had also served on U-409. The two aging submariners hadn't seen each other in more than forty years and spent much of their time together reminiscing about the war and the parts they had played in it.

Wagner was born in Heidelberg in 1914, "about a half year before the First World War," he said. Although he has lived in the U.S. since 1951, he still speaks with a heavy accent.

Trained as a cabinetmaker, Wagner found himself out of work during Germany's post–World War I depression. When he joined the German Navy—the *Kriegsmarine*—in 1934, Germany was only allowed a ten thousand-man navy and a one hundred thousand-man army. But a year later, Hitler broke the Versailles Treaty and began raising troops and building his war machine in earnest.

Wagner was sent to Stralsund, on the Baltic Sea, for boot camp and then to Kiel before being assigned to the minesweeper *Pelikan.* Six months later he transferred to submarine school, and in 1935 he was assigned to his first U-boat—U-3—as a cook. U-3 was one of the obsolete coastal submarines used mainly for training. Wagner, however, wanted to be on a regular submarine, and after additional schooling, he was assigned to U-22 as a seaman. He remained on U-22 until April 1940, when he was transferred to U-24. Not long after that, U-22 was lost at sea. "U-22 left the port and I never saw any of them again. The belief is that it ran over a mine," he said. "I guess I was awful lucky. . . . For two and a half years we're all together. And then they're all gone. It's hard." Wagner was put to work training submarine cadets and later attended navigation school. Then he received a promotion and was assigned to U-409.

Massmann, a resident of Bremen, Germany, was born in Kiel and joined the *Kriegsmarine* in April 1936. He received his officer's commission in 1938 and completed his submarine training the following year. In February 1940, he was assigned to U-17 as watch officer and participated in several North Sea sorties, as well as the invasion of Norway, which took place that April. He spent the next seven months on U-137, and in December 1940 he was given command of the submarine, which was used mainly as a training vessel for submarine officers. In January 1942, he took command of U-409, one of the then-new Type VIIC submarines. The Type VII U-boats were the main weapons used by the Germans in their battle for control of the Atlantic. Measuring 67 meters long and weighing 770 tons, the sub carried a crew of 50 and had a maximum diving depth of 250 meters. Her armament included 14 torpedoes—4 tubes on the bow and 1 on the stern—a 20-millimeter antiaircraft gun, and an 88-millimeter deck gun.

Although Massmann took command of U-409 in January, the submarine wasn't put into active duty until September due to the bitter North Atlantic winter. "We had such awfully strong winters all during the war," Wagner said.

Massmann said early in the war the subs operated in wolf packs, and their main targets were the Allied convoys crossing the Atlantic between England and the U.S. "The most important [of our] activities took place against the east-west convoys," he said. "The whole war at sea was the fight against supplies going to [and from] England."

The battle for the Atlantic had been going on since September 4, 1939—the day after Britain declared war on Germany. That was the day U-30 sank the ocean liner *Athenia,* which was bound from Liverpool to Montreal with 1,400 passengers. Among the 112 dead were 28 Americans. Two weeks later, U-29 sank the British aircraft carrier *Courageous* west of Ireland, and 514 people were killed. During that engagement, British destroyers sank U-39, which became the first German submarine loss of the war. On October 14, U-47 slipped into the British naval base at Scapa Flow, torpedoed the battleship *Royal Oak,* and escaped undetected. The U-boats also were used to mine the sea approaches to England to further disrupt the sea traffic on which the British Isles depended.

But by the fall of 1942, the Allies' new sonar and radar equipment were slowly breaking the stranglehold the U-boats had on Atlantic shipping. When submerged, the U-boats had a speed of only 7.5 knots, and so they had difficulty escaping surface vessels once they had been detected. Armed with depth charges, the ships would follow the sonar readings and drop the TNT canisters, which were set to explode at the submarines' maximum depth. For that reason, U-boat duty ranked among the most hazardous assignments of World War II. Of the forty thousand men who served on German submarines, thirty thousand never returned home.

But for the men of U-409, September 1942 marked the beginning of their great adventure as universally feared, silent hunters of the deep. All too soon their time would end, and the predator would become prey.

Beneath the Mediterranean Sea, north of Algiers, July 12, 1943—At 7 A.M., Massmann's radioman woke him with bad news. They had just made sonar contact with two ships on a westward course. The British destroyer *Inconstant* was escorting the *Empress of Russia,* a former passenger liner that had been converted into an Allied troop carrier. In an earlier time, the detection of a troop ship would have filled the crew of the U-boat with nervous excitement—sleek wolves after a lumbering elk. But 1943 had brought hard times for German submarines. The days when groups of thirty or more U-boats roamed the seas in wolf packs were gone. Now there were only scattered remnants of the packs; many German subs had fallen victim to Allied technology. Many, like U-409, now sailed alone, and survival was a day-to-day struggle. And often the U-boats' survival depended on making a quick escape. If the submarines were detected, surface vessels, with their superior speed, detection equipment, and armament, would doggedly pursue them. By the time Massmann gave the order to dive, it was already too late. The destroyer had "heard" them. U-409 sank to 190 meters and waited.

As German submarines went, U-409 had a short but successful tour of duty during World War II. Between September of 1942 and July of 1943, the U-boat sank five ships—four freighters and a tanker. Mostly she preyed on convoys, using the hit-and-run tactics dictated by its unique design. With their slow submerged speed, U-boats had to do the majority of their sailing and attacking on the surface, going underwater only in close quarters or to escape. Massmann said generally he got his ship as close as possible to the convoy without being seen and then waited for dusk to move in to attack. Then, when the ship was silhouetted on the horizon, her speed and course calibrated, the sub could fire as soon as the target was within range, usually fifteen hundred meters. "When we were in the right position, the boat was brought into the final firing position and the torpedoes were launched," Massmann said. Then he got his U-boat away as quickly as possible.

Although the U-boat could carry up to fourteen torpedoes, she could fire only five before she had to reload. Reloading had to be done underwater and could take more than an hour. The extra torpedoes were stored under planks in the enlisted men's living quarters. "It was a hard life for the sailors," Massmann said.

In June of 1943, U-409 and two other U-boats received orders to proceed to the Mediterranean. Only U-409 made it. "The other two were detected and sunk by the British," Massmann said. It got so that the once-feared U-boat would dive whenever she sighted a surface vessel. On one occasion Massmann sighted a Red Cross ship and immediately gave the order to dive. "We had hardly reached one hundred meters when we heard the propellers of a fast craft coming from the east. Luckily they hadn't detected us," said Massmann. The ship that passed over was probably an Allied destroyer. Another time, the sub was attacked by a British fighter plane, Massmann said, "but due to our very good shooting, he couldn't keep on course with his guns firing so we were able to dive away."

By the summer of 1943, the Mediterranean was a hotbed of naval activity. Operation Husky, the Allied invasion of Sicily, began July 10, and sea traffic both before and after the landings was heavy. The crew of U-409 had to remain vigilant to escape from the aircraft and destroyer screens roaming the coastal waters. "Warfare at that time for submarines was already a very hard thing," Massmann said. As soon as the invasion of Sicily began, U-409 and several other German and Italian submarines were ordered to positions south of the island. On the morning of July 12, U-409 was at a depth of about 40 meters, having just reloaded her batteries, when she was detected by the *Inconstant.* When the submarine reached 190 meters, "then the bombing began," Massmann said.

The destroyers were armed with dozens of depth charges, which could be set to explode at different depths. Because the main force of the explosion was upward, the sailors tried to set depth charges to explode below the submarines. Each canister contained three hundred kilos of TNT, so if it exploded near enough to a submarine, "the whole body of the boat came into heavy motion," Massmann said. "It was not the best of possible situations."

Wagner agreed. "I don't forget it," he said shaking his head.

The bombing lasted almost four hours and eventually took its toll on the U-boat, which began to take on water. "It came in in such masses that it became obvious the only way out was to go up," Massmann said. "It took quite a while."

When the submarine finally reached the surface, the *Inconstant* was waiting and opened fire, killing several of the submariners as they tried to escape the foundering U-boat. Eleven of the forty-nine crew members died. The destroyer picked up the survivors. "I was probably the first one in the water," said Wagner, who received acid burns to his eyes.

After his rescue, he was transferred to a hospital; he spent several weeks there. "I was told in the hospital that I wouldn't see anymore," he said. However, his blindness turned out to be only temporary, and he attributes his recovery to the salty Mediterranean, which helped wash the acid out. "I think that was my luck." In September he arrived in Norfolk, Virginia, and later was sent to a POW camp in Tennessee. "It was a wonderful camp," Wagner said. "We woke up in the morning and there were these big oak trees. It was beautiful."

Massmann, meanwhile, was taken to Algiers, where he was interrogated by the British and eventually turned over to the Americans, who sent him to the U.S. in a ship that was part of a huge convoy bound for New York City. Although a few renegade U-boats still operated in the Atlantic, they posed little threat to Allied shipping. "There [were] alarms, but this was after the U-boats had suffered terrible losses," Massmann said. "The power of the U-boats had already been broken by that time." Eventually he was sent to the same POW camp as Wagner and in January 1944, the submariners were moved to a camp in Phoenix, Arizona, where they remained until the end of the war.

But the end of hostilities didn't mean either man was going home anytime soon. In February 1946, Massmann was shipped to a British POW camp in

Antwerp and underwent extensive interrogation regarding his political convictions. Despite having never been a member of the Nazi party, he was classified as a security risk and transferred to a camp in Germany, where he remained in detention until February 1948.

For Wagner, the end of the war meant a transfer to a town outside Phoenix, where he was made supervisor of a work gang picking onions. Later, he and other POWs with specialized trades were sent to a camp in Oakland, California. There Wagner was able to return to his trade as a cabinetmaker.

On May 16, 1946, Wagner was told he was going home, but instead he was sent to Liverpool, where he spent more than a year working for a brick company and on area farms—apparently it was the British government's way of exacting war reparations from German POWs, while at the same time providing badly needed labor to replace the manpower lost in the war. Wagner finally arrived back in Germany in August 1947. It was a bittersweet homecoming. He found almost total devastation. Although his family was still alive, they had lost all their possessions in the air raids on Hamburg.

He had been gone for five years, and his children barely knew him. "I never [was able to enjoy] my children. Because they were grown up," he said.

With the country in ruins, there were few jobs, and Wagner joined the millions of Germans who were unemployed. Disease also was widespread in postwar Germany, and his wife contracted typhoid fever. When she died, he decided he'd had enough. Although unable to speak English, he immigrated to the U.S., making a new home in the country he had fought against. He moved to Kansas City in 1952.

As it does with many veterans, the war continues to have a strong hold on both men. They're proud of their service aboard U-409. Wagner had the submarine's number on his vanity license plate. For Massmann's visit, he purchased shirts with U-409's wartime emblem—a giant thumb pressing down on a ship.

Both were asked if they had any lasting bitterness from the war. "Not so much about the war," said Massmann, who remained in Germany. "We were fighting against each other as was our duty." But he said what still bothers him is the way they were treated after the war. "We were accused of doing it for Hitler and for all those criminal things," he said. "The whole nation was accused of being guilty of all the things that had happened." In reality, he said, most Germans fought honorably for the same things as the Allies—patriotism and love for their country.

But he feels no animosity toward his former enemies. "We can't feel bitter about the war," he said. "Hitler and his people entirely underestimated the national consequences of starting the war with Poland. And Germany had not the slightest chance of winning a war against a world united in its hatred of Hitler."

For Wagner, the feelings were closer to the surface. Is he still bitter? "In some ways, yes, but it's not wise to talk about it," he said. "The war is over and you can't change it anyway."

Italy

Death on the Rapido

The Rapido River, Italy, January 20, 1944—Warren Anderson was one of the lucky ones. The young sergeant was left behind with the supply packs while the men who owned them—members of Fox Company, 143rd Infantry, 36th Texas National Guard Division, U.S. 5th Army—crossed a narrow river called the Rapido, during the Allied push into Italy in January 1944. Their job was to establish a bridgehead as part of a coordinated effort to break through the heavily fortified German defensive line blocking the way to Cassino.

Although only fifteen yards wide, the Rapido was swift-running and winter-cold. The GIs didn't want to be loaded down with extra gear if their boats overturned during the crossing, so they left their extra equipment to be brought up later. As it turned out, many of them never reached the river. There were no approach roads to the crossing sites, and the soldiers were forced to carry their boats and bridge-building equipment through several miles of mud and mines. Also, there was a thick mist that night, and when the German 88s began falling, a rising pall of smoke. The combat engineers had managed to clear eight-foot lanes through the minefields, but when the artillery barrage began, the soldiers scattered. Hidden in the mud were hundreds of German antipersonnel mines loaded with ball bearings and razor-sharp metal spurs. "It's like a grenade," Anderson said, "but it jumps up in the air six foot and goes off."

Some of the soldiers, disoriented by the artillery and mortar explosions, blundered off the cleared paths into the mine clusters. Some who made it to the river with their boats capsized in the treacherous current and drowned. Others were cut down by automatic weapon fire from the other bank. German mortars blew up the footbridges as soon as they were erected. The few soldiers who actually made it across the river were pinned down by deadly crossfire.

Anderson spent most of the attack in a slit trench, listening to the thunderous shelling. "I was just left there with the supplies," he said. "I was one of the lucky ones." There weren't many. According to one estimate, the two-day operation cost the Allies 143 dead, 663 wounded, and 875 missing and presumed dead—a 56 percent casualty rate among riflemen and company officers. One entire battalion disappeared without a trace. Of the 200 men in Anderson's company, only 20 survived the attack. "I lost a lot of friends," he said.

The invasion of Italy almost didn't happen. In the summer of 1943, the Allies were planning their next step. The North African campaign was ending, but the long-awaited invasion of southern France was still months away. The Allies had already decided to invade the island of Sicily; a victory there would ease their shipping problems in the Mediterranean, but initially, they did not consider a follow-up invasion of the Italian mainland, which many thought would be too costly. Churchill, however, began to push for an Italian invasion, saying possession of the southern peninsula would, among other things, allow the Allies access to several large airfields, which could be used to make long-range bomber strikes against the German-held oil fields at Ploesti, Romania. Also, he said, an invasion might convince the already reeling Fascist government to surrender.

The U.S. wanted to put all its efforts toward the Normandy invasion but finally agreed to exploit the Sicilian campaign with another cross-channel invasion into Italy after receiving assurances from the British that the Allied invasion of France would take place the following spring. Unknown to the Allies, the Italians were ready to surrender but feared reprisals from the Germans. Eventually they began meeting covertly with the Allies to work out a peace agreement.

On the night of July 10, 1943, an Allied invasion force of nearly half a million men began landing on Sicily. Among them was Eddie Epperson, who was wounded during the campaign and still carries a piece of shrapnel in his left arm. Epperson has a lot of memories of the war. Many of them he wishes he could forget. "There was one fella hollerin'," Epperson said. "He had his leg blown off and he was callin', 'Eppy help me, Eppy help me.'" Epperson dragged his wounded buddy beneath a demolished halftrack and tied a tourniquet around his stump, but within minutes he was dead. Later, Epperson and a group of soldiers charged up a hill, seeking some protection from the 88s and mortars that were falling like hail all around them. When they reached the crest of the hill, they found it littered with corpses. "It wasn't nothin' but meat, bloody meat," he said. "Nothin' but meat everywhere."

Sicily was secured by August 17. Two weeks later, on September 3, British and Canadian troops crossed the three-mile-wide Straits of Messina separating Sicily from Italy. That same day, the Italian government signed a secret armistice with the Allies, but the surrender wasn't announced until September 8. On September 9, the U.S. Fifth Army, under the command of Gen. Mark Clark, landed at Salerno. After repulsing a German counterattack September 12 through 16, the Fifth Army began its push up the western Tyrrhenian coast. In October, the Allies took Naples and crossed the Volturno River.

Poor roads, mountainous terrain, and a dogged German defense slowed the Allied advance. As the Germans grudgingly withdrew, they blew up bridges and mountain passes and retreated to prepared defensive positions. One of the strongest of those positions was the Gustav line, which guarded the mouth of the Liri Valley and the main road leading to Rome. The key point on the line was the town of Cassino. Above the town, at the top of Mt. Cassino, was a four hundred-year-old Benedictine abbey, which the Allies believed the Germans were using as an observation post. As German opposition stiffened, Allied leaders who had offered lukewarm support for the Italian campaign became reluctant to commit resources that they felt could be better utilized elsewhere. For that reason, the Italian operations often were plagued by divided leadership and inadequate supplies. Nowhere was that more evident than at the Rapido River.

Most historians agree that the assault across the Rapido River was hastily and poorly planned as well as inadequately supplied. Instead of crossing the river in the amphibious, four-wheel-drive ducks, the soldiers had to use inflatable rubber dinghies and 410-pound plywood scows. The shrapnel and machine gun bullets shredded the rubber boats and blasted through the wooden ones. Also, many of the soldiers were inexperienced with the boats; incorrectly handled, the boats capsized as soon as they were out in the current. Men and equipment were swept away in the rushing water. “There was a helluva lot of confusion,” Anderson said. “They lost a lot of men. I remember them bringing them back over by the truckloads.”

Sam Crookshanks will never forget what the soldiers called the “screaming meemies.” They were a type of German mortar that made a distinctive, high-pitched sound. They were used almost exclusively at night. “They didn't do so much damage, except to your mind. That's what they were working on.” Crookshanks was a corporal with the 194th Field Artillery Battalion; he manned a fifty-caliber antiaircraft machine gun emplacement. In 1944, his company had dug into the base of Mount Porchia and was lobbing eight-inch howitzer rounds into Cassino. His job was to shoot down the German fighters and dive-bombers who were trying to knock out the Allies' artillery positions. His most vivid memories are of the nighttime artillery exchanges—the thunder of the guns, the way they flashed when discharging, lighting up the sky like lightning. He doesn't remember being afraid very long. "At first you are," he said, "but you kind of get over that."

On January 22, 1944, the same day the tattered remnants of the Thirty-sixth Texas National Guard Division were pulling back from the Rapido River, after the costly, abortive attempt to cross, General Clark launched Operation Shingle, the landing of forty thousand British and American troops of the Sixth Corps at Anzio. The invasion took the Germans by surprise and was all but unopposed; however, instead of pushing immediately off the beach, the Allies dug in and fortified the beachhead against the inevitable German counterattack. That gave the Germans time to rush reserves from Rome. Within a few hours, the Germans had the beachhead contained and the Allied troops pinned down under heavy, almost continuous, artillery fire. The Allied troops remained trapped on the beach for four months.

In late March, Crookshanks's outfit was pulled out of Cassino and sent to Anzio. He said, "They dropped us off and no one came back for three days. We were just settin' there for three days hidin'. It was just flatlands. There wasn't really any place to go. There was no protection. Every night you'd dig a little deeper."

Crookshanks was nineteen and working for the Missouri Pacific Railroad in Kansas City when he was drafted in January 1943. Like many veterans of the Italian campaign, he started out in Africa and was part of the Fifth Army invasion force at Naples in November.

At Anzio, he set up his machine gun in a bomb crater and built up the sides of the crater with sandbags. German fighters making low-level strafing runs and observation planes, nicknamed Bed Check Charlie, were frequent targets. The observation planes came at dusk, Crookshanks said, and about 30 minutes later, the Germans would bring out the Anzio Express, a huge artillery piece mounted on a railway car, which was kept hidden in a cave during the day. He never learned how large the rounds fired by the Anzio Express were, but they dwarfed the 204-pound projectiles shot by the Allies' howitzers. "I wouldn't be surprised if they were three times that [size]," he said. The shelling typically continued into the night, slacked off for a while, and then started up again around 4 A.M. The rounds from the Anzio Express made a whistling sound as they approached but went silent just before impact. The GIs at Anzio grew to dread that eerie silence preceding the explosion because they were never sure where the shell was going to hit. "It had a sound all its own," Crookshanks said. "Long as you can hear one, it's alright."

Meanwhile, back at Cassino, the Allies' problems continued. By mid-March the siege had turned into a stalemate and the Germans' defensive positions—the Gustav and Hitler lines—were still intact. On March 15, the Allies launched Operation Bradman. The attack included a three-and-a-half–hour bombing blitz carried out by four hundred sixty bombers, which dropped one thousand tons of explosives. Nearly half the bombs fell within a mile of the center of Cassino for a strike ratio of more than four tons per acre. As soon as the bombing was over, the artillery opened up, and over the next eight hours, Cassino was reduced to rubble. Also destroyed was the Benedictine abbey on top of Mt. Cassino, which the Germans insisted hadn't been used as an observation post.

The German survivors turned the ruined buildings with their gutted basements into a sniper's paradise and continued to hold off the Allied advance. "We lived in foxholes," Anderson said. One of Anderson's responsibilities as supply sergeant was to make sure the men in his company changed their socks every day to prevent trench foot, also called immersion foot, an ailment caused by wearing wet socks for extended periods. Never dry, the soldiers' feet would turn purple and swell painfully. In extreme cases, gangrene set in, and it wasn't unusual for a man's toes to fall off when his sock was removed. More than a few soldiers lost their feet to amputation. Anderson not only had to provide the men with dry socks, he also had to collect and clean two hundred pairs of dirty socks each night.

While at Cassino, Anderson was wounded in the hand and the leg by artillery shrapnel. "I still have them in me," he said. "They never did take them out."

In May, the Allies launched a new offensive; they smashed through the Gustav and Hitler lines, sending troops pouring into the Liri Valley; they captured Cassino, allowed the soldiers trapped on the Anzio beachhead to break out, and captured Rome. In one massive wave the Allies moved two hundred miles up the Italian peninsula. Behind the frontline troops came the support soldiers—men like Ralph H. Saunders, who was with the Fiftieth Finance Division. He came to Italy with his equipment—typewriters, calculators, and field safes packed in watertight boxes. Among his jobs were overseeing GI pay records, providing pocket money for soldiers on leave, and exchanging currency.

Saunders recalls seeking shelter during air raids in petrified lava beds and underground bunkers abandoned by the Germans. Once he was sharing tea and stew with some British Marines when "all of a sudden everything opened up," he said, referring to the Allied antiaircraft guns. "That damn flak is more dangerous than the German guns." Another time he was standing in a chow line when a German plane suddenly appeared overhead, the plane so low he could see the pilot. Everyone dove for cover. It turned out to be a reconnaissance plane. "He just came over the top of the hill," Saunders said. "Scared us. First time I saw one [a German] that close."

His clearest memory is of the eruption of Vesuvius, which happened while he was stationed in Naples. The glowing lava lit up the horizon at night, he said, and the German bombers used the volcano as a sight marker during their night raids. But Saunders also remembers arriving at Anzio and seeing the bodies stacked like cordwood, separated by nationality. "The smell of the dead," he said, "oh it was horrible."

The Allies pursued the Germans north during the summer of 1944. But the Germans didn't panic; their retreat was calculated and methodical. They set up ambushes, blew up culverts and bridges, and repeatedly fell back to fortified defensive lines. One of the last major battles of the Italian campaign occurred three thousand feet above sea level at Mt. Altuzzo, the anchor of the Germans' Gothic line, which ran through the rugged Northern Apennines. Louis Degginger was the supply officer for the 329th Field Artillery Battalion, 338th Regimental Combat Team, 85th Infantry. He supplied ammunition, food, fresh water and clothing to his 105-millimeter howitzer unit.

The Germans had turned the mountains into formidable defensive positions; there were minefields, pillboxes, and log bunkers with overlapping fields of fire manned by the Fourth Parachute Division, the elite German troops in Italy. The bitter fight lasted five days and ended on September 18 with the capture of Mt. Altuzzo and the key Futa and Giorgo passes. The infantry suffered 290 casualties, but Degginger's unit lost only 3 men (out of the 5 killed during the two years they were in Italy).

The Joplin, Missouri, native had been drafted in 1941 at the age of twenty-four. One of his clearest memories of Italy is of going through Giorgo Pass after the battle. "I can remember them hauling out the dead German soldiers," he said. "Jeep after jeep loaded with dead German soldiers."

So It Goes

Gene Rigney has some things in common with former Kansas senator Bob Dole. Both men served in the Tenth Mountain Division, America's elite ski troops, during World War II, and both were wounded in combat. In fact, they were wounded on the same day and on the same Italian mountain. There are differences as well. Dole, a young second lieutenant, was leading his platoon when he was cut down by a burst of German machine gun fire. Rigney, a private first class medic, was hit by shrapnel while going to the aid of a wounded soldier. Rigney spent six weeks recuperating from his wound. Dole's recovery took nearly four years. Dole went on to a successful career in the U.S. Senate, and he made an unsuccessful bid for the presidency in 1996. After the war, Rigney used the GI Bill to get an engineering degree and eventually went to work for the space shuttle program at NASA. He retired in 1987 and moved to Blue Springs, Missouri, in 1998. But for both men, the short time they spent in combat was the most exciting and frightening time they would ever experience. And it's a time Gene Rigney will never forget.

Rigney was born in Salt Lake City and raised in Provo. His father died when he was young, and his mother, unable to support him, sent him to live with his grandparents. His grandfather had emigrated from Denmark to join the Mormon Church but eventually left to become a minister for the Reorganized Church of Latter-Day Saints. Rigney lived with his grandparents in the parsonage.

In 1934 Rigney lost both his grandfather and his mother in a six-month span. An orphan at ten, he moved with his grandmother to a log cabin in Levan, Utah. Young Gene, however, was growing up wild. Eventually his grandmother decided she couldn't handle him and bundled him off to Englewood, Missouri, to live with his uncle, who owned a cafe.

In the mid-1930s, the family moved to Lee's Summit, where Rigney attended the seventh through tenth grades in the Lee's Summit School District. In the early 1940s he moved back to Utah, and after the Japanese attacked Pearl Harbor, he got swept up by patriotic fervor. "I was kind of caught up in the frenzy of the whole thing," he said. "Everybody was gung ho. Course, nobody knew what combat was like. . . . People getting blown apart, getting arms and legs blown off, you didn't think about things like that."

Rigney was inducted in 1943, but poor eyesight got him assigned to limited service. He spent his first year stationed at a hospital in Salt Lake City. Then he found out the army was looking for experienced skiers to join an elite mountain division that was to fight in Italy. Rigney had skied and climbed in the high country of Utah and was welcomed into the Eighty-seventh Regiment of the Tenth Mountain Division. Also in the division was Friedl Pfeifer, a world-class Austrian skier who had immigrated to the U.S. to escape the Nazis. Pfeifer had a brother who was fighting for the German Army and the U.S. high command kept tabs on him to ensure that he wouldn't meet his brother in combat.

(After the war, Pfeifer helped transform Aspen, Colorado, from an abandoned mining town into one of the world's premier ski resorts.)

Partly because he had hospital experience, Rigney was put into medic training. He was sent to Camp Swift, outside Austin, Texas, for advanced training and on December 20, 1944, boarded a train for Camp Patrick Henry, Virginia. On the morning of January 4, the Tenth Mountain Division left Newport News on the USS *West Point*, a converted passenger liner. The *West Point* took nine days to cross the Atlantic and arrived at the teeming Naples pier in between cold rainsqualls. Eventually the division bivouacked east of Camaiore.

After a month and a half of patrols and minor skirmishes, the division prepared for its first major offensive, an attack on Mt. Belvedere, planned for February 19 and 20. In Italian, *belvedere* means a tower or balcony that overlooks a pleasant scene. This scene, however, was anything but pleasant. The German-held side of the mountain was covered with machine gun nests, mortar pits, artillery emplacements, and those weapons most hated by infantrymen: mines.

The Allies had already tried to capture Mt. Belvedere. Burned-out tanks littered the slopes where attacks had been repulsed the previous autumn. The Eighty-seventh's objective was Corona, a demolished town clinging to the side of the mountain.

Rigney and the other men of the First Battalion were dumped out of trucks at the foot of the mountain at 9 P.M. on February 19, and two hours later they began trudging up a muddy, icy dirt road that curved up one slope of Mt. Belvedere. They stopped to rest every hour, and just about the time Rigney dropped off to sleep, he'd hear the dreaded order: "Saddle up, men, we're moving out."

"God, I hated those words," Rigney said.

Although he was walking with thousands of other men, the darkness and eerie quiet made it seem as if he were all alone. After a while he began hearing someone yelling off in the darkness where the terrain dropped away steeply. The words were in English, and the speaker seemed to be in great pain. When he asked about it, Rigney was told there weren't any Allied troops in the area so it was probably a German trying to lure someone into an ambush. But the voice persisted, sometimes yelling for help, other times simply crying out in pain.

Finally Rigney had had enough. He stepped off the road and began walking and sliding down the embankment. It was pitch-dark, but Rigney began answering the voice, and as it responded, he slowly closed the distance between them. As Rigney approached, he identified himself as an unarmed American medic and asked whoever it was (thinking it might be a German after all) to please not shoot him. When Rigney got to the man, he found he was an American artillery spotter for the army air corps. He'd been wounded in the legs by a shell burst, and he was bleeding badly. Rigney patched him up as best he could and then helped him back up the slope, where litter bearers were called up to take the injured man back down the mountain. "He'd have lain there and bled to death if I hadn't gone down there," Rigney said. He was feeling pretty good later that night when he rejoined his company, which had continued up the mountain. The feeling didn't last long.

Rigney's baptism of fire began at daybreak on February 20, 1945, outside Corona. He was sitting on the side of a dirt road watching a bulldozer, which had been called up to clear the road of mines. As he watched, there was a sudden explosion, and he saw the treads of the 'dozer fly apart and the heavy machine lurch into the air. The driver was flung skyward, cartwheeling in slow motion, then falling to land slack-limbed on the wrecked machine.

That image was still with him when his unit moved out. Its objective was rubbled Corona, still held tenaciously by the Germans. As the men neared the devastated town, they began to take sniper fire. Soon word came back that Lee Chew had been hit. Chew was a friendly and popular Chinese American with the second platoon, and Rigney was sent out to help him. Chew was lying face down in the open; he'd been shot while leading a forward element of the second platoon. One of his legs was folded under him at an odd angle, and he wasn't moving. Despite the lack of cover and with sniper fire still zipping overhead, Rigney crawled out to Chew. When he got close, he reached out and shook his boot, asking if he was alright. When there was no response, he crawled closer and lifted Chew's head. A surge of blood and brains spilled onto the ground.

"He'd been shot between the eyes and [the bullet] had come out his temple," Rigney said. "He was the first guy in my company to get killed." Memories like that one still haunt Rigney. "I've seen our guys do some things that still stick with me today," he said. Another incident happened shortly after Rigney crawled back and reported that Chew was dead. The news spread quickly through the company, and men who knew Chew reacted with shock and anger. They already had taken some German prisoners, and Rigney was near three who had been disarmed and were standing, their hands raised in the air, when things suddenly went very wrong. "This little sergeant came running up and shot all of them in the face," Rigney said. Stunned, Rigney bent over the fallen prisoners to see if he could help them, but at first he could find no wounds or blood. On closer examination, he found that one had been shot in the mouth—the bullet had neatly clipped away one of his front teeth—

another had been shot in the nostril, and the third had been shot in the corner of one eye. None of the wounds had bled much because the men had died instantly.

The company completed mopping up Corona later that day. Chew was the only fatality on the American side, but four others were wounded. Seven Germans were reported killed in the fighting, and twenty were captured. However, all those numbers were revised upward as the offensive continued into the evening. "We lost a third of our men killed or wounded that first day," Rigney said.

The division spent most of the next month moving north and consolidating their gains. By the end of March they had moved to the rear for some rest and recuperation in preparation for the big spring offensive in the Northern Apennines. Rigney remembers the weather was warm and mild, and the fruit trees, many of which had been shredded by artillery, were beginning to flower.

The offensive—Operation Craftsman—would involve both the British Eighth Army and the U.S. Fifth Army. According to the plan, the British would attack the Argenta Gap on April 9, and the Fifth Army would move on Vergato three days later. Although the British attacked on schedule, the U.S. forces were delayed when a heavy fog grounded vital air support. Then, early on the morning of April 13, while awaiting the signal to begin the attack, the division received the news that President Roosevelt had died. The attack was postponed another twenty-four hours.

The attack was set to begin at 7 A.M. Both the Eighty-seventh and Eighty-fifth Regiments would jump off at Mt. della Spe, with the Eighty-fifth seizing the high ground to protect the division's left flank and the Eighty-seventh taking the town of Torre Iussi.

Second Lieutenant Bob Dole, who had joined I Company, Third Battalion of the Eighty-fifth Regiment, as a replacement officer, was leading a platoon on Hill 913 on Mt. della Spe on the night of April 14 when a German gunner opened fire. The hail of bullets killed two scouts and tore into Dole's neck and shoulder. For Dole, who would spend the next forty months in army hospitals, the war was over.

For Rigney's first platoon, the battle opened with artillery and an aerial display by army air corps Thunderbolt fighter-bombers, which attacked the German positions. The bombs were mostly napalm, Rigney said. "They'd burn everything for a block long and a block wide. They were fierce." Despite the intense aerial and land bombardment, the Germans still had plenty of fight left in them. Rigney, who started out accompanied by three mules loaded with medical supplies, came under fire as soon as he appeared over the crest of the ridge. A German sniper quickly shot the three mules and then shot an Italian partisan, who had been leading one of the mules, in the leg. The other two partisans, neither of whom spoke English, immediately grabbed their wounded friend and headed for the rear, leaving Rigney to fend for himself. "My mules were dead. My Italians were gone, and there was nobody left to shoot at but me," he said. Rigney saw a shell hole about forty feet away and started for it at a dead run. As he dove into it, he heard something buzz past his ear. From the comparative safety of the crater, he looked back. On the lip of the crater was a ten-inch-long furrow made by the bullet that had just missed him. "They say you never hear the one that gets you. [But] if they come close, you hear them," he said. "I heard it go by my ear."

Later that day, Rigney found himself in an artillery barrage and sought shelter in a gully with three other soldiers. Half a dozen shells landed in the vicinity in quick succession, and then the shelling stopped. Rigney and the others climbed out cautiously; before they could get very far, the shells started falling again, and the men ran back to the gully. "We were in that gully more than four hours," Rigney said. Each time they tried to leave, the barrage would start again. Rigney has a theory about why the Germans wasted so many shells on four stranded soldiers: "I think they thought we had a mortar there," he said.

During one barrage, a shell burst in a tree near the gully. Rigney, who was on his hands and knees "trying to crawl into my helmet," felt something slam into his back. "I remember letting out a big yell," he said. Almost immediately he lost feeling in his arm and for a while thought it had been blown off. He remembers blood spurting over his shoulders and into his hair and face. When he sat up, the blood coursed down his back, soaking his trousers. "It looked ten times worse than I was. I looked like I'd had a direct hit," he said. He decided that if he stayed in the gully, he was going to die. He had timed the barrages and found that "it'd take them three or four minutes to reload." So, as soon as the shells stopped, he and the others took off.

Rigney made it back to an aid station set up in an old barn. Light-headed from loss of blood, he found himself sitting next to a German POW, who was holding his stomach. Instinctively, Rigney drew back his fist to strike the German, who shook his head. "Nein, nein," he said and raised his hands.

"His intestines rolled out on his lap," Rigney said. "He was holding them in with his hands."

After being examined by a doctor, Rigney was told to get on a stretcher to be carried down the mountain. But the only bearers available were German POWs. Rather than risk being "accidentally" dropped off the side of the mountain, he decided to walk down under his own power.

When he arrived at the field hospital, they dug out two pieces of shrapnel the size of a fingernail. The wound was next to his spine. "Another half inch," the doctor told him, "and you'd be paralyzed from your shoulders down." Rigney remembers being shoved unceremoniously into the back of an ambulance with several other wounded soldiers who were heading out of the war. Just before the door was closed, someone tossed in a small box, which hit him in the back of the head. "Here's your Purple Heart," a voice said, and someone slammed the door.

Rigney spent six weeks recuperating from his injury. In that time, the Germans capitulated, and the war in Europe ended. When he recovered, he sent for his barracks bag, which had been left in Italy. In it were dozens of photos and papers rifled from the pockets of dead Germans, several German pistols and watches, and a white camouflage helmet, which he'd found filled with the owner's brains. "I never got it," he said of his barracks bag, noting that most war souvenirs ended up in the possession of rear-echelon soldiers, most of whom never spent a day in combat. So it goes.

After the war, Rigney got his engineering degree and returned in Kansas City in 1950. A product and tool designer, he spent most of his career in the missile and aerospace industry.

Rigney said serving in combat changed his outlook on things. Born and raised in the Utah high country, he had been used to climbing and skiing fearlessly. After the war, he said, "I never wanted to do anything. I never wanted to go skiing anymore. I never wanted to jump out of airplanes." He had a new outlook on life, a new appreciation for the simple pleasures. "I want to be around to watch the sun come up in the morning," he said. "I had all the excitement I needed."

War in the Pacific, Part 2

Ack-ack over Wewak

SOMEWHERE OVER WEWAK, NEW GUINEA, 1943—The B-25 swooped out of the roiling sky for another strafing run. The American gunners weren't particular. They shot at anything—trains, gun emplacements, buildings, people. It didn't matter. Everything was a target. The plane was loaded with explosives as well; everything from one thousand-pound blockbuster bombs to parafrags—parachute fragmentation bombs—which drifted slowly earthward to detonate on impact in a murderous scattering of twisted metal.

As the B-25 banked, waist gunner Sgt. Stew Kluender leaned back from his fifty-caliber machine gun. The pilot asked him to check the fuel level in the plane's 350-gallon tank. Crouching on his hands and knees, Kluender peered into the tank. There was only a little gasoline sloshing around the bottom. Was there enough to make another strafing run? the pilot asked. Kluender said there was.

When he stood up, Kluender noticed a fist-sized hole in the fuselage at about eye level. A second hole was in the other side of the plane, directly across from the first. It occurred to him that a piece of shrapnel had just passed through the plane, missing him by inches. "That's the closest call I know I had," said Kluender. "If I'd been standing up, it'd have gone through my head. It went through one side of the plane and out the other."

Kluender was a thirty-seven-year-old control technician for Cook Paint Company, in North Kansas City, when he was drafted in the fall of 1942. His boss offered to arrange a permanent deferment for him. Kluender declined; he said, "If I didn't consider myself patriotic, I wouldn't have gone. I always said I'd never enlist, but if my number comes up, I'll go." He was sent to St.

Louis for basic training and then to Las Vegas for gunnery school. At the time, he wanted to join the tank corps. He ended up in the army air corps. "I said, 'I don't want the air force.' They said, 'You're going in the air force.' And I said, 'Yes, sir!'" Gunnery school lasted three months and focused on machine gun training. Kluender's next stop was New Mexico, where he received training in bombing and navigation. Then it was on to Greenville, South Carolina, for more gunnery and anything else the army air corps could throw at the new draftees. "They did about everything they could to make you mad," he said. "They wanted to make mean soldiers out of us."

Kluender arrived in Port Moresby, New Guinea—"mosquito heaven of the world"—in mid-1943. He was assigned to the 499th, nicknamed "The Bats Out of Hell" squadron. Port Moresby, located on the southeastern tip of New Guinea, had been first attacked by the Japanese in February of 1942, but it was never invaded. The 499th, a low-level bombing and strafing outfit, used the city as a jumping-off point to attack Japanese bases along the northern coastline of the island.

The twin-engine Mitchell B-25 was the perfect airplane for low-level raids. With a top speed of 275 miles per hour, it was a fast medium bomber with firepower superior to almost anything then in the Pacific. Its armament included eight nose guns, a thirty-five-millimeter cannon, two fifty-caliber guns at the waist and two more in the top turret, which revolved on a 360-degree track, and twin fifty-caliber tail guns. It had a crew of six.

Kluender started out as a top turret gunner and later became a radio operator. That position was also responsible for manning one of the waist guns. The plane's engineer manned the other waist gun. "We flew low enough so planes couldn't get under us," he said. Sometimes that meant skimming the ocean, and the waist gunners often got soaked with spray kicked up by the prop wash.

From Port Moresby, the squadron flew missions over Dobodura, Finschhafen, and Nadzab. On targets like the Nabire airdrome on the south shore of Geelvink Bay, the planes dropped their thousand pounders and then swooped in at tree level. While the gunners strafed the ground, the bomber would release a cloud of parafrags. "When they hit something," Kluender said, "they'd just disintegrate and throw everything every which way." The parafrags were especially effective against ground troops.

The squadron moved its base to Nadzab when that city was secured. From there it attacked But, Dagua, Wewak, and Boram. According to Kluender, Wewak was the worst. "The Japs really had gun emplacements and everything you could think of. We flew over that and the sky just turned black with ack-ack."

As they moved west, the men began raiding neighboring islands, the names of which Kluender has mostly forgotten. "We weren't over there to learn geography," he said. "We were there to clear out the Japs." He did remember the farthest west he got was a little island named Biak. "It's got one distinction. It's got the deepest outhouse in the world," he said grinning. "I think it was twenty-seven feet deep. Now that's deep."

Kluender flew his fiftieth mission just before the campaign for the Philippines was to begin. "I didn't get in on that Philippines stuff. That was rough." But even after he had completed his fifty missions, there were some who tried to talk him into sticking around. But his commanding officer said no. "Any of my boys who've flown fifty missions," the officer said, "that's it."

Was it a relief to be sent home?

"Well, if I'd say no, I'd be lying," he said. But unlike some men, he never felt like he was living on borrowed time. "Always had a little bit of faith [I'd] be back."

Despite the number of combat missions he flew, Kluender never saw an enemy soldier during his tour of duty overseas. "I never saw a Jap, dead or alive, when I was there. I knew they were there because they were shooting at us." For that reason, he can honestly say he doesn't know if he killed anyone in the war. And it wouldn't matter if he did. "Hell, they were shooting at me too," he said.

Kluender returned to the States in November 1944. After the war, he returned to Cook Paint. He retired in 1971 after forty-three years of service.

Kluender said he has no bitter feelings toward the Japanese. "I've known some Japs," he said agreeably. "I can get along with anybody."

Tarawa

DAWN, TARAWA ATOLL, THE GILBERT ISLANDS, NOVEMBER 20, 1943—The landing craft shuddered to a crunching stop more than a half mile from shore. Military strategists, who were supposed to know better, thought the tide would be in, enabling the LCMs (landing craft, mechanized) to get over the brilliantly colored coral reefs ringing the tiny island. But the tide was too low for the boats to get close; the marines would have to wade to shore.

That morning, radio operator Pfc. Robert C. Barackman stepped off the ramp into eighteen feet of water. The heavy radio he was carrying on his back immediately pulled him underwater. Knowing he would drown if he didn't abandon the equipment, he wriggled free of the radio and splashed to the surface. Barackman was in the third wave of marines to land on Tarawa, but there was still heavy machine gun fire coming from the fortified pillboxes along the shoreline. The eighteen-year-old had never before been shot at. As he swam toward shore, he saw the smoking hulks of mortared amphtracks, which had made it over the reef but been hit before they could reach the beach. The bodies of scores of dead marines bobbed in surf turned crimson by blood.

Barackman grew up in Kansas City, Kansas, and graduated from Ward High School in 1942. The Japanese had bombed Pearl Harbor just a few months before, and like most of the guys in his graduating class, he was ready to enlist.

Barackman said it's difficult to explain why he wanted to go to war. "It was a different age. An innocent age," he said. It was a time of intense patriotism, a time when everyone worked together toward a common goal. "It's cornball to say it now," he said, "but when the flag went by, it meant something. And we were proud it meant something."

If you were male and reasonably healthy, you gladly went overseas to fight for the right to be an American. The others, the unlucky ones, had to stay on the home front to work in the war-accelerated factories and tend the victory gardens. "The biggest fear was that a kid would be classified 4-F," he said. "Then [he'd] be an outcast."

The crucial factor, the thing that made that war different, was that Japan was the aggressor, Barackman said. "They bombed us, they killed us, and we were going to finish it." Nearly all the boys in his senior class enlisted. Few of them waited until they were eighteen; they didn't want to risk being drafted into the infantry. Barackman got permission from his mother and enlisted in the Marine Corps in November of 1942. He was seventeen.

He was sent to San Diego for six weeks of boot camp and then on to communications school to be trained as a radio operator. In May 1943, he arrived in New Zealand to join the Second Marine Division, which was recuperating after the Guadalcanal campaign. The marines of the Second Division had been among the first to land on Guadalcanal back in August 1942—the first U.S. invasion of World War II. The Second also would participate in the last invasion of the war—Okinawa on April 1, 1945. Barackman would be there, too, a corporal by then, but in November 1943, he was just about to learn where his first stop would be. He was going to Tarawa.

Things weren't much better when Barrackman finally reached Tarawa's shattered shore. The Japanese defenders kept the invaders pinned down on the beach the rest of the day, and it wasn't until the next morning that he and a group of marines finally scrambled over the seawall. Shelling and sniper fire chased them into a crater that had been scooped out by a sixteen-inch shell about fifty yards inland. Luckily, one of the marines was toting a fifty-caliber water-cooled machine gun, which was immediately positioned on the forward edge of the crater so the marines could return fire.

Unluckily, the marines were low on water. Each had been issued a single canteen on the morning of the invasion and had been assured that fresh water would be brought up soon after the landing. During war in the tropics, water and ammunition were the top priorities for the fighting men. Because of heavy American casualties and stubborn Japanese resistance, fresh water was still unavailable. The marines, many of whom had drained their canteens during the first roasting day on the beach, now faced a day without water in the broiling tropical sun. Worse, there was no water to cool the barrel of the machine gun; the gun would soon become inoperable if the water evaporating from the jacket was not replaced.

Barackman grinned as he told the story. With no canteen water, the marines had to improvise. When the water level became low, the machine gun's tubular jacket, which fit under the barrel, was removed and passed among the twelve marines, who all carefully urinated into the jacket. The procedure was made all the more difficult because they couldn't stand up without exposing themselves to enemy fire. "Being hot and dehydrated," Barackman said, laughing, "[we found] it was awful hard to get enough moisture for the jacket."

The battle for Tarawa lasted four days. American casualties included 980 dead and 2,101 wounded. Virtually all of the 4,690 Japanese defenders were killed. After Tarawa, the Second Marines were shipped to Hawaii to rest, refit, and take on replacements to rebuild the division back to battle strength. Barackman, now a nineteen-year-old combat veteran, was promoted to corporal. His next stop: Saipan.

Women in War

For the Boys

Josephine Clark was a member of the army nurse corps caring for wounded soldiers in a tent hospital outside Cherbourg. Isabel Fritchie was a pharmacist's mate serving stateside in the Waves. Fran O'Brien was a navy occupational therapist helping sailors who had lost their sight or their limbs adjust to a new life. Mamie Mulligan was a "Rosie the Riveter" working the swing shift at the Pratt and Whitney plant in Kansas City.

Women served in various capacities during World War II, both in uniform and out. Although most were far from the front, they did work vitally important to the war effort, such as caring for wounded GIs, tending victory gardens, and replacing men in factory jobs (freeing the men to fight overseas). They worked double shifts and cheerfully accepted the privations of rationing, often while they were raising their children alone. America couldn't have won the war without them.

Josephine Clark

Josephine Zimmerman, born in Ashland, Kansas, entered the army nurse corps as a twenty-two-year-old second lieutenant on October 15, 1942. Her first assignment was at Fort Leavenworth. She had only been there a few months when Alden Clark, the young technician who had taken the X-rays during her entry physical, asked her to marry him, and Josephine accepted. In an unusual role reversal, Alden remained stateside while Josephine headed overseas.

She recalled boarding a ship in New York harbor late in the evening on September 11, 1944, and going to bed. When she woke the next morning, the ship was out to sea, and Josephine had no idea where she was going. "The first day I was seasick, so I stayed in my bunk all day!" said Josephine. "I got my first war experience on the high seas in a sixty-eight-ship convoy when I could hear and see depth bombs being dropped by destroyers. German submarines had been detected in the English Channel. We were on the Atlantic Ocean for twelve days." She said a landing craft "dumped" the nurses on the Normandy coast near Cherbourg on September 24. Although D-Day had been almost four months before, there were still snipers and mines hidden in the fields and hedgerows.

She was assigned to the 165th General Hospital, a tent installation erected in an open field six miles from Cherbourg. The nurses were rarely allowed to leave the immediate area. "We had designated areas that we could go on because they were cleared," she said. Many of the wounded came directly from the front lines. Those with minor wounds were patched up and sent back. The more seriously wounded were evacuated to England. The hospital treated a lot of shrapnel wounds, she said, especially from land mines, as well as numerous cases of trench foot, made worse by the cold, wet weather. "The winter of 1944 was real bad," she said. Things were especially grim during the Battle of the Bulge. At one point, the nurses were told to pack a bag each in case they had to be evacuated during the German offensive. If the Germans had been able to get that far, she said, "we'd probably have been prisoners of war."

Josephine suffered from debilitating migraine headaches, and she left France on a hospital ship before the war was over. But most of her memories are of good times. "There's a lot of memories," she said. "It was exciting in a way; adventurous, enjoyable. I'd never have gotten overseas if it wasn't for the army. . . . It was a very good experience for anybody to have."

Isabel Fritchie

Born in Marshall County, Iowa, Isabel Beye was teaching school when she decided to join the war effort. "I needed more challenge," she said. At first rejected because her vision wasn't twenty-twenty, she finally was accepted into the U.S. Women's Naval Reserves—better known as the Waves—in June 1943 at the age of twenty-five. She served stateside throughout the war as a pharmacist's mate, first in Norman, Oklahoma, and later at a naval air station at Banana River, Florida. "I worked in the dispensary most of the time [in Norman]," said Isabel. "The fellas called me a 'pill pusher.' . . . I loved it." When she was transferred to Banana River, she went to work in the maternity ward and nursery. Her memories of the war are pleasant ones. Unlike some people, she liked the closeness and camaraderie of barracks life. "They were great people. I really liked everybody," she said. "We had a job to do and we felt like we were helping our country."

Fran O'Brien

Boston-born Francis Howard joined the navy in February 1943 and reported to midshipmen school in New Hampshire. "The first thing I did was lose my suitcase on the way up there," said Fran (ninety in 1995). For the next six weeks she didn't have a change of clothes. She had to wash her clothes in her apartment sink and dry them on the radiator.

She received her commission on May 4, 1943. The next day she married Jim O'Brien, to whom she had been engaged for three years. "We never had enough money [to get married], so when we had no money, we got married," she said.

Her first assignment was the naval hospital in Brooklyn, New York. A few months later she was transferred to the Philadelphia Naval Hospital, where, as a registered occupational therapist, she began working with returning sailors who had been blinded or had lost limbs. During training to work with blind patients, the therapists were required to wear blindfolds and walk with canes. "You have to have some feeling about what they're going through," she said. She taught each of her patients how to walk with a cane, eat, and generally become independent. She said she noticed the enlisted men tended to adjust faster to their disabilities; many officers seemed to have more difficulty because they were used to being waited on.

Later, she began to treat amputees. She found that the best way to help them was to allow them to help others at the hospital. "The amputees taught the blind people how to type," she said. They also read to them and accompanied them on trips outside the hospital. The experience changed the way Fran looked at war: "I tell you, I'm a pacifist," she said. "It was a very sad situation," she added, because most of the men she treated were disabled for life. But she's proud of the work she did. "We felt we helped some of them," she said. "I'm glad I was in the service."

Mamie Mulligan

Mamie Clements was born near Lone Jack, Missouri, in 1905. In 1942, the thirty-seven-year-old housewife—by then married to Jerry Mulligan—went to work for the war industry at the Pratt and Whitney plant in Kansas City, Missouri. Mamie was one of the thousands of "Rosie the Riveters" who took factory jobs previously held by men. She worked as a drill press operator. Her task was to ream a hole in a piece of two-inch metal tubing, drilling as many pieces of tubing as she could manage in an eight-hour day. "I had no idea what they were for," she said. "They didn't tell us. We weren't supposed to know what we were making. It was top secret. . . . It was very boring, [but] I knew it was for the boys overseas, so I knew it was worthwhile."

She worked the three-to-eleven swing shift. That allowed her to get her older kids off to school each morning and drop her youngest, who was two and a half, off at the babysitter. Usually she made dinner for her family in advance and ate leftovers when she got home. Her uniform consisted of coveralls and safety glasses. She also had to wear her hair up. Although the work was tedious, she remembers those war years fondly. "It was a very exciting time really," she said.

Mamie worked at the factory until 1944. Why did she quit? "I was waiting for that question," she said, smiling. "I got pregnant."

Although she isn't a veteran, Mamie feels good about her contributions to the war effort. "I think we all tried to do what we could at that time," she said. "People did that during the war. Everybody did what they could."

Broken Boys

Mary Eble will warn you that the stories of her time as an army nurse during World War II aren't very exciting. Then she'll start talking about going overseas on the *Queen Mary,* zigzagging across the dark Atlantic to avoid being torpedoed by German U-boats; setting up a field hospital in England to accept casualties from the D-Day assaults, Arnhem, and the Battle of the Bulge, working twenty-four-hour shifts patching up broken boys, comforting those beyond repair; sitting in the dark, listening to the eerie howl of the air raid sirens, knowing that German buzz bombs and V-2 rockets were falling onto London just a few hours away. It doesn't take long to realize that even for those behind the lines, who saw the enemy not as a combatant, but as a bandaged and bleeding patient in need of care, the war years were anything but dull. For a young woman in her twenties, it was one of the most exciting times imaginable.

Eble (seventy-one in 1992), of Carmel, New York, originally tried to join the navy, but she was turned down because she wore glasses, so she enlisted in the army nurse corps on May 1, 1943. She was first stationed at hospitals in New York City then sent overseas in June 1944. Her destination was England, where she would help set up an entire field hospital to handle some of the thousands of casualties pouring back across the English Channel from the Normandy invasion. The nurses, all of whom had volunteered for overseas duty, were transported across the Atlantic on the English luxury liner the *Queen Mary,* which had been refitted as a transport ship because of her size and swiftness. But the accommodations were anything but luxurious. There were eighteen women assigned to each stateroom, and they all had to share one attached bathroom. "Let's just say [it was] crowded," Eble said. "You stood in line for an hour to get lunch."

The ship was so large, she said, that sometimes she forgot they were even on the ocean, and the liner was fast enough to sail without escorts through the wolf pack–infested North Atlantic. Few ships could keep up with the *Queen Mary.* Eble's voyage took only three and a half days, "and we zigzagged all the way [across the Atlantic]," she said. If there were any enemy submarines on their trail, they never saw them. The ship docked in Scotland, and the women took a troop train south to the spot where they were to set up the 121st General Hospital. The site was twenty miles from the English Channel and five hours by train from London.

Eble was assigned to a ward for men with abdominal and chest wounds. Most were U.S. soldiers—the field hospital received a lot of casualties from the 101st Airborne—and there was the occasional badly wounded Brit or captured German. Often nurses worked twenty-four hours straight, then rested through a period of inactivity until the next batch of wounded arrived. "It was real messy," Eble said. "It was kind of like 'MASH.' " It was also hard work, but they didn't think of it in those terms. "You couldn't feel sorry for yourself when you saw a [boy with a] belly full of dirt that had just come off a battlefield," she said. The hardest part was dealing with the soldiers with catastrophic wounds, including the burn victims and multiple amputees. She is still haunted by a GI who had to be fed through a tube because his lower jaw had been shot away. Most patients didn't stay at the field hospital long. Either they died quickly or were rushed to the States for more specialized care.

The nurses' accommodations in England were spartan at best. They lived nine women to a hut, and each hut had foxholes dug on either side in case of attack. She said the women in her hut only sought shelter in the foxholes a few times. Although the air raid siren became a familiar sound, most of the destruction was limited to the London area. Eble recalled there was a drought in England when the nurses arrived, and "we had a helmet full of water we were allowed a day." They could bathe only every two weeks, and afterward they would wash their clothes in the used water.

Despite her proximity to the war, Eble never saw an enemy plane, never had a close call, never felt personally threatened. Dull stories? Well, maybe, compared to the bullets and blood of combat. But for Eble, it was the shining time of her life. An experience she'll never forget. "I wouldn't trade it for anything," she said.

Air War

Combat and Captivity

SOMEWHERE OVER GERMANY, JANUARY 30, 1944—Tail gunner Bob Grimes was blazing away at the swooping German fighters when his B-17 suddenly shuddered like a blindsided boxer. The intercom immediately went dead, and when he looked out a window, he saw that the plane's right wing was on fire. Several things went through the nineteen-year-old's mind, not the least of which was that he'd better get out of the plane if it was going down. But since they were over Nazi Germany, he didn't want to jump before he had to—not if there was a chance the pilot could get the wounded Flying Fortress back to base in England.

Grimes decided to stay at his gun position, at least for a while, and fired a burst at another fighter as it dove through the bomber formation, spread out above and below him as far as the eye could see. They were at twenty-nine thousand feet, and the ground was hidden by a mass of cottony clouds. Soon, however, he noticed the flames spreading along the wing, and the plane began to wobble alarmingly—usually an indication the pilot was no longer at the controls. He decided to see what was going on. He crawled through the claustrophobic passageway toward the front of the plane. When he reached the plane's midsection, he found a large, ragged hole in the fuselage—apparently a direct hit from a rocket. "Both waist gunners were lying in a pool of blood, they were dead," Grimes recalled forty-seven years later. The radio operator was dead as well.

Grimes decided it was time to bail out. He knew if he waited too long, the plane would go into a spin, and it would be too late. Adding to the danger were the thousands of gallons of fuel still on board, which the fire could ignite at any moment, and two 12,500-pound bombs. In his excitement, he'd forgotten his oxygen mask, and oxygen deprivation was making him dizzy. When the B-17 lurched again, he fell down. He didn't even notice he was covered with blood. He managed to pull himself across the steel floor to the open doorway and remembers looking out into the bright, cold, roaring sky.

The next thing he knew, he was free-falling in a gray twilight zone. He realized that he had been unconscious, but for how long? Was he still in the clouds, or was this ground fog, the unforgiving earth only seconds away? He pulled the ripcord.

Grimes spent three years in the army air corps during World War II, including more than a year in German prisoner-of-war camps after his plane was shot down. Ironically, it happened during his twenty-fifth mission. At the time, airmen who had completed twenty-five combat missions were automatically rotated back home for stateside duty. Instead of going home, Grimes spent the remainder of the war in German-held Russia with his sometimes cruel, but often humane, captors. He saw the best and the worst of Germans—from the young and sadistic *Kreigesmarine* and SS guards, who bayoneted helpless POWs during the infamous Heydekrug Run, to German farmers who risked their lives to hide escaped prisoners from the Nazis as the Third Reich imploded.

But the possibility of ending up as a POW had never entered his mind when he enlisted in the army in 1939. "I ran away from home and joined when I was fifteen," he said. "I probably read too much Mark Twain. I wanted to be Tom Sawyer. I wanted adventure." Although the army allowed him to sign up, Grimes was told he would have to get a letter from his parents attesting that he was at least seventeen. "I was fifteen and probably looked thirteen," he said. In his letter home, he asked his parents to tell the army he had been born in 1921. To help convince them, he added, "If you don't tell them that, you'll never hear from me again." His parents eventually sent the letter. "My mother said, 'If he's in the army, at least he'll be taken care of and eating good,' " Grimes said.

In June 1942, with the war in its sixth month, Grimes was still in the States. He decided to transfer to the air corps. He remembers being warned " 'the average life expectancy in air combat is three minutes.' 'Hey, that sounds interesting,' " he remembers thinking. "I think I'll try it." Since flying was considered hazardous duty, combat flying in the air corps was voluntary, which meant the airmen had things pretty good. "If we didn't get what we wanted," Grimes said, "we'd threaten to quit." Of course, quitting didn't mean quitting the army. Quitting the air corps meant being reassigned to the military police or worse, the infantry. "No one wanted either one, so you continued flying."

After nearly a year of flight and gunnery training, Grimes prepared to head overseas. He thought he was going to the Pacific theater, and, in fact, already had mosquito netting and a jungle kit stored in his pack. But while the planes were revving their engines on the runway, his orders were changed. He was heading to England. Grimes was ecstatic. "I really wanted to go to England in the worst way. I'm a big fan of Kipling and I'd read all the stories of King Arthur."

He arrived at Grafton-Underwood, home of the 384th Bombardment Group (Heavy), 545th Bombardment Squadron, 8th Air Force, in May 1943. The base has the distinction of being the departure site for the planes that dropped the first and last bombs on Germany during the war. More than 1,500 airmen from that base alone were killed in combat over Europe.

Grimes, who had just turned nineteen, became part of the ten-man crew of a B-17 Flying Fortress. Because he was small, he was assigned to the dual fifty-caliber tail guns. The passageway between the plane's waist and tail was narrow, so only small men were chosen as tail gunners. Also in his crew were a pilot, copilot, navigator, bombardier, ball turret gunner, radioman/gunner, engineer/top turret gunner, and two waist gunners. All but the gunners were officers, but Grimes eventually was promoted to sergeant.

His first combat mission was in June 1943—a daylight bombing raid on Nazi-held Antwerp, Belgium. Forty bombers left England in the morning escorted by British Spitfires. The Spitfire's top speed was 400 miles per hour, compared with the B-17's 295 miles per hour, and the faster planes were forced to bank back and forth in order to stay with the bombers. Because that tactic used up so much fuel, the Spitfires only accompanied the bombers part way; they turned back over France. "Half the mission would be without escort," Grimes said. "The Germans got to know that. They'd wait until the Spitfires left and then they'd come in."

The gunners were instructed to shoot at any unknown plane with fewer than four engines that pointed its nose at them. Several Spitfire pilots learned the hard way not to get too close to the heavily armed Fortresses. Grimes said from the side you couldn't mistake the Spitfire's distinctive shape, but you couldn't always tell friend from foe when the plane was coming straight at you. The cheeky British maintained their sense of humor. "They used to say, 'We lost more good men to American gunners than we did to the Germans,'" Grimes said.

He'll never forget his first experience in combat—the German Messerschmitts swooping down upon them like graceful birds of prey, guns flashing, the explosions of flak dotting the sky like deadly white flowers. In a way, he said, it was almost beautiful—and completely unreal. "It was something out of Hollywood," Grimes said. Although a part of him knew the German fighters were shooting real bullets, and he knew just how little protection the B-17 offered—the airmen joked half-seriously that a pellet from a BB gun could pierce the thin metal skin—Grimes wasn't afraid. He was too fascinated by what he was seeing. Only after it was over did he realize "I didn't touch my guns," he said. "I forgot I had two guns to fire." He was embarrassed about it until he talked to a friend, who told him he'd done the same thing on his first mission.

Grimes never did develop a healthy fear of Luftwaffe pilots. He said shooting them down was easy. "The minute you pointed your guns at a German plane, you'd see a burst of smoke and flame," he said. "It just seemed like it was so easy because they went down so nice." But during his seven months of almost continuous combat, he never put in a claim for downing an enemy fighter. He said there were too many other gunners firing at the same plane to know whose bullets actually reached the mark.

Grimes said he was much more concerned about flak. "The flak you couldn't control. It happened, it was there." When a big 155-millimeter shell exploded, he said, it was like a giant hand slapped the plane.

Although aerial combat retained its surreal aspect, Grimes said there was one big difference between fight scenes in the movies and real life—the noise, or rather the lack of it. It's not that there wasn't noise; the roar of the plane's engines tended to drown everything else out. But the crew members all wore aviators' caps with padded earflaps, which served to both protect them from the cold and muffle the engine's roar. So basically, Grimes said, "we had no sound. We're fighting this war and all you could hear was the [muffled] sound of the explosions." Even the racketing sound of his fifty-caliber machine guns was subdued. He said he gets a little nervous when he watches movies about air combat because the sound is much louder. "[Noise] is the most terrifying thing," he said. "We didn't experience any of that because it was deadened. . . . It wasn't that bad when it was happening."

Late 1943 was a grim time for U.S. airmen. Nearly a third of them were being shot down before they completed their twenty-five missions. On August 17, 1943, 230 B-17s bombed the ball bearing works at Schweinfurt, Germany. Production at the huge plant, which produced 70 percent of the ball bearings for Germany's aircraft industry, was cut by 38 percent. But it was a costly raid for the Allies; they lost sixty planes; the Germans, only twenty-five. Grimes's plane was the only one of nine from the squadron to return home. A second raid on Schweinfurt on October 14 disrupted production for six weeks, but the U.S. lost another sixty bombers and their crews. Grimes said many of the German fighters were from the "Yellow Nose Squadron," also called "Göring's Circus" because the pilots painted the planes' noses and landing gear bright yellow and red.

During the raids, the bomber formations were so close that the gunners had to be careful not to shoot their own planes. Sometimes being careful wasn't enough. Grimes said one time a spent fifty-caliber shell fell into the propeller of a B-17, turning the shell into pieces of brass shrapnel that tore through the plane's cockpit and severely wounded the pilot. To Grimes, a B-17 going down was "the most heartbreaking sight of all." "The B-17 was such a beautiful and graceful plane, everyone fell in love with it." And to see it nose earthward and begin to spin, the centrifugal force preventing the crew from bailing out . . . "It was such a heartbreaking sight," he said, "you felt like crying."

Somewhere over Norway, 1943—At his tail gun position, Grimes scanned the ground for targets. Usually the B-17s bombed from nearly thirty thousand feet, but on missions into occupied territory, they never released their bombs unless they had visual confirmation, which meant flying much closer to the ground. "In Germany," he said, "it was a different story." That day the bombers had to come in lower than usual to get beneath the cloud cover. They had been told their target was an aluminum plant, but in reality they would be dropping their ordnance—six thousand pounds per plane—on a Nazi heavy-water plant. Grimes, however, wasn't worried about their main target. That was the bombardier's concern. He was more interested in the targets he could shoot—like trains, German staff cars, and even people. The Norwegians had been warned of the attack by the local underground, so chances were anyone caught out in the open was German. "It was the first time I strafed the ground as a tail gunner," he said. "They said anything that moves is German, so shoot it. . . . It was great."

In December 1943, the U.S. Eighth Air Force and the British Royal Air Force combined to bomb Hamburg. The RAF did night saturation bombing for seven nights while the Americans handled pinpoint bombing during the days. The main targets were the city's port and submarine pens, but as was often the case, most of the city was destroyed in the process, and thousands of civilians were incinerated in the ensuing firestorms.

Grimes's B-17 was in formation, headed to Hamburg, when one of the engines started acting up. Pilot Joe Vander Haeghen told the crew he was only getting half power from the engine. He suggested that they take a vote: either stay with the formation and try to complete their bombing run or abort immediately and get back to England before they ran into any German fighters. They all knew that once the fighters attacked, "to fall out of formation was certain death," Grimes said. The crew decided to go on with the mission. They soon ran into heavy flak over Germany, which knocked out two more of their engines. Now they had no choice but to drop out and try to make it home on the power they had left. Although German fighters were in the area, the bombers were being escorted by long-range P-51 Mustangs, several of which peeled off to accompany the limping Fortress back to the coast. They kept the German fighters at bay until the B-17 reached the North Sea. Suddenly, the bomber was all alone.

Not long after that, their already damaged engine died, leaving them with one working engine. Vander Haeghen ordered the crew to jettison everything that wasn't bolted down, including the guns and ammo. They'd dropped their bombs before leaving Germany, and the bomb bay doors were frozen open. Grimes said the plane was so close to the water that the spray was coming in through the doors and freezing on the metal surfaces.

About the only thing they kept on board was the radio, which they used to send out an SOS. They were unaware that the RAF had begun tracking them as soon as they left the coast, and rescue ships were already moving into position. Grimes recalls Vander Haeghen nonchalantly walking back to the radio room, where the crew was assembled, his cap pushed back, a candy bar in his hand. "I don't think we're going to make it," he said, "so be prepared for ditching." Somehow they stayed aloft and even managed to climb to three thousand feet. They arrived back at Grafton-Underwood forty-five minutes behind the bombers returning from Hamburg. By then, the other airmen were already dividing up their clothing and gear, which was standard practice when planes didn't return from a mission. "That was a close call," Grimes said. "But the thing is, when you're nineteen years old, things don't scare you. Now, I'd be scared to death. Then it was just part of the mission."

The dying continued. Although German fighter pilots estimated it took 3,343 rounds to shoot down a single bomber, Allied casualties continued to mount. When it was all over, the Allies had lost 160,000 airmen and 33,700 planes during the air war over Europe. And as the war pushed deeper into the Third Reich, more and more German civilians had no place to hide from the high-altitude raids. By the end of the war, more than 305,000 German civilians were dead, including 35,000 killed in Dresden on the terrible, fiery night of February 13, 1945.

In mid-January 1944, a newspaper photographer took a picture of Grimes's B-17, nicknamed "We Dood It," and its kneeling crew as a chaplain blessed them prior to a mission. More than a month later, the picture would appear in the *New York Times.* American readers couldn't know that the bomber had been shot down over Germany two weeks before the photo was published. Only three members of the crew survived. "It was the last picture of our crew," Grimes said. Had they survived, they would have all been able to return home after that flight. Grimes recalled, "I got shot down on my twenty-fifth. I had my bags packed, I was ready to leave."

Their mission was to Brunswick, Germany. Grimes recalls they ran into enemy fighters as soon as they crossed the German border, but "our group wasn't hit too bad." Their altitude was twenty-nine thousand feet, and the cloud "ceiling" thousands of feet below protected them from flak. Grimes remembers an explosion—a buddy in an adjacent bomber told him after the war that his plane was hit by a rocket from a German Junkers—and then silence. The plane's intercom system was knocked out, which was bad news for the tail gunner, who was isolated from the rest of the plane. "I had no way of knowing whether we should bail out or not," he said.

Grimes thought about bailing out, but he didn't want to end up a German prisoner if it could be avoided. He'd seen crews bail out of seemingly crippled planes only to see the pilot go into a dive, put out the fire and make it back to friendly territory. "I said, 'I'm staying with it until I know for sure.' "

That didn't take long. "The flames kept getting worse and worse and the plane started wobbling," he said, which usually meant no one was flying the plane. Dizzy from lack of oxygen, he headed for the front of the aircraft, where he passed out. He remembers crawling to the open doorway and looking into the bright blue sky, then everything went dark.

"When I came to, I was falling face down," he said. He was surrounded by a gray mist—clouds or ground fog he didn't know—so he quickly pulled his ripcord. His chute opened, and his descent almost seemed to stop. There was another parachute in the distance, and the two men hollered to each other. "It was such silence," Grimes said, "you could talk in a normal tone of voice." He found out later from his buddy in the nearby bomber that the engineer and copilot had also escaped the crippled bomber, which exploded in midair. Grimes was thrown clear of the wreckage, miraculously uninjured.

Suddenly, three Me-109s came out of the clouds and began circling him. He'd heard stories about German pilots machine-gunning Allied flyers or chopping them to pieces with their propellers, but he had never seen it happen. He was armed with a forty-five, but it wouldn't do much good against the Messerschmitts' machine guns, should the pilot decide to use them.

But Grimes said that most German pilots, like their Allied counterparts, followed a strict code of honor. "They didn't shoot us in parachutes, we didn't shoot them," he said. "There was a lot of chivalry in the air war." He told of one incident in which an American gunner intentionally shot a German pilot, who had parachuted out of his downed fighter. The gunner's reasoning was that since they were over German territory, the pilot would most likely survive to fly again and kill more American flyers. But the gunner was severely disciplined when he returned to base, Grimes said. "They did everything but court-martial him."

This time, he witnessed an example of German chivalry. The enemy fighters circled the chutists for several minutes, radioing their positions to ground spotters. Then, Grimes said, "They dipped their wings and threw a salute . . . and went right back up to the battle. . . . I was thinking to myself, jeez, they're not all bad."

After the German fighters were gone, Grimes knew his problems weren't over. They were just beginning. He had no idea what kind of reception awaited him on the ground. He could see a small village materializing below him. There had been ominous reports of townspeople capturing and hanging downed Allied airmen from telegraph poles in Berlin and Hamburg, where civilian deaths were high, so he kept his forty-five handy. He landed in the village of Obermkirchen "right in the burgomaster's backyard," he said. He estimated his descent had taken twelve to fourteen minutes, which meant he had opened his chute at about ten thousand feet. That meant that while he was unconscious, he had fallen nineteen thousand feet.

Immediately after landing, Grimes was surrounded by a large group of townspeople and armed soldiers. As he handed over his weapons, several old women in the crowd shook their heads and wept. He knew a little German and recognized the words "so young." For the first time he realized that his face had been burned in the explosion. "It [must have] looked terrible," he said, but the wounds were superficial. He also noticed that he was covered in blood, but it belonged to the waist gunner he'd fallen on in the plane. But the German women didn't know that, and he was touched by their sympathy for him. "They were actually crying. They thought I was wounded," he said. "Those people are crying for me. I'm thinking, where are those vicious Germans?"

Frankfurt, Germany, February 1944—Grimes's first two weeks in captivity were spent alone in a bare cell in Dulag Luft, the main interrogation center located in the heart of devastated Frankfurt. He'd seen Frankfurt only a few days before, but then his view of the city had been from thirty thousand feet. "Between the twenty-fifth and thirtieth [of January]," he said, "we bombed Frankfurt three times." Solitary confinement was an effective tactic, he said.

By the end of the two weeks, "you're talking to the walls, you're talking to the bed posts." When they finally came for him, he was ready to talk. The interrogation room, he recalls, had a large swastika flag draped on the wall and a uniformed German officer, who greeted him in perfect English. He would see the scene recounted many times in movies after the war. "I have more respect for Hollywood than I did before the war," he said.

Grimes had been told in training to answer no questions, to give only his name, rank, and serial number, but that was too much to ask from the nineteen-year-old. "I didn't tell them anything of importance," he said, "but I wanted conversation." The German officer began the interrogation by telling Grimes that he'd lived in New Jersey for five years before the war, working as a commercial skywriter. However, he had actually been a spy and had used cameras mounted on his plane's wings to photograph military bases along the East Coast. Then he asked Grimes at which base he was stationed in England. Grimes replied that he couldn't say. But when the officer showed him an aerial photo of Grafton-Underwood, with the distinctive GU at the end of the runway, Grimes raised his eyebrows. "He [the German] smiled because he got his answer," Grimes said. The officer also asked Grimes about a new secret weapon the Allies were supposedly testing. Nicknamed "The Grapefruit," the weapon was a bomb with wings that extended, which was designed to glide a mile for every one thousand feet of altitude, theoretically enabling the Allies to bomb cities thirty miles miles away. The only problem was, when the bombs were tested in combat, the wings fell off. "None of them did what they were supposed to do," Grimes said. He told the German he knew nothing about them. Despite the pleasant tone of the interrogation, Grimes had no illusions about the Nazis' ability to get information if they really wanted it. "Anybody would tell anything if pushed far enough," he said. Fortunately for him, the officer didn't think he knew enough to be worth the effort. "Not even once did he threaten me," Grimes said. "I was sorry that it ended because I was really enjoying it."

In mid-February, Grimes and hundreds of other captured airmen were crowded into boxcars and shipped across Germany toward German-occupied Russia. They were allowed off the train only once during the ten-day trip—one night in Berlin, during an RAF bombing raid, they were served cups of coffee by the German Red Cross—so those who had managed to keep penknives used them to cut holes in the floors of the boxcars, which they used as makeshift latrines. "The guys who couldn't had a very miserable trip," he said.

When the train arrived at Stalag Luft 6 on the Lithuanian border, the camp commandant told them their war was over. But as far as Grimes was concerned, a new phase had just begun. Now his efforts would be devoted to escape. "I was one of the main tunnel diggers," he said. "I was the smallest guy, so I was always the tunnel initiator." In scenes straight out of *The Great Escape,* Grimes spent much of the time underground, burrowing like a mole through the sandy soil, and because of the high water table, usually he worked half submerged. But none of the tunnels led to freedom. The soil was so marshy that it was impossible to adequately brace the tunnel walls against the weight of the trucks that passed back and forth in the camp. Within a few months, the camp was undermined with aborted tunnels, which would often collapse. Every time a tunnel was discovered by the guards, there would be punishments and reprisals—bed boards used to reinforce the tunnels would be confiscated, and Red Cross parcels would be withheld—but that didn't stop the digging. Work would always begin on a new tunnel. The Germans' attitude seemed to be one of grudging tolerance. They knew tunnels were being built, they expected the flyers to try to escape, but so long as no one was getting out, they let the work go on. At least it kept the prisoners occupied, which was indeed the case. "It makes time pass very quickly," Grimes said.

In July 1944, the Germans began evacuating Luft 6. The Russians were in the middle of their summer offensive, and it wouldn't be long before they reached the camp. The airmen were loaded onto boxcars—packed so tightly they had to stand— at Heydekrug and transported half a day's journey to Memel on the Baltic Sea. There they were herded onto a rusty coal boat, on which the Russian hammer and sickle were still visible on the funnel, and forced to climb single file down a ladder into the ship's hold. Thousands of prisoners were crammed in like sardines, and once the hatch was closed, they were thrown into complete darkness.

For Grimes, it was one of the worst experiences of the war. No one could move, and the heat and the smell were almost unbearable. Sanitary arrangements consisted of a bucket that was hoisted up and down the ladder—often the contents were spilled on the men below, who were unable to move out of the way. For the sick, suffering from diarrhea and vomiting, there was no extra room. Everyone suffered. "You really started to feel like an animal," Grimes said, "a trapped animal."

The men also had to contend with the fear of being bombed by their own planes or blown up by one of the thousands of mines sown by Allied aircraft in the Baltic. The prisoners were at least fifty feet below the waterline, Grimes said, and "it wasn't a very well-built boat to begin with." The trip took nearly three days, during which they had no food or water. At the Swinemunde docks, they were loaded back onto boxcars and transported to Kiefeheide, a small farming community near the Polish frontier.

The airmen didn't know that there had been some recent changes in the German POW system. Until April 1944, the *Wehrmacht*—the German Army—ran the POW camps. But in response to the "great escape" from Luft 3, Hitler not only ordered the execution of fifty men involved in the escape, he also put all of the camps under the jurisdiction of the Gestapo.

The airmen, shackled to one another at ankles and wrists, got off the train in groups of five hundred, and Luftwaffe guards from Luft 4—their destination—began herding them from the train station toward town. As townspeople crowded the cobbled streets, they were joined by soldiers with dogs, young *Kreigesmarine,* and SS guards. Many of them had rifles with bayonets.

Grimes doesn't know if what happened next was an act of inspired cruelty by individuals or a case of organized violence intended to break the spirit of the POWs. Regardless, the helpless airmen were about to begin a run for their lives. The prisoners were unshackled and ordered to run all the way to camp, a distance of several miles. To spur them on, the soldiers set the dogs on them and prodded them with bayonets and rifle butts. As the prisoners ran through the narrow streets of Kiefeheide, the townspeople lined up to curse and spit on them and yelled encouragement to the German soldiers. Many of the POWs, already weakened by malnutrition and illness, began falling by the wayside with the dogs tearing at them. Others were beaten or bayoneted as they lay exhausted, unable to move. Some of the *Kreigesmarine* would yell the names of German cities bombed by the Allies each time they stabbed POWs with their bayonets.

The POWs did their best to help each other, carrying or dragging those who couldn't keep up. Some of the stronger prisoners moved to the outside of the columns to protect the weaker prisoners in the center. When they finally reached the camp, some of them had as many as fifty bayonet wounds. They were the lucky ones. Grimes said they never found out how many didn't survive the infamous Heydekrug Run. "We just know there were an awful lot of missing."

If the POWs thought life had been hard at Luft 6, they were in for a shock when they reached Luft 4. They quickly found out things were much different with the Gestapo running things. There were no longer any coordinated efforts to escape, Grimes said. "They said, 'Anybody escaping now is killed.' They meant it and we knew it." And no one wanted to be caught outside the barracks after dark when they set the dogs loose. "They weren't like *Hogan's Heroes* dogs," he said dryly.

"You tend to forget the unpleasantries and only remember the good things. But it was a totally boring time. A day lasted a week, and food was always a problem. There was always hunger," Grimes said. "There was no such thing as a meal. The bread would come in, hopefully every day. We called it sawdust." A loaf generally had to feed seven to ten men. The morning meal consisted of ersatz coffee. "Somebody said it was made of burnt acorns. That's what it tasted like." Grimes took up smoking to take away the taste of the coffee and buffer the hunger pangs. Lunch was a "potato soup" made of ancient-looking dehydrated vegetables. "They were all full of maggots," Grimes said. "The new guys would pick out the maggots. The old guys would just close their eyes and eat." When a horse died, there would be a little meat in the soup. In the evening, usually there would be another bread ration and more ersatz coffee. "I didn't weigh a lot to begin with," Grimes said, "but we all lost a lot of weight. . . . The Germans, the guys that were guarding us, weren't getting fed much better than us," he said, but a few of them risked their lives to slip the prisoners an extra loaf of bread or a little barley in their soup.

And then there was "the uncertainty of not knowing when they would give the orders to get rid of all prisoners," he said. "That was the worst part. Not knowing what was going to happen."

In February 1945, the Russians were closing in again, and the camp was evacuated. The prisoners were marched all the way to Hamburg, and by spring they were being held in a deserted pottery factory in Annaberg, on the Elbe River. During an Allied air raid, the last of the guards ran off and Grimes and a buddy, Vic, who could speak some Russian, escaped into the countryside. After hiding out for a few days, they decided to head east—away from the advancing Allied troops.

Grimes had too much bitterness bottled up inside to leave the war just then. "I hated those bastards and I wanted to get it out of my system." He and Vic spent several days cutting German communication lines; eventually, tired and hungry, they wound up at a farmhouse outside Annaberg. The airmen told the old farmer if he'd hide them from the Nazis still roaming the area, they'd put in a good word for him when the Russians arrived. The man took them in, fed them, and let them hide in his family's barn when a retreating German infantry division passed by. When the Red Army arrived on April 23—Grimes's birthday—Vic told the Russian soldiers that the farmer was a good Communist who had sheltered Russian POWs. "His farm was the only one that wasn't burned," Grimes said.

At first Grimes helped the Russians round up German soldiers—until he found out that any Germans with SS tattoos were being summarily executed, and other German soldiers were being shipped to Russia as slave labor. Grimes saw more atrocities committed in the two months he spent with the Russians than he had during more than a year as a German prisoner of war. "The Russians treated them [German civilians] horribly, raped women. . . . They were savages. They were just like animals." Once he and Vic were with a group of Russian soldiers when one of them, without provocation, started firing a machine gun at a house. They could hear a woman screaming inside, but when the Americans complained to the Russian officer, he just looked bored. "Who cares, they're only Germans," he said. "That's what they did in Russia."

Living with the German farmer and his family had helped Grimes get rid of his bitterness. He had come to realize that he didn't hate the German people, who, in many ways, were like his loved ones at home. But when Grimes and his friend were ready to leave the Russians, the Russians weren't ready to let them go. Even then the Russians didn't trust the Americans and refused to let them cross the Elbe River. Finally, in June 1945, a U.S. officer negotiated their release and that of thirty other Allied POWs. After two long years of combat and captivity, Grimes was finally headed home.

Dreams of Flying

Above Modena, Italy, February 14, 1944—Lt. Paul Hoover's B-17 had just reached the target zone when a flak burst sent a piece of jagged metal chewing through his number two engine. Moments later, his bombardier released six thousand pounds of high-explosive valentines over the target—a railroad yard. Hoover's B-17 remained in tight formation as the Flying Fortresses banked over the ocean and headed toward their home base at Foggia.

But Hoover was having problems. Although his number two engine was out, the propeller continued to spin. The greater the plane's speed, the faster the propeller spun. He had seen the propeller of another B-17 go into an uncontrolled spin on a previous mission. The propeller had eventually overheated and broken away, slicing through the cockpit and sending the plane spiraling into another bomber, knocking them both from the sky. The twenty-three-year-old pilot decided that wasn't going to happen with his plane. He was still over the Mediterranean, about twenty miles from the Italian coast, when he dropped out of formation. He leveled off at eight thousand feet and cut the plane's speed from 160 to 135 miles per hour. His number two prop slowed down.

Everything went fine until they were just south of Rome. There they were supposed to make a ninety-degree turn to avoid passing over German-held territory on their approach to Foggia. However, the navigator miscalculated, and before they knew what was happening, they were directly over a nest of enemy antiaircraft guns. Flak exploded on all sides of the plane, punching fist-sized holes in the fuselage. "They shot the tar out of us," Hoover recalled forty-eight years later. "Those fragments would go through aluminum like paper." Three members of the crew were wounded—the tail gunner, the bombardier, and the copilot—but Hoover managed to avoid a direct hit, and soon they were out of range. Then, twenty minutes from Foggia, another engine quit. Hoover finished the flight on two engines. "That was probably one of my worst missions," he said.

He didn't know just how close a call he'd had until he was safely on the ground. That's when he noticed a piece of shrapnel embedded in the back of his seat. It had sheared through the metal cockpit and cut neatly through his parachute strap, missing his body by inches. "It's a wonder it didn't take my backbone out," he said.

Hoover had always wanted to fly. As a child, he had been inspired by Charles Lindbergh's nonstop, solo flight from New York to Paris in the *Spirit of St. Louis.* The oldest of ten children, he grew up in Eureka Springs, Arkansas. His family was poor, and when he was fifteen, he got a job with Franklin D. Roosevelt's Civilian Conservation Corps to help support his family. In 1940, he went to Little Rock and joined the army. His father had fought in France in World War I with a field artillery unit, and Hoover followed in his footsteps, joining the Thirty-first Field Artillery Battalion, Seventh Division. He made staff sergeant nines months to the day after his enlistment. But he never forgot his dream of flying.

In 1942, he was faced with a decision: He could go for an officer's commission in the army or give up his stripes and thirty-two dollars a month to become an air cadet. He decided to join the army air corps. He was sent to flight training in Texas, and in late 1943, he picked up a brand new B-17 in Grand Island, Nebraska. His orders were to proceed to England to join the Eighth Air Force. His plane had a minor brake problem, and he stopped over in Syracuse, New York, for repairs. While he was waiting, he received a new packet of orders. His plane was one of fifteen B-17s being rerouted. He was to go south through Florida, and when he reached South America, he was to open a second packet of orders marked *secret.* Hoover opened the packet as soon as he and his crew left the U.S. coast: they were heading to Italy.

Hoover's crew became a replacement outfit for the Ninety-ninth Bomb Group of the Fifteenth Air Force stationed at Foggia, a once-bustling Italian town that had been bombed to rubble by the Allies. "It had been blown to pieces by both aircraft bombing and field artillery," he said. "We were not welcome there."

When Hoover arrived—January 9, 1944—Salerno and Naples had been liberated, but much of the rest of the peninsula, including Rome, was still in enemy hands. The rugged Italian terrain concealed numerous German 88s and tanks (buried to their turrets), and the heavily fortified Gustav Line, anchored by 1,700-foot Mt. Cassino, had stalled the Allied advance.

Not long after his arrival, Hoover was informed that his new B-17 was being given to one of the ranking officers. He received a replacement plane. "I had the oldest airplane in the place," he said, "but it had the best engines." The B-17 was arguably the finest bomber of World War II. Superchargers on its four engines gave it more power than other bombers, and pilots considered it an easy plane to fly. "It was easy to land, and it was fairly easy to fly in formation," Hoover said. When taking off, you simply set the controls for a climb. "You didn't have to slam the wheel around or the pedals [to get off the ground]. It didn't take a lot of physical effort to fly the airplane."

Hoover's first combat mission was a railroad marshaling yard in Prato, Italy, on February 9. He described the five-and-a-half-hour mission as "routine," with plenty of flak but no enemy fighters. His second mission, to Poggibonsi, Italy, targeted another rail yard. "What they were trying to do is break up transportation, rail transportation," he said. That mission attracted the Luftwaffe, and Hoover, at the extreme rear of the formation, had to stay on course as waves of Messerschmitts tattooed the planes with fifty-caliber machine gun rounds. "[We're] the tail end of the whole group. We're really being shot at first. It was a tight spot, but it's like all the rest of them. It's important."

Was he scared?

"You knew that you had enough to do just to fly the aircraft in formation," he said. "You're professional enough at that point not to [panic]. I was responsible for nine other fellas, and I had to take care of them."

On February 25, 1944, Hoover's bomb group took part in a raid on Regensberg, Germany, the site of a huge ball bearing and Messerschmitt plant. The bombers went without fighter escort—there were no fighter planes with sufficient range to accompany the bombers all the way into Germany and back—and came under attack as soon as they reached the northern edge of the Adriatic Sea. The attacks continued steadily, and according to the flight log Hoover kept during the war, the squadron lost twenty-seven of fifty-one planes on that mission. "It was just unreal that you'd lose that many in one attack," he said. Later, Hoover and his crew received the Distinguished Flying Cross for their part in the successful mission.

During the next few months, Hoover participated in bombing missions in southern France, Germany, Hungary, and Yugoslavia. He also participated in four raids on the Ploesti oil fields in southeastern Romania, considered the most heavily defended air target on earth at that time. Following one Ploesti mission on April 5, he noted in his log, "Flak and a lot of fighters." "It was another one of those tough missions," he said. "We never did have an easy mission to Ploesti."

By early June, Hoover had completed forty-nine combat missions; he needed just one more to be eligible to rotate back to the States. His commander asked him to volunteer for a shuttle mission to Poltava, Russia, and Hoover (and his crew) accepted. Once they reached Russia, they made a bombing raid on Romania, then returned to Poltava before taking part in a final mission during their return flight to Italy. Hoover arrived in Foggia with fifty-two missions to his credit.

He returned to the States later in 1944 on a converted passenger liner, relieved that his war was over and grateful for the combination of luck and divine guidance that had kept him and his crew alive. "The good Lord took care of us. There were no deaths in my crew. We had men shot up, but no deaths."

After the war, he stopped flying but stayed in the air force, working in communications and electronics. He wasn't called back to active duty during the Korean War. "I hadn't flown as a bomber pilot in five years," he said, "so they didn't recall me." Hoover retired at the rank of lieutenant colonel in 1966. "It was a great career for me," he said. Later, he went back to school and used G.I. benefits to get a degree from Syracuse University. He never got a civilian pilot's license, hasn't touched a plane's controls in years, but sometimes he still thinks about flying and the war that gave him the opportunity to realize his dream. "I don't really think I was the best pilot who ever lived," he said. "But I liked to fly."

Thirty-five Missions and Home

Fear. It's something you live with in war. The fear of dying, of being horribly maimed. Fear of the unknown. Bob Wood knows all about fear. As a B-24 bomber pilot, he flew thirty-five missions in Europe during World War II. Budapest, Munich, Bleckhammer, and Vienna weren't just scenic European cities. They were important military and industrial centers of the Third Reich.

The sites of oil refineries, railroad marshaling yards, bridges and naval bases, all were targeted by the Allies for obliteration. Wood still remembers the anti-aircraft guns, the pounding flak, planes exploding in midair, the senseless, random death. There was always fear. You handled it. You never let it get in the way of doing your job. But it was never far away. "I never was comfortable," Wood said. "I was scared. Anyone who said he wasn't—I never met him or he's a damn liar."

On one mission he was flying behind the lead formation. They had just reached their initial point (IP)—a landmark, such as a town or the fork in a river, about twenty miles from their target and easily identified from above—when the sky up ahead was suddenly filled with smoke and debris. Wood remembers telling his copilot that was the biggest wall of flak he'd ever seen. "That's not flak," the copilot said. "That's airplanes."

Wood said once a plane was on the final bomb run, which usually lasted from six to eight minutes, the pilot flew at a steady altitude, which gave anti-aircraft gunners time to find their range. On this trip, the lead plane of the doomed formation had apparently been fixed on the wrong target then stayed too long on the bomb run while the crew looked for the right one. Wood said he learned from the experience. "That day I fully made up my mind that I wasn't going to be scared," he said. "If you're going to get it, you're going to get it."

Wood graduated from Harrisonville High School in Cass County, Missouri, and moved to Kansas City to attend the Fry Aviation Institute. Eventually, he got a job in San Diego building B-24 Liberators. There he got to know the heavy bomber inside and out and even was allowed to fly one once. He was inducted into the army air corps February 1943 and attended Drake University as an aviation student. In March 1944, he graduated from multiengine flying school in Texas and requested assignment to a B-24 squadron because of his familiarity with the bomber. The request was quickly approved. "They were not popular," Wood said of the B-24s. "The B-17s were the ones the movies were about. If you asked for a B-24, you got it."

Unlike the sleek Flying Fortresses, the Liberators were ungainly, to say the least. Nicknamed the "Pregnant Cow," the plane was built so low to the ground you had to stoop to climb through the bomb bay doors. But when it came to delivering ordnance to Hitler's backyard, the B-24 had few equals. Fortresses were better engineered, could fly at higher altitudes, and were more durable—"They could take a little more flak than us," Wood admits—but the Liberators were faster and had significantly larger bomb capacity. They were the draft horses of the Allies' strategic bombing campaign in Europe. They weren't pretty, but they got the job done.

Wood and this crew arrived at the Pantanella air base in Italy on the Adriatic Sea in August 1944 and were assigned to the 464th Bomb Group, 779th Bomb Squadron, 15th Air Force. About a week prior to their arrival, Wood said, the bomber command had suspended attacks on the Ploesti oil fields. The sprawling oil refinery, called the "fuel tank of the Wehrmacht," had been a target of U.S. bombers since July 12, 1942, the date of the first U.S. bombing raid on Europe in World War II. During that low-level raid, thirteen B-24s attacked the vast oil complex but did only slight damage.

A year later, it was a much different story. On August 1, 1943, 177 Liberators flew beneath German radar and into heavy flak; 53 bombers were shot down, and 310 airmen perished, but production at Ploesti was temporarily slashed by 40 percent. Five airmen were awarded the Congressional Medal of Honor, and all the crews received the Distinguished Flying Cross. By the late summer of 1944, Ploesti was a smoking shell, all but useless to the Nazis. The Fifteenth Air Force had turned its attention to other targets, with which Wood soon would become acquainted.

Wood, who started his tour as a lieutenant and eventually reached the rank of captain, recalled that the tent he and his crew were given on arrival had belonged to a crew that hadn't made it back from a mission. They had to clean out the missing men's personal effects. "That was a nice welcome," he said. Later, Wood and several members of his crew visited an old Italian barber, who had set up shop under an olive tree and was giving the airmen haircuts. Using his Italian-speaking engineer as a translator, Wood asked the barber how he felt about losing the war—the Italian government, having overthrown Mussolini, had signed an armistice with the Allies in September 1943. "I didn't lose the war," the barber replied mildly. "I'm at home and you're still fighting."

Wood's first mission, on September 1, was a raid on a railroad marshaling yard in Szajol, Hungary. Wood, his radio operator, and his tail gunner flew with a veteran crew on what turned out to be "a milk run," a term airman used to denote easy targets. There was no flak, and they dropped their load of twenty five hundred-pound bombs with no complications.

Wood admits that army air corps duty was somewhat different from the other branches of service. There wasn't a lot of formality during combat missions. Uniforms were a rarity. The standard airman's clothing included long underwear, a heated flight suit, boots, and the trademark leather bomber jacket. Titles were often ignored. Wood's crew just called him Chief. Air corps food was generally better than the K- and C-rations the infantry had to live on a good part of the time. Wood said one time they had to eat corned beef every day for two months, but it was always hot. There was a regular beer quota, and once Wood's air base received a delivery of vanilla ice cream powder. Since there was no ice, they had to experiment. "Vanilla ice cream flavored pancakes aren't too bad," he said.

On September 10, Wood and his crew got some bad news: They were going to Vienna. With Ploesti out of the mission rotation, Vienna was a primary target (only Berlin itself was better defended). Vienna had a large oil refinery and was protected by huge antiaircraft guns mounted on railroad cars. "When they said you're going to Vienna," Wood said, "it was a bad deal." However, when the plane was still about an hour away from the IP, its number one engine shut down. Wood was forced to "feather" the engine—a process in which the pilot turns the plane so that the stalled propeller blade is parallel to the wind—which cuts down on drag and helps maintain air speed. With only three engines, he and his crew dropped out of formation and headed for home.

Wood flew his first few missions with seasoned pilots, who stressed the importance of maintaining air speed and altitude. Once you lose either, you're courting disaster. He recalled one time he was on the ground watching a plane come in for a landing. The leading edge of one wing had been shot up, and the plane had lost speed. As he watched, the plane's nose came up, the engines stalled, and the plane crashed on the tarmac. There were no survivors.

Flak from antiaircraft guns was a constant companion. "The damn stuff hit the airplane," Wood said, "it sounded like hail on a tin roof." During a mission to Munich, which took them over the formidable Alps, Wood's crew saw a plane explode in midair, an apparent flak casualty. A mission summary written by a crew member described the incident: "At the IP we noticed a group just going over the target. Then, for the first time, we saw a plane blow up. There wasn't much to describe—just a burst of flames and then parts filling that part of the sky." To combat the antiaircraft guns, the waist gunners threw out chaff—long rolls of shredded aluminum—which was designed to confuse the Nazis' radar. Enemy fighters were another obvious threat. During a mission to bomb a marshaling yard in Bratislava, Czechoslovakia, Wood ran into a squadron of Me-109s shortly after completing his bomb run. One of the Messerschmitts flew directly across the Liberator's nose. "I was close enough that I could see the pilot, and that's too damn close," Wood said. Junior McKenzie, the tail gunner, was credited with shooting down two of the fighters.

Not all of their missions were considered successful. During one raid into northern Italy, bad weather obscured the target. In an effort to get credit for the mission, they went looking for a "target of opportunity." They found what they thought was a ball bearing factory and bombed it to rubble, but later reconnaissance photos showed that it had been an abandoned brick factory, which wasn't very high on the bomber command's list of strategic targets. Not surprisingly, they didn't get credit for the mission.

Wood has seen Hollywood's depiction of the air war, and he said movies like *Memphis Belle* were "pretty realistic," although he and his crew never had a single plane they considered their own. "You just took what was assigned to you," he said. They had their share of close calls—like the time a chunk of spinning shrapnel barely missed their startled tail gunner, and the mission where Wood had to land with a blown nose tire. But "Wood's Crew," as they referred to themselves, survived thirty-five missions with only one injury, which occurred when their navigator decided to make sure the heater was working properly by sticking his finger into the whirling blades.

Wood spent less than a year overseas. Although airmen were required to log fifty missions before they were rotated home, particularly dangerous missions counted double. And the men also received extra rotation points when they had to fly over major battlefields and when they were promoted. Wood received his fifty points on his thirty-fifth mission and was out of the service and home by V-J Day. "We were in and out pretty fast," he said. "I just had to be in the right place at the right time."

"Now for You the War Is Over"

Marvin Boyce has forgotten a lot over the last fifty years. For one thing, he has no memory of jumping out of his crippled B-17 over Germany. "You don't have time to think," said the former pilot, recalling that clear, midsummer day in 1944. "It's all reflexes. You just respond to the situation." But he does remember telling his copilot to get the hell out of the plane. And after his chute popped open, he remembers the breathtaking view of the Alps, the rolling countryside, the complete absence of wind, the intense silence and peace as he floated earthward. And most of all, he remembers the voice. Although he was alone, the voice broke the silence. It was not a voice in his head. He heard it, as clear as if someone were drifting beside him.

He doesn't embellish the story. He says it matter-of-factly. There was a voice. He heard it. And it said to him: "Now for you the war is over." He didn't have long to contemplate the words. Moments later, a Me-109 roared past his boots. "I remember jerking up my feet," Boyce said. "Right behind him was a P-51." The Mustang poured fifty-caliber rounds into the Messerschmitt, which crashed in flames. Then the Mustang's pilot swung his plane back around toward Boyce, tipped his wings, saluted, and peeled off. Boyce said he never felt so empty in his life. "That's when it hit me," he said. "By God, I bet I don't get a hot meal tonight."

Boyce was shot down on July 19, 1944, and spent ten months in a German POW camp before being liberated by the Russians on May 1, 1945. A native Texan, Boyce joined the army in early 1942, figuring he'd be assigned to the defense of the Gulf Coast. Instead, the army sent him west. He spent his first year in the infantry. He'd worked as a baker after graduating from high school, so the army made him a cook. "I did all the baking for our company," he said.

Unlike some pilots, Boyce had not had a longtime interest in flying. Joining the air corps was a means to an end. "I wanted to be an officer," he said. With pilots in short supply, the army air corps lowered its entrance requirements, enabling Boyce to get into flight school. Soon he was flying B-17s. "It was the queen of the sky and anyone who ever flew it will tell you that," he said. "It was a beautiful airplane. . . . A B-17 could take a beating and still get back."

In June 1944, he arrived in Molesworth, England, and was assigned to the 358th Squadron, 303rd Bomb Group of the 8th Air Force. His first mission was on July 5, a milk run to a German-held airfield in Belgium. A low overcast forced his crew to bomb by radar, he said. He recalls little flak and no enemy fighters over the target. He was not so lucky on his third mission. The target was in Munich. That's when "the hell hit the fan," Boyce said. His squadron bombed Munich five times in seven days. Each mission was a ten-hour flight. "It was hard," Boyce said. "You had to be in tiptop shape. . . . The flak was very heavy at Munich," he added, noting that more planes were lost to flak than to enemy fighters. "That flak was deadly."

Boyce's fifth mission to Munich—his ninth overall—was on July 19. It was a joint mission with the Fifteenth Air Force based in Italy, involving about fifteen hundred Allied planes—both fighters and four-engine bombers. Twenty-seven of those planes were lost. Boyce's was one of them. He remembers coming off the target after releasing his bombs and seeing several Messerschmitts, which had slipped through the Allied fighter net, coming at him at six o'clock, twenty-millimeter nose cannons blazing. As the fighters swept past, the B-17 shuddered. The tail gunner and a waist gunner were both killed, and Boyce's copilot was wounded in the leg and foot. Engine number one was smoking; there was a fire in the main compartment; and part of the tail was shot away. The controls weren't responding, so Boyce ordered the crew to bail out. The seven surviving crewmen jumped into the thin atmosphere twenty-five thousand feet above the earth.

Boyce landed in a wheat field. He hoped to make it into an adjacent forest and evade capture, but as soon as he got out from under his chute, he saw some civilians armed with pitchforks and hoes had gathered nearby and were watching him warily. Boyce stood still, uncertain what to do next. Eventually other civilians joined the group. One who had a Luger approached and motioned for Boyce to follow the group onto a road that led into the forest.

Back in England they had heard reports of civilian vigilantes killing downed airmen, so Boyce was understandably nervous. "I didn't know what they were going to do, kill me or what," he said. But before they got very far, some soldiers came along in a truck and took him into custody. Later, Boyce learned that civilians had hanged two of his crewmen. Boyce and about eighty other captured airmen were taken to a train station and shipped to Frankfurt. Along the way, civilians lining the tracks pelted the train with stones and spat on the prisoners when they got off.

Boyce was put in solitary confinement in a cell six feet by nine feet and given only bread and water. After four days, German guards took him to a small interrogation room with a window. Outside, Boyce could see groups of twelve German soldiers each marching past. Minutes after a group passed, he would hear a volley of gunfire. The interrogating officer said if he didn't tell them what they wanted to know, he would be shot as a spy. The German spoke flawless English. Later, Boyce learned he had been born in the U.S. He asked Boyce about his mission, the aircraft he flew, the type of bombs they dropped. Boyce refused to answer the questions. "In a way you're scared," he said, "but you know, if this is the way it's going to be . . ." The German officer took out a folder with Boyce's name on it. In it was everything they knew about him, including his hometown, the names of everyone in his family, and even where he went to high school. But apparently they had no information on him after he left for England. Eventually, Boyce was returned to his cell, and soon afterward he was on his way to what would be his home for the next ten months: Stalag Luft 1.

The camp was located 120 miles north of Berlin, near the town of Barth on the Baltic Sea. It housed about 13,000 American and British officers, all airmen. Boyce said that was to their advantage since the Germans had a higher respect for officers than they did enlisted men and tended to treat them better. "We came out better than probably any prison camp in Germany," he said.

Boyce was assigned to room nine, an enclosure measuring sixteen by twenty-four feet that housed eighteen men. When the others found out he was a former baker, they immediately made him the room's official cook. Food at the camp was fairly plentiful but was sorely lacking in variety. The staples were rutabagas, a thin barley soup, potatoes, sauerkraut, and black German bread extended with finely ground sawdust. That was supplemented by such rare delicacies as coffee, sugar, powdered milk, crackers, peanut butter, and Spam, which the prisoners received in their regular Red Cross packages. But as the war wore on, their food allotment decreased, Boyce said. "We were getting a little hungry towards the end." The men in their room lost an average of seventeen pounds each. When food became scarce, Boyce came up with the idea of serving his fellow prisoners earthworms. He dug them up inside the compound and deep-fried them in boiling margarine. "Tasted good, boy," he said grinning.

Life in the camp was reasonably comfortable. Every morning and evening the prisoners were required to assemble outside the barracks to be counted, and the rest of the time they were left to their own devices. They weren't required to work, and they cooked, ate, and slept in their rooms. At night the doors to the barracks were locked from the outside, and the compound was patrolled by guard dogs and swept by high-powered lights mounted on the guard towers. There were occasional attempts to escape from the camp, but few, if any, were successful. Boyce said room nine took part in one attempt in March 1945 at the request of the prisoners' senior officer. They dug a hole beside their fireplace, and when it was deep enough began a tunnel that was to go under the compound. They carried the dirt outside in their pockets and pants cuffs. One day they went into the hole and found that the Germans had filled in most of the tunnel. Oddly, there were no reprisals for the escape attempt. "[The Germans] never said a word," Boyce said.

One evening that spring, the Germans bolted the doors of the barracks as usual, and the prisoners settled in for another long night. They had a scavenged radio, which the Germans either didn't know about or ignored, and that night they heard BBC reports that the Red Army was closing in from the east. Eventually, someone noticed that the compound was quiet: No dogs were barking, and no searchlights were sweeping the ground. The Germans had gone by the time Russian troops reached the camp. "They just left everything," Boyce said. "They just took off."

Boyce and most of the men from his room joined the Russians as they pushed west. It was a sobering journey. He said the Russian soldiers, most of whom were in a constant state of drunkenness, carried no supplies other than a few wagons piled with ammunition and barrels of vodka. They lived off the land, which usually meant that they pillaged every little town they came upon, and they raped and killed indiscriminately. Eventually the Russians met the British Army, and after V-E Day, Boyce hitched a ride on a Halifax bomber going to Brussels. He went back into the plane's tail and sat, mute, surveying the desolation below. "You just sit there. It's unbelievable, all the horror and the hell," he said, shaking his head. "God, look at this. But I was part of it."

Dark Days, Good Days

SOMEWHERE OVER GERMANY, DECEMBER 23, 1944—The German fighters came out of nowhere, heading directly toward B-26 tail gunner Wendell Fetters. Fetters, a twenty-year-old staff sergeant, told his pilot that a squadron of Messerschmitt 109s and Focke-Wulf 190s was on their tail in a "company front" formation—a tight cluster, four or five planes deep. Fetters let loose with his dual fifty-caliber machine guns. "I shot down one [a Messerschmitt] and scared the hell out of two," he said, recalling the incident fifty years later. The rest of the fighters roared past, riddling the bomber with bullets and killing the pilot on the first pass. The plane was soon enveloped in flames. "I turned around and everyone was gone," Fetters said. "I decided it was time to leave." He was the last of the crewmen to bail out. He landed in a tree, breaking his left ankle, and was captured by the Germans on Christmas Day.

Milton Shalinsky, a navigator with the 385th Bomb Group, 8th Air Force, was shot down near Hamburg on June 20, 1944. As luck would have it, the day before, Josef Göbbels, Hitler's propaganda minister, had announced to Germany's civilians that it was their duty to kill any downed airmen they found. Shalinsky and his waist gunner were captured by a German farmer and taken to a jail in a nearby village. On the way they were paraded before a group of brown-shirted Hitler Youth who threw rocks and spat on them. The civilians turned him over to the German military, and he said the only time he was mistreated was when he tried to talk to his waist gunner. A soldier heard him and jabbed him several times in the stomach with his rifle butt. He kept quiet after that.

Paul Shull, a bombardier with the 34th Bomb Group, 8th Air Force, was on a mission to bomb a German oil refinery when his B-24 was shot down on November 30, 1944. He recalled that the pilot brought the plane in from a high altitude to avoid the flak, held steady while Shull dropped the payload, and then took immediate evasive action. But he wasn't fast enough. A burst of flak hit the plane's left wing, "put a hole in there about the size of a man's head," he said. The plane was at least four miles high when the order came to bail out. Shull didn't exactly like the idea, but he said, "I'm here to tell you, when you got no choice, it's awful easy to do."

Although all nine crew members quickly exited the plane, Shull did not see any of the others while he was floating down or after he landed. He'd heard the stories about civilians killing downed flyers, so he wasn't totally unhappy when soldiers were waiting for him as he hit the ground. At the German headquarters, he saw four airmen's vests hanging on the wall. They were stained with blood, and a German officer who spoke English explained that they belonged to four of Shull's crewmen; he said, "The German civilians got to them before we could, and they run them through with pitchforks."

John Weaver had his own encounter with German civilians when he was shot down during his twenty-fifth mission on April 11, 1944. A pilot with the Ninety-second Bomb Group, Eighth Air Force, he was captured by a group of civilians, who decided to hang him. He was already bleeding—"It's hard to get shot down and not get hurt," he noted—and unnaturally calm as they put a noose around his neck. "I don't remember being terrified," he said, adding that he was probably in shock.

Luckily, members of a Luftwaffe unit showed up and rescued him. He was taken to a house and laid on the floor. He recalled that papers were spread beneath him so his blood wouldn't get on the rug. But the elderly woman who lived there still managed to show her displeasure. Weaver said she would sweep around him, and when no one was looking, she would give him a little whack with her broom. Weaver didn't really blame the German civilians for taking out their anger on the Allied fliers. Between the saturation night bombing by the British and the daylight bombing by the U.S., Germany's civilian population suffered greatly during the war.

The men went through varying forms of interrogation after their capture. Shull said the Germans put him in a small cell by himself. He noted that one of the hardest things was being isolated. When the actual interrogation began, he said, they seemed to know a lot more than he did. "They told me stuff that I'd even forgotten about."

Shalinsky also was impressed by how much German intelligence knew about his crew. The Germans knew each man's name and had personal information about him, including his hometown, where he went to grade school, and the army training programs he had attended.

Weaver said during his first combat mission, his crew tuned in the Nazi propaganda station and heard the announcer welcome the pilots on the mission by name. "That [was] kind of unnerving," he said.

Fetters was shot down while on a mission to bomb a Rhine River bridge that the Germans were using to supply troops during the Battle of the Bulge. "We lost sixteen airplanes out of twenty-six," he said. He said during his interrogation, the German officer tried to entice him with things he thought Fetters would crave. There were two large bowls on the table: one was filled with Camel cigarettes and the other with Oh, Henry candy bars. He refused to talk.

The Russians finally liberated Fetters, Shull, and Weaver in May 1945. Shull admitted there were times when he was more afraid of the Red Army than he had been of the Germans. "Everybody was drunk [and armed]," he said. "I never seen such a mess in my life."

Shalinsky said as the war neared an end, the Germans became friendlier with their captives. Not long before the camp he was in was liberated by "Patton's bunch," the prisoners were told they could have their first hot shower in more than a year. But once inside the showers, they became nervous because many of them had heard stories about prisoners being gassed at German concentration camps. "Everyone was very relieved when water came out," Shalinsky said.

Weaver remembered that the camaraderie among the POWs kept him going. "Your fellow prisoners are your brothers. You really look after each other. . . . There was a necessity for friendship. In my own mind, although they were the dark days, they were also the good days," he said. "I made some friendships that I wouldn't trade for anything."

The Tuskegee Airmen

A squadron of red-tailed P-51 Mustangs was escorting a bomber mission in the Mediterranean in 1945 when a group of enemy fighter planes attacked the formation. One of the Mustang pilots, Lt. Charles McGee, got on the tail of a Me-109, which immediately took evasive action. McGee followed the twisting, turning Messerschmitt to a low altitude and gave it a burst from his machine guns. The German plane went down in flames. "Just three or four minutes it was all over," McGee said. "I was fortunate enough." That type of aerial combat wasn't unusual in World War II. But there was something different about McGee and the other pilots in his squadron. They were black. And before they could fight in the war, especially from behind the controls of America's premier fighter plane, they had to fight the prejudice of many of their white countrymen.

They were members of the group now known as the Tuskegee Airmen, named for the Tuskegee Institute in Tuskegee, Alabama, where they had trained. Originally formed as the Ninety-ninth Pursuit Squadron on January 16, 1941, until recently they were little more than a footnote in most history books. "It's a story still not known by many people," said retired army Col. Kenneth Wollford, another Tuskegee veteran. "We're a nonentity."

Wollford said that it's not widely known, but blacks have been involved in every American conflict since the Revolutionary War. However, with only a few exceptions, blacks were limited to doing menial jobs and manual labor. That began to change in 1939 with the passing of Public Law 18, which provided for the large-scale expansion of the army air corps. A provision of the law authorized the establishment of training programs in black colleges to employ blacks in various sectors of air corps support services. "Overnight the doors to aviation were opened to us," Wollford said; however, he added, it was a "very tiny crack."

The Tuskegee Institute was designed as a training center for black pilots and support crews. Wollford said the forty-week Civilian Pilot Training Program was an experiment approved only reluctantly by the U.S. government in response to pressure from a few congressmen and the black press. "It was a venture that was designed to fail, [but] destined to succeed," he said. Few whites believed that the experiment would work. The predominant attitude then was that blacks lacked the aptitude to grasp the mechanics of flying. That notion was based partly on a fifteen-year-old study by a student at the army's war college, which concluded that blacks had smaller brains, which prevented them from absorbing the technical information necessary to fly an airplane. That belief prevailed despite the fact that a number of blacks had become accomplished civilian pilots. McGee said the military in general viewed blacks as shiftless and lazy. "This was official air force policy from the top on down," he said.

The Tuskegee Airmen changed all that. Nearly a thousand black pilots earned their wings at Tuskegee, and four hundred fifty of them served overseas, where they compiled an impressive combat record. "They blew the myths out that blacks couldn't learn to fly," McGee said. Flying Curtis P-40s, the Tuskegee pilots—later the Ninety-ninth Fighter Squadron—were sent to North Africa, where "they weren't really welcomed with open arms," he said. None of the commanders wanted the all-black squadron in their group, and after-action reports were written downplaying their combat role in an effort to get them reassigned to coastal patrols.

In January 1944, they were assigned to the Twelfth Air Force and sent to

Italy. There they provided air support for the Anzio beachhead and were credited with shooting down seventeen German planes in three days. If many of their own countrymen didn't respect their efforts, the enemy certainly did. The Luftwaffe pilots called them *Schwarze Vogelmenchen*—Black Birdmen.

Pilots of the 99th flew with both the 332nd Fighter Group and the 477th Bombardment Group. They had the distinction of never losing a bomber to enemy fighters. "No other group can boast of that," Wollford said. In June 1944, the 332nd moved to the 15th Air Force to take up duties as bomber escorts for raids on Ploesti and other industrial targets in Europe. At the same time the pilots switched to the Republic P-47 Thunderbolts, and later they began flying America's top fighter, the P-51 Mustang.

McGee said each escort group adopted a different tail color so the bomber crews would be able to recognize them. The 332nd painted the tails of their Mustangs red, earning them the nickname the "Red Tails." "It was an identification both for us and the friendly bombers we were escorting," he said.

Despite the growing respect the airmen earned, there remained racial divisions in the army air corps and other branches of the military throughout the war. Segregation extended to the support personnel as well. Only black mechanics and nurses were assigned to the Tuskegee units. In contrast, McGee said he found Europe refreshingly free of bigotry toward blacks. Even the Germans he met seemed unprejudiced. When he and the other pilots did encounter racism, it was usually from white Americans who wanted to impose the same segregational practices they were accustomed to back in the States. For example, the black pilots weren't allowed to use the same rest and recreational facilities in Italy as their white counterparts. Instead, separate facilities had to be built. That situation changed after the war, when President Harry Truman signed Executive Order 9981, which authorized the integration of the U.S. armed forces. "He believed all along that the experiment would succeed," Wollford said.

After 143 missions, McGee returned to Tuskegee to become a flight instructor. He stayed in the military and flew one hundred combat missions during the Korean War. He also flew combat missions in Southeast Asia a decade later, but then he was in the cockpit of an F-4 Phantom jet fighter. His switch from propeller to jet engine was, he said, "one of the greatest joys I ever had."

D-Day

Overlord

On June 6, 1944, the Allies conducted the largest amphibious invasion in history: the D-Day landings at Normandy. The invasion force, code-named Operation Overlord, included a six thousand-ship armada that stretched for miles. Ten divisions made the initial assault, and fifteen thousand airborne troops dropped by parachute and glider behind enemy lines to attack strategic targets inland.

The breaching of Hitler's Atlantic Wall was a massive undertaking that depended on a number of factors, including strategic planning, uncertain weather, and blind luck. The weather was probably the biggest gamble. With a low-pressure system building out to sea, forecasters were predicting low clouds, high seas, and poor visibility over the Normandy coast from June 5 to 7, when the tides would be right for the invasion. But forecasters anticipated a brief window of opportunity on June 6, when there would be improved weather in Normandy before the storm closed in again. It was a huge gamble, but the Allies had little choice. By early June there were nearly two million fighting men in England, and thousands knew the invasion was imminent. It was only a matter of time before German agents figured out the location. Besides, the Allies reasoned, the Germans would never expect an invasion in such bad weather. And they were right. On June 5, the weather was so foul the Germans kept their own patrol boats in port. Normandy's commander, Erwin Rommel (nicknamed "the Desert Fox," for his defense of North Africa, for which he had earned praise from his enemies and criticism from his Führer) went home for his wife's birthday. Many of his subordinates left their commands to attend war games in Rennes, Brittany.

The Allies had gone to great lengths to persuade the Germans that the invasion wouldn't take place at Normandy. In Operation Fortitude, they used false radio traffic, dummy landing barges and tanks, and even recorded sound effects to divert German attention to phantom armies and their supposed targets, such as Norway and Calais. Hitler's instincts told him Normandy was the likely invasion site, but he had the entire Atlantic coast to defend, his troops had already been depleted by devastating losses in Russia, and resources were stretched thin. He kept the bulk of his seventy-eight divisions, including his Panzer units, within striking distance of Calais.

The Allies' luck on D-Day ranged from good to catastrophic. At Utah Beach, dust and smoke from the naval bombardment, plus a strong current near the shore, caused most of the landing craft to beach a mile south of their designated landing zone. There, as luck would have it, the German defenses were weak, unlike at the original landing site, where two enemy batteries had survived the preinvasion bombardment and would likely have taken a heavy toll on the assault troops. Most other coastal defenses had been knocked out, and the Fourth Infantry Division made it to shore with little difficulty. The beach was secured by 8 A.M., and by dusk, the division had 23,000 troops ashore at a cost of only 197 casualties.

At Omaha Beach the luck was almost all bad. Unlike Utah, with its gently sloping beaches, Omaha was overlooked by 150-foot bluffs, which gave its defenders an unobstructed view of the landings. Despite saturation bombing and a 35-minute naval barrage, many of the well-camouflaged, concrete-reinforced gun emplacements survived the attack and were operational as the landing craft came within range. "Bloody Omaha" became a grim killing ground for troops in the U.S. 29th and 1st Infantry divisions. Among the hardest hit was A Company of the 29th's 116th Regiment, which arrived with 197 troops and suffered 96 percent casualties within minutes of the landing.

Bob Maier enlisted in the navy on January 11, 1943. He was sent to the Great Lakes for basic training and then to the University of Illinois, where he learned to overhaul diesel engines. "I wanted to go to PT boats," he said, "but they wouldn't let me because I wasn't twenty-one. I was eighteen." He was sent overseas on the *Queen Elizabeth.* In Scotland, he was trained to work on British LCFs, converted landing crafts one hundred feet long with mounted flak guns. Later he was sent to England to set up an LCF maintenance shop.

At the time, he said, it was obvious the Allies were preparing for an invasion. "I think England would have sunk with the weight of equipment if it hadn't taken place," he said. Then they started asking for volunteers. "We knew it was coming off then." He was among those who volunteered. "I joined the navy to fight a war. I wasn't going to sit there at a base."

He was originally assigned to LCF-31, but a friend asked him to trade assignments. His friend went to Normandy on LCF-31, Maier on LCF-3. After the invasion, Maier learned that his friend's ship had hit a mine on the way in. Many of her crew, who wore only flotation belts, were flung unconscious into the sea. Only half of them lived to tell of it. "LCF-31 was the only ship of our group that was sunk," Maier said. His friend was among the dead.

The job of the LCFs was to protect the invading troops from enemy planes. But Allied planes flew thirteen thousand missions, compared with one hundred sorties by the Germans, and quickly established air superiority. Maier said, "The only [enemy] planes we saw were two German Messerschmitt 109s. They came right over the top of us. . . . We also shot at a couple British Spitfires" that came in too low for immediate identification. They missed both planes.

LCF-3 arrived off Omaha in the early morning darkness. Out to sea, the USS *Nevada,* which had been raised from the mud of Pearl Harbor, fired fourteen-inch shells over the LCF's mast. "When they went over," Maier said, "it sounded like a freight train." Maier's job was below the deck, keeping the engines running. Every once in a while he'd go to a hatch, stick his head out and try to see what was happening on the beach. All you could see was "smoke and confusion," he said; however, he does remember watching destroyers move within one thousand yards of the shore to fire point-blank at the enemy pillboxes raking the beach. "They must have [been dragging] bottom," he said.

Things got more harried at night when the Luftwaffe was most active. Maier remembered it was nearly impossible to sleep with the frequent air raids and guns firing and bombings. A French cruiser sitting next to his ship was a frequent target. Bombs, Maier said, would "drop in between us and the French cruiser. It was kind of scary." As expected, the weather deteriorated after the beaches were secured that night. Soon the ships in the armada were in a full-fledged storm. The crew of the LCF had no authority to head out to sea to ride the storm out, so they decided to beach the LCF next to an American LCT (landing craft, tank). As the ship was going in, he said, "one of the ships ahead of us hit a mine. You could see a big piece of [the ship] float up in the air and land on our deck." It wasn't much better on the beach. Every time the surf came in, other beached ships would wash up against the LCT, causing the rivets in their ship to pop out and ricochet from wall-to-wall like bullets. "We were scared," Maier said. "We didn't want to get killed in our own quarters." Eventually they had to jump ship. They waited for the ships to come together and then, as their LCF came apart, leaped onto the LCT and then onto a Canadian LCI (landing craft, infantry). "If you missed your jump," Maier said, "you would have landed between the ships." Later, the LCF crew was allowed onshore to see the French countryside. On one of their trips, they strolled blithely through an uncleared minefield.

After Normandy, Maier was sent back to the States for small-boat training and then sent to the Pacific, where he transported troops and supplies to the Philippines, Guam, Saipan, and Okinawa. By then the Allies were preparing for an invasion of the Japanese home islands. That was the invasion everyone was dreading, he said. "I'm not sad at all about the A-bomb."

When Mel Schneider enlisted on July 15, 1942, he had to change his birth certificate. He was only sixteen. "I was a pretty wild kid," he said. With the war only seven months old, basic training was brief and to the point, he said. "They needed warm bodies." They especially needed recruits for the navy's armed guard, who manned the antiaircraft guns on merchant marine vessels. Schneider said their entry requirements weren't very strict. He was accepted when he showed them he could swim the length of a pool. "We were gunners. We were the military presence on those vessels. . . . It was very boring duty, but very necessary."

After serving on several runs across the Atlantic, he was sent to intelligence school and eventually to England—officially as a member of the armed guard—to prepare for D-Day. After the invasion, he would be assigned to a three-man intelligence team sent inland to guide airborne troops back to the beach. On D-Day, Schneider was transported across the English Channel on a ship designated "ferry command," he said. "We were the command [ship] for all supplies on the beach." That day they dropped anchor off Omaha and directed the unloading of supplies and troops. They also picked up the bodies of dead GIs as they floated by. Because of his intelligence background, Schneider wasn't assigned to a gun. "We were more or less passengers," he said. "We were back-up." Their ship stayed off the coast of Normandy for six months. "We got bombed once. They dropped antipersonnel bombs," he said. "Two merchant seamen were wounded."

Alvin Hammer enlisted in the army air corps in November, 1940, and became a flight engineer on a B-24 with the 837th Bombardment Squadron of the 487 Bombardment Group. Unlike the ground troops, the army air corps was kept busy during the weeks leading up to D-Day with almost daily sorties over France and Germany. Their targets, often chosen to mislead the Germans about where the invasion would take place, included airfields, coastal gun emplacements, airplane factories, and marshaling yards. The bombers were usually escorted by Mustang fighters. They had to be a lot more careful about who and what they bombed after D-Day, he said. With thousands of paratroopers operating behind enemy lines, "we wanted to make sure we weren't dropping bombs on our own people." He recalled the flak was especially bad during the initial invasion. "The sky was just filled with [it]."

Hammer, who rotated home after completing thirty missions, had one close call during his tour of duty. He was at the plane's waist gun during one mission, he said, when "I had the gun blown away" by a flak burst. That was the "closest I ever came to anything. I was very fortunate. . . . They had a rough time [on the ground]."

Bloody Omaha

Omaha Beach, Normandy, France, June 6, 1944—LCT-29 pitched in the heavy surf, heading for the smoky beach. It was ninety minutes past H-hour. The first waves of men had hit the beach at 0630, and an hour and a half later they were still being butchered. Those who had survived the initial onslaught hid behind beach obstacles or in the meager shelter of the low, stone seawall. In position on the bluffs, the Germans had rifles and machine guns playing over every inch of sand, and they killed anything that moved. Other machine guns, mortars, and heavy artillery were aimed at the incoming landing craft. The troops huddled inside were wet, cold, seasick, scared. They had to shout to be heard over the roar of the diesel engines. Those near the front and sides could hear bullets and shrapnel hitting the hull and steel ramp.

On board LCT-29 were the implements of war—howitzers, half tracks, and jeeps—and the troops of the 58th Armored Field Artillery, which was attached to the 116th Regiment of the 29th Infantry Division. The 29th was untested in battle. Although it had been one of the first U.S. Army divisions sent overseas, reaching England in October 1942, it had been held back for the planned invasion of Europe. The division's long stay in England had earned it the derisive nickname, "England's Own."

As the LCT neared the beach, 2nd Lt. Vince Baker stationed himself near the ramp. Once it dropped into the water, he would be one of several soldiers manning ropes to guide the vehicles around any nearby shell craters. "It was fine going in," Baker recalled fifty years later; however, the landing craft's navy driver had been in the invasion of Italy where he "got the hell shot out of him and he was kind of itchy." Anxious to drop his cargo of troops, he started letting the ramp down prematurely. That wasn't good, Baker said, because "there were a jillion machine guns firing from the beach" and the ramp provided the troops' only protection. Baker didn't have long to worry. One moment he was crouched near the lowering ramp; the next he was hurtling through the air as a mine exploded beneath him.

Baker was living in Lyons, Kansas, when he enlisted in the National Guard. He received his commission in March 1943. For a while he was an obstacle course instructor in the Seventy-seventh Replacement Depot, and in November headed overseas on the *Queen Elizabeth* to join the Fifty-eighth, a light-armored artillery battalion.

In May 1944, the Fifty-eighth was sent to Slapton Sands on England's Channel coast to participate in Operation Fabius, the top-secret final amphibious rehearsals for the invasion of Omaha Beach. "I don't mind telling you," he said, "they were screwed up." But Fabius was a marked improvement on Operation Tiger, the rehearsal that had taken place a month earlier for the assault on Utah Beach. Amidst the confusion, nine German U-boats had attacked a convoy of fully loaded LSTs off Slapton Sands. Two of the landing craft had been sunk and another severely damaged, and 749 soldiers and sailors had died in the attack—more than three times the number the Fourth Infantry would lose at Utah on D-Day. Both the attack and the casualties were kept secret for years after the war.

Shortly before the invasion, Gen. Omar Bradley, commander of the U.S. ground forces taking part in D-Day, visited the Twenty-ninth. The general arrived at 0500 in a black LaSalle limousine and had a voice that reminded Baker of his grandmother. During his pep talk, Bradley told the soldiers if they started to worry, they should "turn around and look out in the Channel and you'll think the city of Chicago's out there."

Later he turned to Gen. Charles Gerhardt, commander of the Twenty-ninth Infantry, and asked which artillery would be supporting the division. When told it was the Fifty-eighth, he turned back to the men and said, "Barney, where the hell are ya?" Col. Bernard McQuade, commander of the Fifty-eighth, identified himself and saluted. "Damn, it's good to see ya," Bradley said, grinning. "It just makes me feel better about the whole thing." Then he turned back to Gerhardt. "You've got the best damned artillery the United States Army has to offer," he said.

Baker remembers feeling almost weightless. "It [the explosion] blew me up in the air. I felt like an eagle soaring." His lifebelt inflated while he was airborne. But when he landed in front of the LCT, he said, "I figured the propellers were going to finish me off." He passed out, and when he regained consciousness, he was floating, his feet resting on the sand bottom. The landing craft was swamped and deserted, but it wasn't completely empty. One of the navy crewmen had managed to remain with it, and he helped Baker climb aboard. The water was knee-deep inside the LCT, and none of the vehicles had been unloaded. Baker had lost his rifle, but he still had his watch, which he carried in a condom. The sailor offered Baker a nearly empty bottle of bourbon. Baker took a drink and started to hand it back, but the sailor shook his head. "I've had plenty," he said. "Finish it off." Baker managed to find his outfit, which was still on the beach pinned down by machine gun fire. Colonel McQuade was trying to rally his men.

Before the invasion, the colonel had talked to them about what they should expect on the beach. "I'm not worried too much about anything except the damned machine guns," he said. McQuade was convinced the air and naval bombardment would be unable to knock out the individual nests and pillboxes, which, from their vantage points on the bluffs, would be able to trap the invading troops on the beach in a murderous cross fire. "He also said it was stupid sending the C.O. in the first wave," Baker said. McQuade's words proved prophetic. As the soldiers slowly moved forward, Baker saw McQuade go down; he'd been hit in the chest by machine gun fire. At first, Baker said, "I thought he'd stubbed his toe on something." He watched as the colonel struggled back to his feet and then went down again. "He was a helluva commanding officer," Baker said. "I took the battalion colors to his wife after the war." She lived in Brooklyn with two little kids. "It was a sad day."

By 1030, small groups of soldiers had climbed the bluffs and begun infiltrating the German defenses, knocking them out one by one. By the end of D-Day, Omaha Beach was secured, but at the cost of nearly 1,000 29th Division casualties, 850 of whom were members of the 116th Regiment. In the next four days, the 29th Division suffered 2,210 casualties, including 280 killed, 896 missing, 1,027 wounded and 7 known captured. The 1st Infantry had 1,638 casualties, including 124 killed, 431 missing, and 1,083 wounded. The 82nd and 101st Airborne Divisions, which parachuted behind enemy lines, also were hit hard. In the first four days of the invasion, the 101st had 2,619 casualties and the 82nd 1,235.

German casualties on D-Day can only be estimated. According to some estimates, the Germans suffered 4,000 to 9,000 casualties from the Allied air and naval bombardment alone. Several German divisions on the Normandy coast, particularly those facing the landing zones for the Americans (Utah and Omaha) and the British (Gold, Juno, and Sword), virtually ceased to exist. By June 30, German losses totaled 47,515.

At the end of D-Day, Baker's war was far from over. Afterward, working as a forward observer assigned to a tank unit, he was wounded five times and received two Bronze Stars for valor. His first Bronze Star was for helping bring down artillery fire on an enemy force, preventing a counterattack during the capture of a hill on October 2, 1944. He also established a defensive-fire zone that enabled the Americans to hold the hill. The second Bronze Star was for helping knock out a German tank with a bazooka outside Frankfurt, Germany, on March 18, 1945. Baker, who went on to serve a term in the Missouri General Assembly after the war and spent ten years as an associate circuit judge before retiring in 1991, downplayed the awards. "Decorations to me really don't mean a helluva lot," he said. Too many medals went to the undeserving and too few to the real heroes to put too much stock in them, he said. But they had some practical worth, he admitted. "Actually, they meant five points, each one, toward going home." And for the survivors of D-Day, going home meant just about everything.

Glider Pilot

The aging former glider pilot met the reporter at the door and ushered him into the living room of his modest home in Gladstone, Missouri. The year was 1985—the fortieth anniversary of the end of World War II. The war was on Jim Campbell's mind. Campbell, who had just turned sixty-nine, was tall and spare. A photo of him taken in 1944, just before the disastrous airborne invasion of Holland, showed a strapping young soldier brandishing a Thompson machine gun.

"I'm a retired bread salesman, Manor Bakers, Teamster's Union," Campbell said, displaying a mischievous grin that turned into an infectious laugh. "Got a good retirement from 'em. I was born and raised in Bonham, Texas, named after James Butler Bonham, one of the heroes of the Alamo," he said. "I went to Austin College and they had a program called civilian pilot training that was sponsored by the government. I always wanted to fly, so I took that and got my private pilot's license.

"The war was comin' on and I knew I was gonna be drafted, so I enlisted 'cause I wanted to get in on the flying end of it. This new program came up, glider pilots, and I said, 'Ahh, that sounds good.' "

The glider pilots eventually ended up in Fort Sumner, New Mexico, 150 miles east of Albuquerque, in midsummer. "This one day, by golly, it was hotter than the hinges of hell and I was out there on KP duty. Great big old

32-gallon pots—we had to clean 'em—and this buckass sergeant, my God, he was out there complainin' about this and that. Nobody liked him. Nobody.

"It was early afternoon and our orders came down. We were flying staff sergeants and we outranked that buckass [laughs]. I gave him the signal [he raises his index finger] and went over to the PX and bought a nickel beer."

The pilots were transferred to a desert base in California to learn "sail plane flying. It's comparable to a glider," he said. "We were towed into the air and after getting on wind currents and updrafts and downdrafts, stayed up as long as we could, stayed nearby our runway. Finally, when we ran out of altitude, we came in and landed."

After graduating from the glider program, Campbell was sent to Louisville, Kentucky, where he began training in the glider he would fly into combat in a few short weeks: the Waco CG4-A. The CG4-A was a medium-sized glider with an eighty-three-foot wingspan. It could carry up to fifteen fully armed soldiers, plus a pilot and a copilot. It had a tubular steel fuselage and metal struts, but the rest was just plywood and canvas. It contained no armor or armament. The hinged nose opened up for loading, and it could carry equipment in the troop compartment.

Campbell was assigned to the 79th Squadron of the 436th Troop Carrier Group, 101st Airborne Division. He was sent to New York to board a ship to England. "I went over on the *Queen Mary*," he said. "The *Queen* had no escorts. She was so fast. Radar, sonar or whatever, my God, she could outrun any submarine." It took four days to cross the turbulent Atlantic, and the ship docked at Gurroch, Scotland. From there, the men took a train to Membury, west of London. They spent a lot of time in London during their final training exercises. Mostly, Campbell said, they partied with the local girls, who, with their husbands and boyfriends absent, were drawn to the Yanks like metal shavings to a magnet. Campbell also did some sightseeing. "This one time I decided I wanted to see The Sir Winston Churchill. My God, 10 Downing Street was so guarded, but I bullshitted my way in to see him. These bobbies said [affecting a bad British accent], 'Ah, you can't go in.' I said, 'Well, what the heck. I'm an American. His mother was an American. . . .' So, I talked my way in and it just tickled him to death [laughs]. I said, 'Well, I just wanted to say hi [laughs].' He just enjoyed it no end."

Sunrise over Normandy, France, June 6, 1944—The American C-47, skimming the ground at 150 feet, was dodging flak bursts. Trailing behind the plane were two gliders, one staggered ahead of the other, on taut nylon towlines. Campbell, then twenty-seven, was piloting the rear glider. His copilot sat next to him in the glider's nose. His cargo was five combat troopers and a jeep.

Sergeant Campbell scanned the countryside below. He needed a flat, open area to land, and he would get only one chance. But he could already see obstacles below. "Evidently, the German intelligence knew this thing [D-Day] was going on, so they put fence posts up. Well, hell, that was no problem." The towropes were attached so the gliders wouldn't bump into each other. The lead glider had a 100-foot rope, and the second, a 175-foot rope. "The fella ahead of me naturally cut off first. He saw these fence posts and landed in between." But as Campbell watched, the glider disappeared in an explosion of flame and debris. There were no survivors.

"I cut off shortly thereafter and I was still in the air, but, man alive, I had to do something and do something in a hurry." What had looked like fence posts from the air were what the Allies came to call "Rommel's Asparagus"—stakes strung with barbed wire and mined with high explosives. Campbell used his wing flaps to cut his speed and searched for an open field. He found a small meadow bounded by a hedgerow and brought the glider in. "I got out alright, kinda messed up the undercarriage of the glider. . . . I came up against a [hedge]row, which maybe saved our lives 'cause we could jump down and have a little protection from the trees. Got seven of us down and a jeep."

When everyone was out, the combat troops piled into the jeep and headed east toward their designated assembly area. Campbell and his copilot went west, back toward the beach (about ten miles away). Both men were armed with Thompson machine guns, forty-five-caliber sidearms, and hand grenades.

As they were walking, they saw "all these paratroopers with their throats slashed that were hung up in the trees," Campbell said. Apparently the German SS troops in the area had been busy. Campbell recalled that when he was stationed in Membury, there had been a group of Native American soldiers at the camp. They bunked together, cooked their own food, and everyone pretty much left them alone. They looked like soldiers you didn't want to mess with. "There was about eight or ten of 'em at Membury. They were paratroopers. By golly, they were a mangy, scroungy [bunch] and they were all by themselves."

Soon the Allied paratroopers, who'd been killed while they hung helpless in trees, weren't the only grisly sights Campbell saw as he made his way to the rendezvous point. He began seeing dead Germans, their heads and upper torsos thrust into the body cavities of dead horses. He immediately thought of the Indian paratroopers. "I tell you, those American Indians saw what was going on there and it was like Custer's last stand. By God, they took care of those Germans. . . . Boy, I'll never forget that."

Campbell made it back to the beach without firing a shot. He would have similar luck in each of the combat missions he flew. His second, the invasion of Holland—Operation Market-Garden—in September 1944, was catastrophic in terms of casualties among glider pilots. "Some of 'em were shot down, but most of 'em were [killed] getting down on the ground. You just had to get down the best way you could." His final mission was into Wesel, Germany, on March 25, 1945. Campbell was one of the lucky ones. "I got through it all without a scratch," he said.

He traveled home on the USS *Aikin* Victory ship, a troop and cargo transport. By then he was a first lieutenant and already had orders to report to California to become aide-to-camp to Maj. Gen. Lewis Brereton, commander of the First Allied Airborne Army, to help plan the glider invasion of Japan. The plan was for the gliders to be launched from aircraft carriers. But first Campbell had thirty days' leave, and in the summer of 1945, he went home to Texas. He was there when the war ended. V-J Day. August 14. His birthday. "Oh boy, I was real happy," he said, emotion creeping into his voice. "It was quite a celebration for my birthday."

Raymond Johnson and his wife, Rhoda, wrote to each other daily while Raymond served on the USS *San Francisco.* Photo by Jeff Kirchhoff, *Lee's Summit Journal,* 2001.

Albert Schultz served with the 832nd Engineer Aviation Battalion, which was attached to Patton's 3rd Army. The drawing is of Schultz as a captain in France in 1944. The artist, Peter DuMitru, served in the battalion. Photo by Jeff Kirchhoff, *Lee's Summit Journal*, 2001.

Dee Nicholson and her father, Buddy Stagner, witnessed the attack on Pearl Harbor. Photo by author, 1991.

Stewart Kluender served as a gunner on a B-25 in the Pacific. Photo by author, 1985.

Harold Meyer was a driver with the 466th Amphibious Truck Company, and Nadine Meyer served stateside in the marines. Photo by author, 1985.

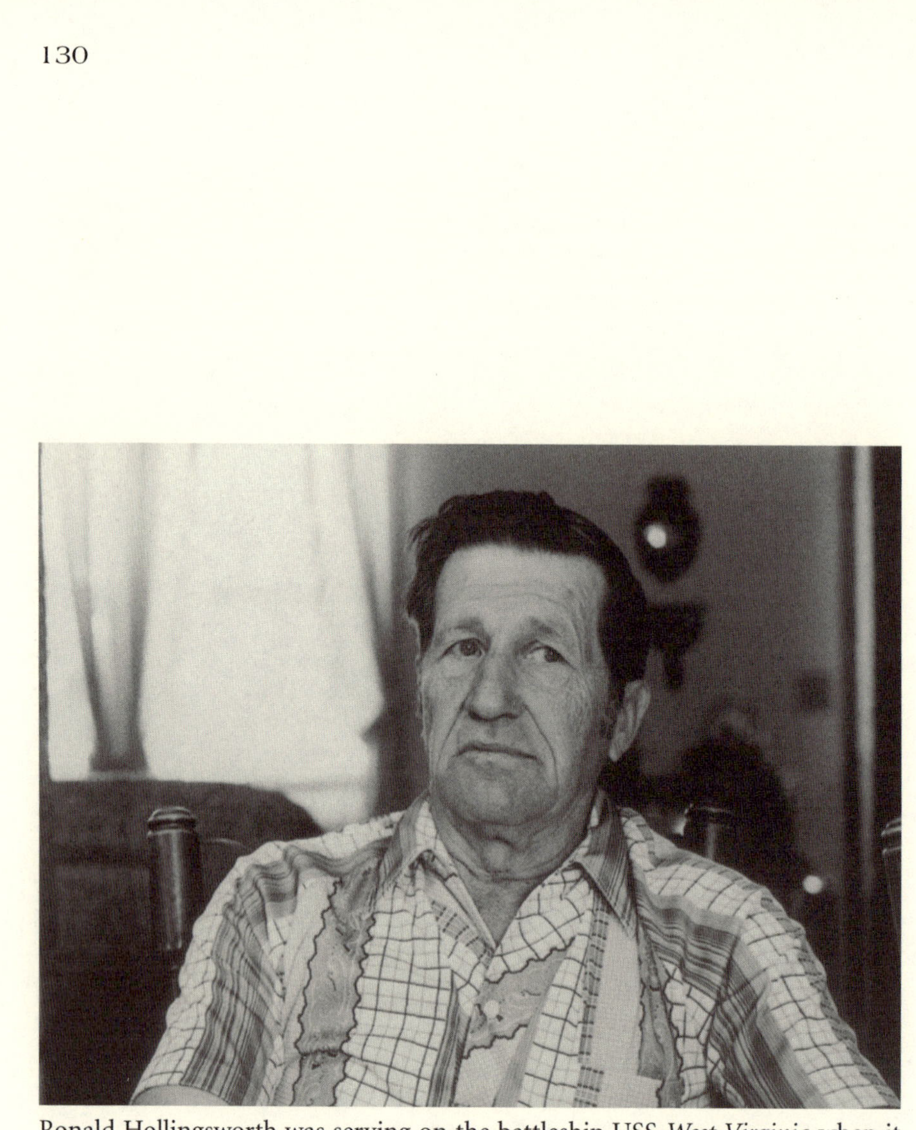

Ronald Hollingsworth was serving on the battleship USS *West Virginia* when it was sunk at Pearl Harbor. He later served on the cruiser USS *Minneapolis,* which took part in the carrier war in the Pacific. Photo by author, 1985.

Oscar "Runt" Pruessner was a gunner on a Sherman tank in the Sixth Armored Division of the Third Army. Photo by author, 1985.

Jim Bennett spent most of his four-year tour with the Fifth Marine Division in the Pacific and took part in the invasion of Iwo Jima. Photo by author, 1985.

Pat Flanagan (right) and Les LeTourneau survived the attack on Pearl Harbor. LeTourneau was a member of the 251st Coast Artillery Antiaircraft unit, and Flanagan was aboard the USS *Ward* which sank a Japanese mini sub prior to the attack. Photo by author, 1985.

Tudie Brisciano was a deck gunner on the destroyer USS *Hadley* fighting off kamikazes, baka bombs, and suicide boats during the invasion of Okinawa in April 1945. Photo by author, 1985.

LeRoy Dir fought with the 101st Airborne at Bastogne during the Battle of the Bulge; his mother, Francis, had a dream about her son on the day he was reported missing in action. Photo by author, 1989.

Leo and Jean Burrow traveled to Belgium in 1989 to visit the area where Leo had served as a loader with the 749th AAA Gun Battalion. Photo by author, 1989.

Bill McMullen served in the Coast Guard on the attack transport USS *Arthur Middleton* during the invasions of Tarawa, Saipan, and Leyte. Photo by author, 2002.

Bob Sommer was a tail gunner on a B-17 that was shot down over Germany in 1945. Photo by author, 2002.

After his patrol was pinned down, and his leg nearly blown off by a mine, George Rhodes Jr. used a grenade launcher to knock out an enemy machine gun nest. Photo by author, 2002.

Marvin Boyce's B-17 was shot down over Germany in 1944. He spent ten months in a German POW camp before being liberated by the Russians. Photo by author, 2002.

Finis Saunders, seen here with his wife, Betty, was a crewman on a B-29 that had to ditch in the ocean after an attack on Nagoya in 1945. Photo by author, 2002.

Vince Baker, a forward observer for the Fifty-eighth Armored Field Artillery, was wounded five times and decorated twice for valor during combat in Europe. After the war, he became a state circuit judge. Photo by author, 2002.

Mamie Mulligan was a "Rosie the Riverter" on the swing shift at the Pratt and Whitney plant in Kansas City. Photo by author, 2002.

Ken Morton served as a radio technician on the destroyer escort *Ulvert M. Moore* during the invasion of Luzon in the Philippines. During the campaign, the ship shot down three enemy planes and sank an enemy submarine. Photo by author, 2002.

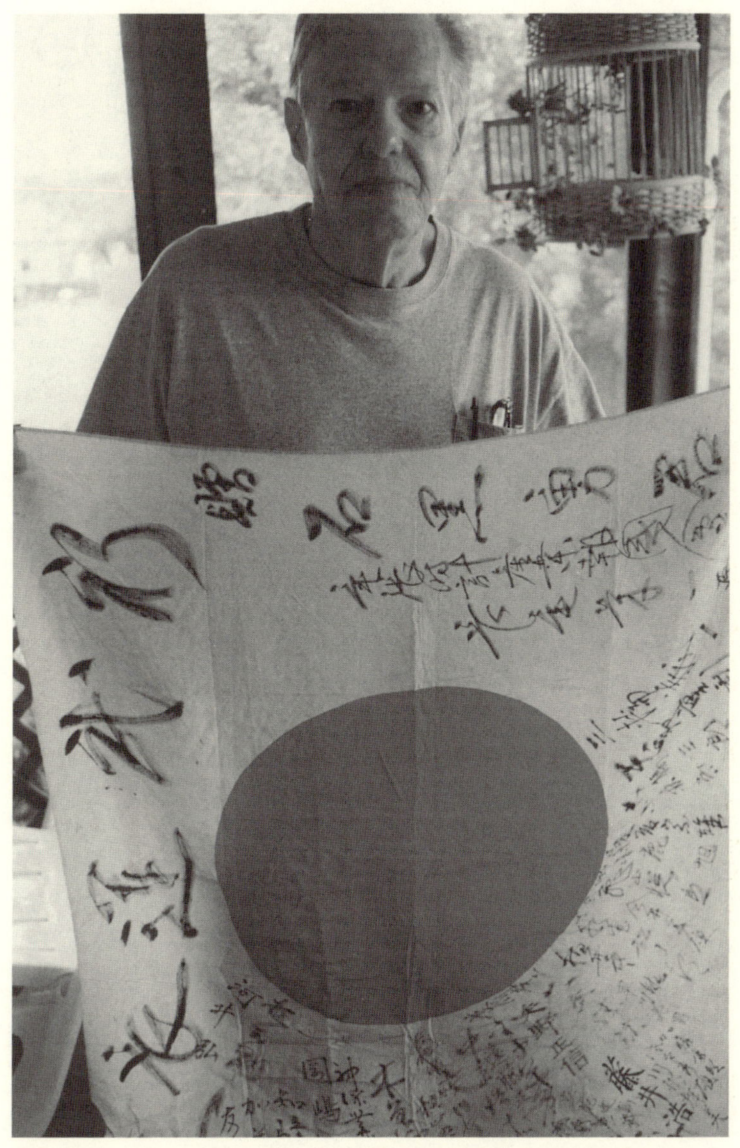

Bob Seek was a platoon leader with the Eighth Marines during the invasions of Saipan and Tinian. The Japanese battle flag he is holding was taken from an enemy casualty. Photo by author, 2002.

Byron Banta was a company clerk with the Fifth Armored Division as it raced through Europe during the final months of the war. Banta served with front-line troops. Photo by author, 2002.

Mike and Betty Norris met while both were serving in the marines. Photo by author, 2002.

War in the Pacific, Part 3

Tropical Paradise

NEW CALEDONIA, JUNE 1944—Everett Browning was driving a jeep through the jungle the day the ground shook and the sky caught fire. "It rocked the whole island and lit it up like a candle," he said, recalling the day forty-six years earlier when five hundred tons of American ammunition had exploded. "It was a heck of a blast." Although the exact sequence of events was never known, military investigators surmise that a bomb with a live fuse was somehow shipped overseas. When it was rolled out of the back of a truck and down a ramp, it collided with other bombs waiting to be fused and loaded onto waiting U.S. warplanes and set them all off. "Two men were killed and just bits of them were found. [They] just disintegrated," Browning said. Browning, a member of the 209th Military Police Company, was on his way to pull guard duty at the ammunition depot, which was located in a secluded valley at the foot of the mountains. "I narrowly escaped," he said. "I missed that by ten, fifteen minutes."

You could say luck followed Browning's military career, but if you'd asked him back then, he'd have called it bad luck. Browning enlisted as a construction ground crewman in the army air corps in September 1942. When he returned home, he found an induction notice in his mailbox. "They held me to the draft," he said. "Greetings from the president of the United States." He had hoped to serve in the air corps because he liked being around airplanes and had heard that promotions were more frequent in that service than in the others. Besides, working on a ground crew, which mostly involved building runways, was safer than being a pilot. "I wanted to stay on the ground," he said. He got that much of his wish. On Halloween night, 1942, the twenty-two-year-old was sworn into the army.

He was sent to Camp Wolters, near Mineral Wells, Texas, for thirteen weeks of infantry training and then to Pennsylvania, where he received orders to ship out to the European theater. While waiting for the ship, a member of his battalion contracted scarlet fever, and the whole battalion was quarantined for thirty days. By the time the quarantine was lifted, his orders had been changed. In April 1943, Browning's battalion landed on the French island of New Caledonia, in the South Pacific.

New Caledonia fit the description of a tropical paradise. South of the equator and about six hundred miles east of Australia, the island has a warm, mild climate and lush vegetation. Later in the Pacific War, it was used mainly as a place for battle-weary soldiers to rest and recuperate. "It was comfortable," Browning recalled. "It wasn't overly hot."

While most of the battalion joined the 43rd Infantry, eventually taking part in the Bouganville and Saipan invasions, Private Browning was put to work unloading supply ships. "Fortunately, I was held back. Seventy-five percent of my buddies were sent directly into combat. Punk kids," he said. "I was real fortunate. I was just real lucky." In June 1943, while still on New Caledonia, he joined the military police. "I was primarily a downtown intersection road patrol [officer]," he said. One of his duties as an MP was to escort ambulances from the docks to the island hospital. "I saw a lot of my buddies [come in] injured," he said. He also worked closely with the French police and pulled his share of stockade duty. The prisoners were mostly American GIs being held for infractions such as being AWOL and crimes such as murder. "Some of them were just habitual," he said. "They'd rather be in the stockade" than in combat.

Browning spent two years and ten days on New Caledonia, and then the 209th received orders to proceed to the Philippines. One of his most vivid memories is of sitting on a troop ship in the Admiralty Islands, smack on the equator, the temperature a sweltering 114 degrees, waiting for other troops to arrive so they could proceed to Leyte. In June 1945, they landed at Cebu City, the second largest city in the Philippines. The city had been liberated, but pockets of Japanese soldiers were still holding out in the vicinity. "We were close enough we could hear the ammunition going off," Browning said. While in the Philippines, he saw a lot of Adm. Bull Halsey. "I saluted that old boy many times."

One night in August, a large group of soldiers was watching a movie outdoors when the film was suddenly turned off, and an announcement came over the camp loudspeaker: all personnel were to report to their duty stations. When they arrived, they were told the Japanese had surrendered. The war was over. "The whole town went wild, the Filipinos and the GIs," recalled Browning, who had just earned his sergeant's stripes. "After being over there thirty-four months . . . I was greatly relieved."

Browning did pick up a scar during the war. While he was unloading a truck, he cut his shoulder on a bolt protruding from the tailgate. His only illness was from a "nonmalarious mosquito bite" that laid him up in the hospital after the war was over. He remembers lying in the hospital with a 104-degree fever listening to the official Japanese surrender ceremonies broadcast from the deck of the USS *Missouri* in Tokyo Bay in September 1945. He ate Thanksgiving dinner at Leyte and spent Christmas Day on a train in Ogden, Utah. "They let us off the train long enough to eat Christmas dinner at the depot," he said.

He was mustered out of the army on December 30, 1945, exactly thirty-eight months after entering the service. He returned to his hometown of Lee's Summit and went back to his old job at the R. B. Rice Sausage plant. Although he had vowed he would never carry a gun again, he ended up carrying one for thirty-two years as a security guard at the Bendix plant in Kansas City. He retired in 1983. Sometimes he still thinks about the war. Mostly they're good memories. Like the tropical night in December 1945, steaming home in a crowded troop ship, the war won, the lights of Midway Island off in the distance, moonlight glittering on the water. "Oh, it was a beautiful night. The ocean was just like a mirror."

Gyokusai on Saipan

SAIPAN, JUNE 17, 1944—Night in the tropics falls quickly. Cpl. Robert C. Barackman barely had his shovel out before it was pitch black. He and his buddy Carlos Begay, a full-blooded Navaho, dug a two-man foxhole in the humid darkness and waited for morning. The Second and Fourth Marine Divisions had landed on Saipan two days earlier, and the U.S. invaders were slowly working their way inland. The Japanese were giving ground grudgingly, and casualties on both sides were mounting.

Barackman's company was part of the advancing front line. It was supposed to secure a nearby hilltop before nightfall, but intermittent skirmishes with Japanese snipers had slowed the men down, and the company was forced to dig in about three-quarters of the way up the slope. The Japanese attacked that night in the first of several suicide charges they would make on Saipan. The worst of these attacks came about three weeks later during the night of July 7–8, when thousands of Japanese soldiers and civilian workers, many of them drunk on saki, died charging American positions. It was the largest mass suicide of the war. The Japanese called such raids *gyokusai* (death with honor). But the first such charge was on a much smaller scale with no more than a few hundred soldiers taking part. Their main objective—before dying for the emperor—was to break through to the beach where the U.S. supplies and ammunition were being stockpiled. They never made it to the beach. Barackman was trying to find a comfortable position in the hastily dug foxhole when the Japanese charged. He immediately brought his rifle up and began firing at the dark, howling shapes descending on them from the ridge.

A bullet sliced past his right cheek and plowed through the muscle of his shoulder. He recalled it felt like someone had swatted him sharply with a ping-pong paddle, but the impact knocked him flat on his back, and his right arm was rendered useless. He looked up just as Begay took a bullet in the brain, which killed him instantly. Without making a sound, the teenager sprawled backward. Barackman unholstered his forty-five and pulled Begay's body on top of his own. He saw three Japanese soldiers jump over the foxhole without stopping. The sound of the fighting diminished, and soon Barackman was alone. Although he couldn't move his arm, the pain wasn't too bad, he recalled. His strongest memory is of the hours following the attack, hours lying in a muddy trench with a dead man on top of him, not knowing where the Japanese were, wondering if more were coming. Only seven members of his company survived the attack. Despite the obvious danger, they called each other's names throughout the night to see who was still alive. "It was a very long night," Barackman said. "There were a lot of prayers. A lot of prayers."

Barackman was nineteen and on a ship bound for Saipan when he heard about the Normandy landing on June 6. That was when he began to realize the full extent of America's military might. He found it almost unbelievable that the U.S. could mount two major invasions on opposite sides of the world only nine days apart. "It was just mind-boggling," he said. "I thought we had every ship in the world out with us, [but] Saipan was peanuts next to Normandy."

The U.S. invaded Saipan on the morning of June 15, 1944, after a heavy naval bombardment and attacks by navy fighters and dive-bombers. The idea, Barackman said, was to charge in while the enemy was still pinned down and confused, but it rarely worked that way. The most fearful time, he said, was the fifteen-minute ride to shore on the landing craft. There were usually ten boats in each group. They would circle endlessly until ordered to proceed to the beach, then, like a single entity, the landing craft would turn toward shore and head in side by side. By the time the squad leader yelled, "Lock and load!" bullets were whining off the steel hull. "That's the moment of truth," Barackman said. "You know there's no going back. . . . That's when the rosaries come out and the prayers are mumbled. That's real fear." It took the marines twenty-four days, at a cost of more than three thousand lives, to take the island. The Japanese lost more than twenty-seven thousand soldiers and civilians.

One American casualty was a guy named Shapiro. When Barackman got to him, his leg had been blown off by a mortar and was lying just out of reach of his outstretched hand. He died within minutes, but Barackman can still hear him hollering for someone to please hand him his leg. "He wasn't in pain. He just wanted me to kick his leg over to him, so he could put it back on," he said. "It was crazy."

Actually, there were one or two good things about the Japanese bullet that wounded Barackman: It passed through his shoulder without so much as scratching a bone (and after it healed, it never bothered him again. "It was a real clean bullet wound," he said). It got Barackman off Saipan, where fighting would continue for three more grueling weeks.

The Japanese who made it past Barackman's position were stopped long before they reached the beach, and the attackers were wiped out. After the long, fearful night of the suicide attack, Barackman and the other survivors of his company were picked up by a patrol and taken back to the beach. Barackman was evacuated to a Red Cross hospital ship anchored a few miles offshore and transported to a field hospital on Guadalcanal. From there he was sent to New Caledonia for some much-needed R and R. Barackman rejoined his division in the middle of the invasion of Tinian, a tiny island south of Saipan. After Tinian was secured on August 2, 1944, the Second Marines returned to Saipan to rest up for the last major invasion of World War II. They didn't know it then, but it also would be the bloodiest fight of the Pacific War.

No Quarter

For Bob Seek, World War II was the worst of times and the best of times. As a platoon leader with the Eighth Marines, Second Division, he saw the most ferocious fighting imaginable on Saipan and Tinian. But it was also a time of friendship, camaraderie, and bonding of an intensity that only veterans of combat experience. "There's a bond between marines that I'll never forget," he said. "I wouldn't be here today if it wasn't for other marines."

Seek enlisted in the Marine Corps in 1942 during his senior year of high school. When he left for boot camp in San Diego, he was two weeks shy of his eighteenth birthday. After basic training, he was sent to a marine air station at El Centro, California, and assigned to guard duty at the camp's ammunition dump. It wasn't exactly what Seek had in mind when he joined the marines. With a cousin missing in action at Bataan, he was anxious to head overseas and fight the Japanese. Later, as he was trying to survive on the killing grounds of Saipan, he would look back on those quiet months in the States with more than a little nostalgia. He especially remembered the funny things that happened.

One time a buddy, Cpl. Charles Raymond Davis, was stationed at the main gate, checking in marines returning from liberty. A car pulled up. Inside were two pilots, obviously inebriated. In the back seat was a large sea bag. The sea bag was moving. Corporal Davis asked the lieutenants what was in the sea bag. From the movements and sounds coming out of it, he'd decided it was a woman. "Just some dirty laundry," one of the pilots said. "Well," Davis said, "will you tell it to lay still?" Everyone started giggling, including the sea bag. And what did the corporal do? "He passed them on in," Seek said, laughing.

Then there was the time he and a couple of friends drove into town for a bite to eat. They arrived at a restaurant at the same time as a guy named Humphrey Bogart. The actor, who was filming a movie in nearby Yuma, asked the young marines if they were having dinner. "He insisted we eat with him and paid for all our food," Seek said.

He finally shipped out with the Eighth Marines in September 1943. When they arrived in the Pacific theater, they immediately began training for what would become the amphibious invasion of Saipan. Seek, who was a corporal by then, was assigned to the frontline troops. As his troop ship neared the island, he began to hear the boom of the big guns from the assembled naval armada pounding Saipan. The island also was bombed and strafed around the clock by navy planes. Seek was convinced nothing could survive that onslaught. "We wouldn't even have to worry about a mosquito," he said.

On the morning of the invasion, Seek was assigned to go in with the first wave of amphtracks. He remembers being about six hundred yards from shore when he saw a navy fighter begin a strafing run. Immediately the plane began taking ground fire and pulled up. It continued climbing straight up until it seemed to pause in midair and then, almost gracefully, fell back and crashed into the sea. Seek didn't see a parachute. About that time, Seek said, "the reality set in that it [the fighting] wasn't going to be all over." Moments later, the water around the landing craft began erupting in huge geysers. "We was under fire all the way in—mortar fire," he said. "[We] lost a lot of people on the beach." The fighting on Saipan was characterized by almost unparalleled ferocity as the marines slowly rooted out the stubborn Japanese defenders. No quarter was asked or given. "They was all determined to kill you," Seek said. "And they would all sacrifice their lives to do it."

There also were thousands of Saipanese civilians on the island. Although they were considered Japanese citizens, their ancestry was mainly Polynesian and Spanish, and many were practicing Catholics. Prior to the invasion, the Japanese government had indoctrinated the civilians about U.S. Marines. They had said the marines would kill their men, rape their women, and eat their children and recommended that they kill themselves rather than be taken prisoner. More than eight thousand civilians committed suicide. Many families gathered along the island's cliffs and despite entreaties by the marines, threw their children and then themselves into the rock-strewn surf hundreds of feet below.

Seek said his unit was about 50 percent Catholic—he was Baptist—and many of them went into combat with their crucifixes outside their shirts. When they encountered civilians, he said, often they were able to convince them to surrender because the civilians didn't believe anyone wearing a cross was capable of the terrible things they had been warned about. "So it saved a lot of lives," he said. "I don't think it saved any Japanese [soldiers'] lives," he added. "Very few Japanese surrendered."

Bullets and explosives weren't the only dangers the marines had to contend with, Seek said. "The elements cut you down as much as anything." Malaria was rampant on the island. When Seek arrived on Saipan, he weighed a beefy 192 pounds. After a few weeks and several bouts of malaria, he was down to 147. He remained thin throughout most of his time in the Pacific. "When I came back," he said, "they called me Sergeant Bones."

He said much has been made of the alleged physical superiority of the Japanese Imperial Marines. Seek, who fought regular army troops on Saipan and Imperial Marines on Tinian, said while the marines may have been physically larger, they weren't necessarily superior. "I didn't find [the marines] any different than the Japanese Army," he said. "I never saw any difference in their abilities. . . . As far as bravery or combat efficiency [is concerned], I didn't see any difference. . . . It don't take bigness to kill you. It don't take much pressure to pull a trigger." Seek said most of the American soldiers were physically larger than the Japanese, but that isn't why the U.S. prevailed. "We didn't depend on body strength to whip the Japanese. We depended on firepower."

Although he never had to test his strength against a Japanese adversary, Seek had his share of close calls. One occurred when he was on patrol during mopping-up operations on Saipan, which was declared secure on July 9. By then he was a platoon sergeant, and he and his men were trying to find a Japanese radio that was still operating in a mountainous area. Every time the

Americans' B-29s took off on bombing missions from the captured airfield, the Japanese holdouts would radio a warning. Seek and his runner—an enlisted man assigned to deliver his messages—were crossing a valley, pushing through elephant grass seven feet high, to join their captain on another ridge when they stumbled onto three armed Japanese soldiers. "I was going through that grass and I stepped on him," he said. "We didn't have any qualms about eliminating them. They didn't offer to surrender."

Another time his platoon was sent on a flanking maneuver against an enemy machine gun nest. Thirteen soldiers strung themselves out in a column and began going downhill. As Seek passed a rock formation, he saw the muzzle of a Japanese machine gun sticking out of a slot in the outcropping a few feet away. The machine gunner must have seen him at the same instant. "I was so close, he fired over my shoulder," he said. "Two of them behind me got killed." Seek, however, wasn't injured, and the machine gun was quickly knocked out.

Seek's luck held when he went out to rescue a wounded buddy named Don Nyman. As he moved forward, an Imperial Marine officer jumped up and fired an automatic pistol at him. Seek instinctively turned sideways. Whether that's what saved him he doesn't know, but the bullet missed. When the officer tried to fire again, the pistol jammed. Then the man reached for a grenade, and Seek cut him down. Ever mindful of the value of souvenirs, Seek relieved the dead Japanese marine of his pistol and shoulder holster and then found Nyman and carried him back to the American lines. Decades later he telephoned Nyman and asked if he remembered a guy named Bob Seek. "If I live to be a 150," Nyman said, "I'll never forget Bob Seek."

Seek was seriously wounded only once. At first, it didn't seem serious. He was on Tinian when a Japanese grenade exploded nearby, filling the air with small but lethal pieces of jagged metal. He felt a sharp pain in his hand. A tiny sliver of shrapnel had embedded itself in the knuckle of his left ring finger. The injury seemed so minor he didn't even go to the aid station. That was a mistake. Soon the wound had festered, and the infection had gotten into his bloodstream. "My arm got as big as my leg," he said. When he finally went to the aid station, his arm was so swollen, they had to cut his shirt off. The medical officer took one look and said, "Corporal, that arm has to come off."

"Like hell it does," he replied. "I was afraid to go to sleep," he said. "I was worried I'd wake up with no arm." Eventually he was evacuated to a field hospital on Saipan. There, he lay flat on his back in a cot while his arm and hand were immersed in a solution of hot water, lye soap, and bleach. "I had my hand in that water for over a week," he said, "twenty-four hours a day." Slowly the infection subsided. After a while, Seek said, he could actually "milk" the infection out by squeezing his upper arm. The pressure would push the hardened, rubbery pus out his knuckle. He could push several inches of it out at a time. During his treatment, one of the doctors came over to him. "You know," he said, "if you'd let me take your arm off, you wouldn't have to go through this."

One more story: Charles Davis, the friend who had let the inebriated pilots bring the woman onto the El Centro marine base in a sea bag, was heading to shore in an LST during the invasion of Okinawa when the transport was struck and sunk by a kamikaze. The corporal spent eleven harrowing hours in shark-infested waters before being rescued. Dropped off on the island's southern coast, Davis was soon arrested by MPs, who were rounding up deserters, and placed on a prisoner ship bound for the stockades in the Philippines. Davis's explanation was ignored. Eventually, however, inquiries were made, and his story checked out. Shortly after that, Seek said, Davis was summoned from the brig. "He went up and ate with the officers the rest of the trip."

Hell on Peleliu

PELELIU, THE PALAU ISLANDS, SEPTEMBER 15, 1944—The landing boat made its final circle and headed toward the beach. Jack Young huddled with his fellow marines, his stomach knotted, his fingers clenched on his carbine. His pack was filled with caps, fuses, and concussion explosives, which didn't exactly ease his mind. Water geysered near a landing craft trapped on a coral reef. Soldiers were leaping over the side. Those who threw their gear and guns away were able to swim to shore. The others were dragged under by their equipment and drowned.

Gray smoke hung over the beach like low clouds, and the breeze brought the smell of cordite, the thump of exploding shells, the blat of small-arms fire, the rattle of machine guns. Then the landing craft stopped, the ramp splashed down, and Young was jumping into the warm, waist-deep water, moving past the floating dead, charging up the beach toward the lines of blasted, twisted barbed wire. Time to get to work. It was dawn and the First Marine Division was invading a six-square-mile patch of coral named Peleliu, east of the Philippines. "It was well fortified," Young said. "There was a lot of shelling. We were all scared. It was hell, really. The first three days were hell."

Bloody Nose Ridge, Hand Grenade Hill, Shuri Castle. To Young, the names evoke bittersweet memories of the two years he spent island-hopping in the

Pacific during World War II—memories of messy deaths and battlefield heroism, of close calls and paralyzing fear. Memories a man couldn't get away from, even more than four decades later. Even if he wanted to. "You'd be standing there and your buddy would disappear, drop dead," Young said. "Any day you lived through out there was a close call."

Peleliu was of major importance to the Japanese because it had the largest airfield in the Palau islands. North of the airfield was Umurbrogol Mountain, a series of steep coral ridges honeycombed with old phosphate mining caves. The Japanese had enlarged and fortified the caves and equipped them with steel doors that slid open to allow artillery pieces to be rolled out on tracks and fired. When fire was returned, the guns were pulled back and the doors slammed shut.

The island was defended by sixty-five hundred crack troops under the command of Col. Kunio Nakagawa. During the naval and aerial barrage preceding the invasion, the Japanese hid in their underground fortifications, waiting. When the marines landed on the west side of the island alongside the airfield, the Japanese came out of hiding and saturated the beaches with mortars and artillery and machine gun fire.

Young was an eighteen-year-old demolitions specialist with the Thirty-ninth Demolition Platoon and he spent his first day on Peleliu pinned down on the beach by snipers and machine gun–manned pillboxes. His job was to open holes in the barbed wire, which the Japanese had strung across the beaches, and to blow up as many gun emplacements, concrete blockhouses, and machine gun nests as he could find. "They were good," Young said of the Japanese. "They had plenty of time to prepare for [the invasion]."

The marines took the airfield the second day, but they couldn't put it to use because the Japanese artillery, entrenched along the heights of Umurbrogol, blasted anything that moved. The Japanese, having failed to annihilate the invaders on the beaches, withdrew to prepared defensive positions. When those positions were overrun, the survivors hid in a network of interconnected caves and emerged to attack the Americans from the rear, usually at night.

The fighting was fierce and often hand to hand. While moving inland, Young discarded his carbine for the heavier, but more accurate, Garand M-1, that he found with a dead marine. The assault on Umurbrogol was a nightmare. The saturation bombing had destroyed most of the scrub vegetation, leaving a moonscape of jagged coral, wood debris, and very little in the way of cover. The mortar rounds, which the Japanese launched from hidden positions above, exploded and sent up shards of broken coral. The area became known in marine lore as Bloody Nose Ridge. "It took a lot of men to clear it. Cost a lot of lives," Young said. "We'd get so far up and we'd get pushed down."

There were attacks and counterattacks. The marines slugged their way up the ridge, yard by yard.

After more than a month of fighting, the last Japanese-held ridge was taken. Three days earlier, Colonel Nakagawa shot himself. Peleliu was conquered, but at a terrible cost: more than fifteen hundred soldiers had been killed, and another six thousand wounded. More than ten thousand Japanese soldiers and civilians had died. Later, many questioned whether the cost had been worth it, saying the island could have been bypassed, isolated from resupply and allowed to wither on the vine. Young's unit was one of the many that suffered heavy casualties. He said they received replacements on a regular basis during the campaign, but "when we left the island, we were still seventeen men short." But for Young and his fellow marines, the worst was still to come on an island called Okinawa.

Angaur

Cpl. John Michael Garber decided it was worth breaking the rules to save his life. Garber, a driver in the Eighty-first Infantry's quartermaster company on the island of Angaur in the fall of 1944, was heading to the scene of a recent jungle battle. He had the unpleasant job of gathering the dead American soldiers and transporting them back to the base camp for identification. "They sent me up the hill to clean up," he said. To reach the battleground by truck, he had to follow a rough path winding through thick jungle overlooked by steep coral pinnacles pocked with caves. The army had established a speed limit of five miles per hour on the path because the trucks and jeeps overturned easily on the rutted, hairpin turns. Garber was worried about one curve in particular. "There was a Jap sighted-in on that curve," he said. The camouflaged sniper, who was using armor-piercing bullets, would aim at the white star painted on the U.S. trucks' doors. During the Angaur campaign, eighty-five drivers died at that one turn, which was aptly named Dead Man's Curve.

Garber decided he wasn't going to be another notch on a sniper's gunstock, so he elected to ignore the speed limit. As he went into the curve, he heard the thunk of an arriving bullet, followed an instant later by another. He kept driving and within moments was back in the comparative safety of the jungle canopy. "I was going too fast, I guess," he said of his brush with eternity. He noted that no one else in the truck seemed to mind he was speeding. "I was doing twenty. Nobody said a word."

Garber (seventy-two in 1990), a retired heavy equipment operator, was born in Sabetha, Kansas, near the Nebraska border. One of nine kids, he grew up on a farm and learned how to drive at an early age. After the war started, he helped build an airstrip in Colorado and a munitions plant in Parsons, Kansas, between stints as an over-the-road truck driver. In 1942, his luck ran out, and he was drafted. "I didn't think they'd take me," he said grinning. "I thought they had to have good men."

He and fourteen thousand other recruits were the first soldiers sent to newly built Camp Rucker in the southeastern corner of Alabama. Named after Confederate general Edmund Winchester Rucker, the camp provided sixty-five thousand acres of varied terrain, including large ranges for artillery training, smaller ranges for small arms and automatic weapons practice, tactical maneuvering ground for infantry units, and a lake to practice amphibious landings. Garber and his fellow soldiers became part of the reactivated Eighty-first Infantry "Wildcat" Division, which had participated in the Meuse-Argonne campaign during World War I. The new division expanded the U.S. fighting strength to more than three million men by mid-1942.

The thing Garber remembers most about his seventeen-week stay at Camp Rucker was the sweltering Alabama summer. "I never thought we had a place like that in the world," he said. Because of his driving experience, he was assigned to the quartermaster company, which was in charge of supplying the division with everything from food and clothing to ammunition and gasoline. "I wanted to be a pilot," he said, "but I didn't have the education." But that didn't exempt Garber from the rigors of full combat training as an infantryman. After leaving Camp Rucker in March 1943, his division went on maneuvers, slowly working its way west. At San Luis Obispo, on the California coast, the Eighty-first spent five months in amphibious training before shipping overseas in the summer of 1944. A final amphibious rehearsal was made on Guadalcanal just prior to the division's first combat mission—the invasion of Angaur.

On September 17, 1944, two days after the 1st Marine Division stormed the beaches of Peleliu, the 81st Division landed on Angaur, six miles to the south. Both islands were part of the Palau group, east of the Philippines. The 321st and 322nd Regiments landed on the northern beaches and met little initial enemy resistance because the Japanese had concentrated their main strength on the south end of the island. The original plan was for the two regiments to meet and form a larger beachhead before the combined force smashed southward. But the terrain in the northwest proved too rugged to be taken quickly, so the invasion planners decided instead to attack in two different directions. While the 322nd swept west, overrunning Saipan Town and driving the Japanese into the northwest hills, the 321st would drive inland and then wheel south, destroying all but a small pocket of resistance on the southeast coast.

Garber stepped onto the island a couple days after the invasion and spent most of the time ferrying supplies to the forward troops and bringing back the dead. "Whatever had to be done," he said. "When I was attached to the infantry, I was hauling the kitchen." The "clean-up" detail after the battles wasn't a job a person got used to, he said. "It [the truck] smelled so bad. I said, 'Anybody wants my truck, they can have her.' " He kept a carbine in the truck, which he never fired, but the sound of artillery was a constant reminder that the war was never far away. "I could hear the guns going off and hear [the rounds] going over us."

On September 20, with the Japanese divided and unable to mount a sustained attack, the island was declared secure. While the 321st mopped up in the south and workers hastily built a B-24 airstrip that would later serve as a staging area for the invasion of the Philippines, the 322nd set about destroying the remnants of a Japanese garrison in the northwestern hills. The Japanese soldiers there were fighting to the death, and it took thirty-five grueling days, and many casualties, before the 322nd cleaned out the last enemy cave.

Meanwhile, Garber and the rest of the Eighty-first were sent to Peleliu to reinforce the First Marines, who were encountering heavy opposition as they moved through the island's outer defensive perimeter. On Peleliu, Garber drove supply trucks and pulled night guard duty. One night stands out in his memory. He had fallen asleep on guard duty and awoke to deafening explosions and the earth moving beneath him. It took him several seconds to realize that the ground was shaking from the antiaircraft guns firing nearby. "I was so scared, I didn't know what to do," he said. But no bombs fell. It turned out to have been a single Japanese plane, probably on a reconnaissance mission, which quickly left the area pursued by an American fighter. "After he followed him off the island," Garber said, "he blew him up."

The last enemy resistance on Peleliu was mopped up on November 27, 1944. According to casualty figures from both islands, the 81st Division had 542 killed and 2,736 wounded. The 1st Marines had 1,257 killed and 5,274 wounded. More than 10,700 Japanese died defending the islands. Only 344 were taken prisoner.

After the Palau campaign, the Eighty-first was shipped to New Caledonia for a rest, but the men were soon training again, this time for the planned invasion of the Japanese home islands. Those plans were scrapped after atomic bombs were dropped on Hiroshima and Nagasaki and Japan surrendered. "The atomic bomb saved a lot of lives," Garber said. When the war ended, the Eighty-first was sent to Aomori, Japan, as part of the U.S. occupation force. Garber remembered that the Japanese civilians treated the American GIs "real nice, real nice. They didn't want this war either."

Leyte

LEYTE, THE PHILIPPINES, OCTOBER 24, 1944—Stayton Parr remembers heading toward Red Beach in the belly of an LST. The twenty-four-year-old LVT crew commander and driver recalls the ships behind them in the gulf firing at the shore, the huge shells whooshing overhead into the fortified hills. "There was really some blasting going on," said Parr.

When the LST was about a mile from the beach, it stopped and dropped its ramp, and the seventeen-ton LVTs plunged into the blue Pacific. "That was a thrill because you first went underwater, and you were under a while before your back end went down and you evened out," said Parr. His craft fully loaded with thirty-six combat troops—the equivalent of 5,800 pounds of cargo—he headed toward the beach. Between artillery explosions he could hear the sound of bullets hitting the sides of the armored vehicle.

After unloading the soldiers on the beach, Parr and some of his fellow LVT drivers headed back to sea for more troops and supplies, while others stayed onshore to tow trucks, jeeps, and field guns out of the mud created by a recent eighteen-hour monsoon. Some of the LVTs accompanied the combat troops heading inland. "I don't think you'd call us a front-line outfit," he said, "but we were in the front lines."

The outfit was the 727th Amphibian Tractor Battalion, one of several tractor battalions that became integral to the success of the island-hopping campaign in the Pacific. The LVT Model IVs—known to their crews as tractors or by the affectionate nickname "water buffaloes"—resembled nothing so much as the bottom half of a tank that had been sheared off at the turret. With a rear-loading ramp, the amphibious, tracked vehicles could both transport troops and equipment between ship and shore and negotiate the sand and swamps that mired most wheeled vehicles. They were armed with mounted fifty-caliber and thirty-caliber machine guns.

Parr, born and raised on a farm a few miles north of Blue Springs, Missouri, was a tool setter at Lake City Ammunition plant when he was drafted in 1942. He was sent to Fort Knox for basic training, which included two weeks of combat maneuvers in the Kentucky hills with German-speaking instructors "who made your life miserable," he said. Initially stationed at Fort Knox as an instructor, Parr taught soldiers how to operate and maintain trucks and tanks. He stayed there until March 1944, when they sent the battalion to Fort Ord, California, where the men began amphibious training in Monterey Bay.

In June they received their orders to head overseas. They were sent to San Francisco and boarded the *Willard A. Holbrook,* a U.S. Army transport, and on June 16 sailed under the Golden Gate Bridge. The soldiers, to boost their morale, came up with sayings for when they would eventually return—things like "Back alive in '45," "Back in heaven in '47" and "Golden Gate in '48." But some men, like Pfc. Tommy Cook, confided to Parr that they had a bad feeling that they weren't ever coming back. The trip over was uneventful, except for some natural phenomena they encountered. First they saw a huge waterspout, which the ship's captain took hasty steps to avoid, and later some St. Elmo's Fire, a ghostly blue-green light that lit up the ship's rigging and the fingertips of anyone who held his hand up in the air. It also produced an oddly pleasant tingling sensation. Seamen consider St. Elmo's Fire—named after the patron saint of the high seas—a sign of good luck. The *Holbrook* arrived in Hollandia, off the coast of New Guinea, in early July and immediately began training for the invasion. The men left New Guinea on October 13 and joined a convoy heading to Leyte. On October 20, 1944, U.S. troops stormed ashore. A few hours later, Gen. Douglas MacArthur landed near the town of Palo and made his famous declaration: "People of the Philippines, I have returned."

On October 23, as U.S. troops fought their way inland, the greatest naval battle in history began in Leyte Gulf. During the four-day battle, the Japanese lost twenty-six ships, including four aircraft carriers and three battleships. The U.S. lost one light carrier, two escort carriers, and three destroyers. The defeat crippled the Japanese Navy, which afterward was no longer able to mount major naval operations. The battle also marked one of the first organized uses of kamikazes during the war.

Not long after the invasion, Parr and some other men were on the opposite side of the island near a village called Calubian. There they traversed a crocodile-infested river to resupply the Twenty-fourth Division and transport the wounded. One day, near the end of the campaign, Parr was assigned to pick up a Japanese prisoner and take him back by water to Calubian. On the return trip, a Japanese Zero hurtled down the river and strafed the area. Luckily, he missed the LVT. The tractor crew was so surprised that by the time the men got to their guns, the Zero had disappeared. "We were kind of lax," Parr said. "We thought things were over with."

The battalion suffered no fatal casualties during the campaign, although several men were wounded. Cpl. Rade Allen and his two-man crew were credited with killing up to sixty Japanese soldiers after their LVT was disabled by a land mine. Instead of abandoning the vehicle, they remained at their machine guns, opening a hole in the Japanese defense perimeter for the advancing infantry. The men were awarded the Bronze Star for their actions. "We were very fortunate in many ways," Parr said of the battalion. "I can't believe we came out of it as well as we did."

Then, on Christmas Day 1944, a P-47 fighter attempting to take off from Tanauan Field crashed into an LVT. The accident killed five men from the 727th, who were returning from church services. Among the dead was Pfc. Tommy Cook.

War in Europe, Part 1

Making History

NEAR FALAISE, FRANCE, LATE AUGUST 1944—T-5 Byron Banta was riding in an armored column heading to Paris when he passed a wrecked German command car. He told the driver to pull over. "The command car was off to the side. It had been hit," he said. Banta, a company clerk, knew the car must have belonged to a high-ranking officer, and if it hadn't been searched, there might be important documents still in it. He ran to the car and looked inside. He could see two bodies. "The driver and the officer in it had both been killed," he said. "You could see that both were dead." He saw a leather case on the front seat. He grabbed it and ran back to his halftrack. As he got in, the command car burst into flames. Banta opened the case and found detailed German maps of France, Belgium, and Germany. The maps were much better than any the Americans had. "I had the best set of maps in the battalion," he said. "I had the German maps and I could read German, so I did just fine. From then on out, I enjoyed my service very much. Because I knew where I was and where I was going," he said. "The maps, they made all the difference."

Banta (eighty-three in 2001), was born in Sullivan, Missouri, about sixty miles southwest of St. Louis. "I grew up right in the middle of the Depression," he said. He remembers his father, a schoolteacher, reaching into his pocket and taking out a few dollars and change—the family's entire life savings. "He handed me a nickel to buy a loaf of bread," he said. Banta got his first suit when he graduated from high school in 1936.

He was in college at Southeast Missouri State when he received his draft notice in December 1941. "I listened to the president declare war and then went home for Christmas vacation, and my draft notice was waiting for me," he said. He requested and received a deferment until the next February, when he was scheduled to graduate with a degree in history. He went into the army in March 1942. Although he had a college degree, he wasn't interested in being an officer. "I really didn't have any desire to go into the OCS [Officer Candidate School]," he said. He was told most of the officers ended up being assigned to infantry divisions. "I really didn't want to go into the infantry."

Instead, like other midwesterners from Kansas, Oklahoma, Missouri, Minnesota, Nebraska, Iowa, and the Dakotas in 1942, Banta was assigned to the newly activated Fifth Armored Division. The army's philosophy seemed to be that if you came from the Heartland, you probably had some experience with a tractor. And "if you could drive a tractor," Banta said, "you could drive a tank."

Banta was assigned to the Thirty-fourth Tank Battalion, Combat Command A, Fifth Armored Division, Ninth Army. The combat command included four tank companies, four companies of armored infantry, one service company, and one headquarters company. Also attached to it were a mobile field artillery unit, a medical detachment, a reconnaissance unit, and a maintenance company. Banta was assigned to the service company. "I was a company clerk," he said. He kept track of such things as who was on weekend pass and who was in the hospital. "Just the ordinary daily workings of the battalion I was in."

After its activation at Fort Knox, the division was sent to California, Banta said. "That was when they were afraid the Japanese were going to invade California." The men spent much of their time there holding maneuvers in the desert. Later the division was sent to Tennessee, then to Pine Camp, New York, and then to Pennsylvania before finally boarding a troop ship bound for England. They landed in February 1944 and were based in Swindon, just west of London. Because there was no room for armored divisions on D-Day, the Fifth was assigned to operate the embarkation camps for the huge American invasion force. Tank drivers and gunners, infantry troops and clerks were put to work cleaning, maintaining, and cooking in the sprawling camps, which emptied overnight in early June. The Fifth was soon to follow the invasion force; it landed on Omaha Beach in August 1944.

Clerks in some divisions were rear-echelon troops, safely behind the front lines. Not so in the Fifth Armored Division. Banta said the service company traveled with the combat troops in the armored columns. "I was on a half-track and my typewriter went right along with me." One of his jobs was to write a daily report, which went directly to headquarters, detailing company strength and the numbers of men wounded and killed. It was right after the

Allies trapped and destroyed several panzer divisions in the Falaise Pocket, in August 1944, that Banta found the maps in the German command car. The maps, he said, determined what he would do for the rest of the war and even after it. Since he was one of the few in his battalion who could read German, he was allowed to keep the maps. He also received new duties, which included being sent to places "because I could find my way around." One of those new duties was graves registration. "The unit was moving all the time," he said, so they needed someone who could collect soldiers who had been killed in action (KIAs), take them to the designated collection point, and find his way back to his unit.

Banta had to inventory each KIA; that included searching each body for personal effects, which were put in a ditty bag that was attached to the corpse. On one body he found two thousand dollars, which the soldier had apparently won at a crap game. He said he never worried about money or other valuables disappearing because each person who took possession of the body was required to sign for it. Then it was their responsibility. That ensured that the "ditty bag traveled with the body all the way," he said.

After each battle, Banta would take a truck, pick up the bodies, and transport them to the collection points, which usually were open fields beside a main road. He said he transported German as well as American soldiers. "You took all the KIAs, regardless of their nationality, back to the collection point." About dealing with death, he said, "You became accustomed to it. I learned a long time ago, when you picked up dead body, you had to love it. You can't lift up a KIA at arm's length. You had to really love the body," he said. "You had to really take hold of him."

Banta was a T-5, which "was kind of a glorified corporal," he said. Like other soldiers he was issued a weapon. "We had a carbine, but I never used it." One time, he was in the front seat of a truck that was following a column of tanks. As they drove, they could hear snipers' bullets ping off the tanks in front. "The German snipers kept the tanks buttoned up tight," he said. After a while, the driver told Banta to return fire with his carbine. Banta shook his head. "I said, 'If I get that gun, we're dead," he said. "As long as I didn't have a gun, we weren't any danger to them.

"The only injury I ever had was self-inflicted," he added. It happened one night as he was watching an aerial attack while standing on a trailer hitch. "I slipped off that thing and skinned myself from my shin to the top of my knee," he said. "It just took that hide off the front of that shin. . . . Boy, that hurt."

But his proximity to combat ensured more than a few close calls. During the Battle of the Hürtgen Forest in November 1944, the men stopped one night in an area they thought was safe and dug their foxholes. It wasn't long before

German 88s began bursting among them. "They had zeroed in the place we had stopped, the Germans had," Banta said. "I was in one of the few foxholes that didn't receive a direct hit." The tanks also were a favorite target of the Luftwaffe. "We were constantly strafed by the German air force," he said. Luckily, "we didn't stay anyplace long. We were always on the move." During the Battle of the Bulge, they were north of the Ardennes, in Eupen, Belgium. "We had been in contact just before that and had got shot up pretty bad," Banta said. In fact, most of the battalion's tanks had been knocked out of action. But when the Germans counterattacked in December, the Americans were so short of artillery that they towed the disabled tanks to the front and used them as stationary artillery.

In early 1945, the Fifth Armored crossed the Luxembourg border into Germany. Later, it crossed the Rhine River on a pontoon bridge north of Cologne. "I had the wonderful experience of crossing the river in a jeep between two tanks," he said. "That jeep rode about ten feet above the water across the Rhine River." When the war ended, Banta said, "I was in the middle of the Elbe River, thirty miles from Berlin, when they called us back."

After the war was over, Banta's German maps kept him busy. On one mission for U.S. military intelligence, he was sent to Dresden to pick up a scientist who had been involved in Germany's rocket program. At the time the Allies were in a race with the Russians to round up all known Nazi scientists, ranging from the rocket scientists who had helped develop the dreaded V-2 rocket, to the chemists who had developed the poison gas used to murder millions of Jews. The U.S. didn't want them working for the Russians, so they clandestinely brought them to America, cleansed their Nazi dossiers, and put them to work in what would become America's space program and chemical warfare research. In the top-secret Project Paperclip, sixteen hundred German and Austrian scientists were brought to the U.S. between 1945 and 1973. Many, despite their Nazi pasts, became respected members of the scientific community. Former Nazi rocket scientist Wernher von Braun became the director of the NASA center in 1960. Another Nazi rocket expert, Kurt Debus, became the first director of the Kennedy Space Center.

Banta's orders were to pick up the scientist, his wife, and two children. The translator who went along told the family they could only bring what they could carry. Banta said the family offered him a twelve-piece set of German silver, but he couldn't accept it because all the men were under strict orders not to take anything from the Germans. "I couldn't take it. Left it for the Russians," he said. He added that he never knew the name of the scientist, but "he was likely put to work in the [U.S. space] program."

Banta saw a lot of bad things during the war. One of the worst was the Buchenwald concentration camp. Located on a hill four miles outside Weimer, Germany, Buchenwald was one of the largest of the Nazi death camps, at one time housing as many as sixty thousand slave laborers. When it was liberated in April 1945, the population was only twenty thousand. Banta had grown used to seeing dead bodies, but it was different at Buchenwald. "You could see the ovens and the bodies that were stacked up in front of them," he said. "It was an eye opener. You just couldn't see how . . . one man could treat another man they way they did. But they did."

Banta, who married while in the service, left the army in November 1945 and went to Washington University to get a master's degree in history. After he graduated, he moved his family to Marshall, Missouri, and began teaching at Missouri Valley College. He stayed there thirty-seven years, retiring in 1983. He never had a desire to go back to Europe after the war. "I hadn't lost anything over there and I didn't see any need to go back."

To Banta, World War II was an adventure. His adventure. "I think my education made it that way," he said. "I looked at it as an opportunity to see places I never dreamed I would see." While a part of him realized the inherent danger of the situation, "I never thought about that. I never thought about getting hit or killed." What he thought about, he said, was the small part he was playing in the historic events taking place. "I figured I was now involved in making history."

Combat Engineer

The year 2000 was bittersweet for Albert Schultz. The highlight came that December when the Lee's Summit resident received a letter from Senators Christopher "Kit" Bond and John Ashcroft informing him that he would receive a replica of the Jubilee of Liberty Medal. The medal, which was issued by France to the Allied soldiers who took part in the D-Day landings during World War II, arrived in the mail in January 2001.

The low point had occurred a couple months earlier after Schultz attended the last official reunion of the 832nd Engineer Aviation Battalion in Nashville. What had started as a battalion of about 160 enlisted men was down to 25 survivors. Although individual members would likely stay in touch, no more official reunions were planned. "There wasn't enough fellas left," Schultz said. What the Germans couldn't do during the war, time has achieved.

Schultz (eighty-five in 2001) was the unit commander of the 832nd, which was a combat engineer corps similar to the Seabees in the Pacific. The battalion, which participated in five campaigns, built airfields for the Ninth Air Force.

Schultz was working as a sales manager for an appliance store in Kansas City, Kansas, when he received his draft notice in February 1941. At his induction, they asked him what he wanted to do in the service. When he noted his sales background, he was told curtly, "We ain't got room for salesmen." Instead, he was assigned to the combat engineers. At the time, he and the other draftees were told they would only be needed in the service about a year. But when the Japanese attacked Pearl Harbor, that changed. "Now you're in for the duration," he was told.

Shortly after being assigned to the engineer corps, Private Schultz was told to take a truck, drive to a gravel pit, and fill the truck with gravel. "At that moment," he said, "I knew that wasn't what I wanted to do." So Schultz applied for and was accepted into the OCS. The training was tough, he said, but he was aided by having taken three years of ROTC in high school. "That helped me get through officers' school," he said. As a newly minted second lieutenant, he headed to Biggs Field in El Paso, Texas, to join the just-organized 832nd. The battalion was trained to build permanent concrete airfields and temporary pierced-plank airstrips. Pierced plank was a type of metal matting punched with circular holes that could be laid quickly and could accommodate all but the heaviest bombers. "We could put one in in forty-eight hours," Schultz said. "The boys got so they could do it in their sleep."

In June 1942, Schultz got married. Two months later he was heading to England. "I didn't see my wife for three years after that," he said. With orders to go overseas, the battalion had to fill its ranks with raw recruits. Many came from the East Coast and had little basic training. "Some of the fellas hadn't fired a rifle," he said. "Actually, they didn't get any rifle practice 'till we got to England. . . . At that time we were using World War I equipment," principally the thirty-caliber Springfield bolt-action rifle. Later they were issued the thirty-caliber M-1 semiautomatic.

After the ten-day trip from New York to England aboard the USS *Siboney*, the battalion was put to work building concrete runways for B-17s of the Ninth Air Force. That continued until the spring of 1944 when they were mobilized for the D-Day invasion. The 832nd arrived on Omaha Beach on June 10. Although the fighting had moved off the beaches by then, there were still pockets of German defenders in the area. After wading to shore from the landing craft, the men had to wait on a nearby hill until the area that had been chosen for their first airstrip could be taken. "We didn't go over right away because the Germans still had possession," he said.

The Germans didn't go easily. In fact, Schultz remembers getting orders to be prepared to pull back and abandon the beachhead if things went badly. "Fortunately, it didn't work that way, [but] it was scary," he said. "I think the United States kept that quiet." Schultz believes the main reason they were able to break out from Normandy was the arrival of Gen. George Patton's Third Army. "I just thought General Patton was one of the best fighting generals we ever had," he said. "I admired him." With his trademark scarf and ivory-handled side arms, Patton was an imposing figure as he rode past the troops. "He never stayed around long," Schultz said. "He was good at tank warfare," he added. "He knew how to handle them and get the job done."

After the breakout, the 832nd was attached to the 3rd Army and followed Patton through France. Schultz remembers passing through devastated St. Lô. "It was nothing. It was pulverized," he said. "It was horrible." The 832nd was with the 3rd Army during the Germans' Ardennes offensive in the early winter of 1944. Schultz doesn't remember much about that time. "We were busy building airfields," he said.

Although the engineers were usually behind the front lines, they weren't necessarily safe. Shortly after D-Day, the Germans unveiled their newest terror weapon, the V-1 "buzz bomb." A subsonic flying bomb powered by a ram jet engine, the V-1 was used mainly against civilians in London. The buzz bomb got its name from the buzzing sound it made as it flew overhead. Schultz remembers seeing and hearing the London-bound buzz bombs flying over. As long as you could hear the engine, you were safe, but when the engine suddenly cut off, that signaled the bomb was about to crash. One time, he said, a buzz bomb went down near one of the 832nd's construction crews, killing several men. "Unfortunately they were in the wrong place at the wrong time," he said.

Another time, a group of engineers was sent out to find a site for a new airfield. The group, which was traveling in a halftrack, went down the wrong road and was captured by the Germans. Later, the engineers were repatriated in a prisoner exchange. Since U.S. policy was to send all released POWs back home immediately, the engineers got an early trip back to the States. "They lucked out," Schultz said.

He had a close call of his own. It happened while he was standing in a doorway of a just-captured German officer's quarters. Schultz was wearing his helmet, which had a white stripe painted on the front to let the enlisted men know he was an officer. However, the stripe also provided a good target for snipers.

While Schultz was standing there, a sniper took a shot at him. The bullet splintered the wood just above his head. "I jumped into the building real quick," he said. "A little lower and I would have been a dead duck."

The 832nd followed Patton all the way into Germany, which is where the engineers were sent when the war in Europe ended. By then, Schultz had gone from a buck private all the way to major. He stayed in the army reserves until the Korean War began. When he was given the option of reentering active service and being sent to Korea or leaving the reserves, he chose to leave, partly to care for his wife, Louise, who had been diagnosed with multiple sclerosis. "I would have liked to go to Korea," he admits, but in the end decided against it. "I thought I'd done my thing already." After a successful career in commercial real estate, Schultz retired in 1975.

On the wall of his apartment is a pencil sketch of him done by artist Peter DuMitru, who was a soldier in the 832nd. The sketch was done in 1944, while the battalion was in France. Schultz, who was a captain at the time, was sitting in his command tent when DuMitru walked in and started drawing. After the war, DuMitru created an insignia for the 832nd—an armed soldier with a shovel on his back riding a winged tractor. The tractor, which has a face and hands, is holding a piece of pierced planking. Above it are the words *Aviation Engineers.* For years the insignia was used on the 832nd Association's newsletter. DuMitru also designed a memorial plaque to the 832nd, which hangs in the regimental room of the U.S. Army Engineer Museum at Fort Leonard Wood, Missouri, "He was a great artist," Schultz said of DuMitru. "He was really an asset to our battalion. Unfortunately, he passed away [in 1999]."

Like many World War II veterans, Schultz looks back on the war as a once-in-a-lifetime experience. He wouldn't want to go through it again, but he's glad to have served his country. "I didn't mind being in the army. I had a good experience," he said. He's never been back to Europe. "I really didn't have any desire to go back," he said. "I had all I wanted."

Lucky Breaks

Don Wood had his share of lucky breaks during World War II. He managed to survive four months of combat, earning a Bronze Star in the process. And after the war, he played a minor role in the historic Nuremberg Trials.

Wood (seventy-three in 1999) quit school to join the merchant marines and later was drafted into the army. Sent to boot camp in Texas, he enrolled in paratrooper training, but "the Battle of the Bulge was going on then," he said, "so they cancelled all paratrooper training and put us all in the infantry." Wood was sent overseas on a Liberty ship bound for England. Although three-quarters of the passengers were seasick during the trip, Wood wasn't bothered at all. "I never missed a meal," he said. "I almost did once when I was watching a guy at the wrong time."

After a brief stop in England, the soldiers landed in France in December 1944 and were rushed to the Ardennes front as replacement troops for the 376th Regiment of the 94th Infantry Division. By the time they arrived, the division already was moving forward with the Germans in retreat. Wood was assigned to a machine gun outfit. He remembers his first night in combat distinctly. He had the job of ammo bearer for a thirty-caliber machine gun and remembers running, hunched over, from position to position across the irregular terrain with tracers ripping the air only inches above his head. One time he stumbled. "I bet I ran fifty yards on my knees," he said, "and nobody passed me. . . . That was my first night in combat and boy was I scared."

Wood earned his Bronze Star during fighting in Germany on the night of March 21, 1945. With his company pinned down by a machine gun, his squad leader "volunteered" him and several others to draw the enemy fire away from the main body of troops. So Wood, carrying his own machine gun, crawled about two hundred yards to the middle of a field, set up the gun and opened fire. The enemy machine gun then turned toward Wood's group, allowing his company to move out and eventually destroy the German position.

Later Wood had an even closer call during street fighting in a bombed-out German town. There were enemy snipers in one of the buildings, and Wood jumped into a shell hole to get out of the line of fire. A buddy, however, warned him that the snipers had a bead on the crater, so Wood hastily retreated behind a wall. Seconds later another soldier jumped into the crater and before Wood could warn him, "they put a bullet right through his head."

A call went out for a medic, and when one came to the soldier's aid, a sniper killed him as well. "I was kind of upset about that," Wood said. He found a discarded rifle and carried it and his own to the top of a nearby building to see if he could find the snipers. When he looked over the edge, he saw the German snipers surrendering. "They came out with their hands up after they killed those two guys," he said. "I didn't think that was the time to give up." So, he opened fire on the surrendering Germans, who immediately dropped to the ground in panic. He emptied his rifle and then picked up the other weapon and emptied it. And missed. "I shot twenty-two times and I missed every one of them," he said shaking his head. Later there were questions about who the

American gunman had been, but Wood kept silent. "I never got anything out of that 'cause I never owned up."

Once he was running across a field when an enemy position opened up on him. "I could see the bullets pecking toward me," he said. When the explosions of dirt reached his feet, he leaped forward "like Jesse Owens" and emerged somehow unscathed. He's convinced that "the next one would have got me."

After the war, Wood's outfit was sent to Czechoslovakia as part of a multinational peacekeeping force on the Russian border. A few months later, he was transferred to Nuremberg, where the war crimes tribunal was in session. Assigned to guard detail and outfitted in an immaculate uniform, which included white leggings and gloves, he was stationed outside the courtroom doors, at the gate where official vehicles entered the trial complex, or, sometimes, inside the courtroom.

Once, he recalled, he had to pull his forty-five on a Russian officer who didn't have the correct pass and tried to force his way through the gate with his car. "We were having trouble with the Russians all the time then," he said. The only famous person he remembers seeing during the trials was Hermann Göring, once Hitler's right-hand man. Eventually sentenced to death by hanging, Göring escaped his sentence by swallowing a cyanide capsule on October 15, 1946.

After the war, Wood owned and operated a men's wear store. He retired in 1976. He said he wouldn't trade his war experience for anything—just so he doesn't have to go through it again. "It was some of the best times and the worst times," he said.

Shadows

Forty-four years after the end of World War II, Leo Burrow went back to Belgium. The retired auto mechanic took his wife, Jean, and they stayed with her cousin, who lives in Brussels. They toured a crystal factory in Liege, bought a copper milk can in Brugge, and visited the glass-roofed Galerie St. Hubert in Brussels. They went to Wiesbaden in West Germany, where Leo was stationed after the war and walked around downtown Frankfurt and the cobbled streets of Cologne. And they went to Eben Emael, the fortress where Leo served as a loader for the 749th AAA Gun Battalion, an antiaircraft unit guarding the Meuse River and the Albert Canal from Nazi fighter planes during the war. The beet fields were still there. "Every little town you saw was more beautiful than the last one," Jean said. "We saw so much. . . . It was a wonderful trip."

The Burrows arrived in Brussels on June 8, 1989. Jean's cousin, a retired submarine commander, owns a house located in an affluent part of the city, but the Burrows said the entire country seemed to be thriving. "Everybody had nice cars over there. Everybody looked very prosperous," Jean said. "We saw no poverty, no gangs. The streets weren't littered."

It was Jean's first trip overseas, and she was entranced. So was Leo, but for different reasons. For him, returning to Europe brought back swarms of memories of a half-forgotten war: of lost years, lost friends, the kindness of the Belgium people, the camaraderie of battle. It opened a door he'd kept locked for forty years.

It made him remember.

In 1942, Leo was twenty-two. He lived in Lee's Summit and worked at Longview Farms milking cows. In those days he was a much-pursued bachelor, said Jean, who didn't meet Leo until after the war. "The girls had been running after him for years," she said smiling. "At least that's the story I got." That September, Leo was drafted into the army and sent to Fort Bliss for basic training. He was to have been sent to North Africa as part of a replacement outfit, but he contracted the measles, and so, after he recovered, he was sent to Akureyri, Iceland, instead, where he joined the 749th. He saw his first action loading seventy-pound shells into the nine-millimeter antiaircraft guns. "That's where he gets those big arms," Jean said proudly.

"We got six German planes up there," Leo said.

He was one of three brothers serving in the armed forces during World War II. An older brother was serving on a navy tanker in the Pacific. Leo's twin brother was stationed in the Aleutians.

In May 1944, the 749th was sent to England to prepare for D-Day. Leo's outfit went to South Wales for training by English instructors on the use of newly developed radar-equipped antiaircraft guns. Unlike the old field finders, the radar was much more accurate, he said. And the flak rounds of the new guns exploded automatically with no fuses requiring cutting. The 749th landed at Omaha Beach about five weeks after the Normandy invasion. From there they went to Paris and Holland and soon were leading the infantry in the 1st Army's push toward the Rhineland.

Often the men in Leo's outfit had to fight the elite SS troops. One night a company of SS soldiers stumbled onto their camp. The surprised Americans surprised the Germans even more and were able to take many of them captive. "We got twenty-eight of them in one night," Leo said. "They were pretty thick."

When they reached Eben Emael, the fields were full of sugar beets. "We slept out there in our pup tents all winter," he said. He remembers the women of the town walking to their camp in cloth-wrapped wooden shoes during the bitter Belgium winter to do the soldiers' laundry. They did it simply out of kindness toward their American liberators, and the soldiers repaid them with soap and candy bars. "That's all we had," Leo said. "They didn't have any soap or candy, so they were glad to get it." The 749th's job was to protect the strategically located Meuse River and the Albert Canal, located a few miles from Holland's border with Belgium, from German fighters. "We did get a lot of German planes," Leo said. "They'd come in strafin' us."

Later Leo was transferred temporarily to the 17th Airborne Division as a rifleman to provide ground support for the 155th Field Artillery, which was firing across the Rhine at the city of Wesel, Germany. Within a few weeks, the war was over. Leo left the service in late 1945 with four battle stars from campaigns in Northern France, Central Europe, and the Rhineland. He said his unit suffered few casualties. "We were just lucky," he said.

Some of Belgium was as Leo remembered it, but much was not. Gone were the blasted cities, the burned-out tanks, the scattered, unburied dead. The new Belgium was clean, orderly, and prosperous, like much of Europe. Momentos of their trip fill their Lee's Summit home: crystal vases; the copper milk can Leo bought for seventy-five dollars in Brugge; a cuckoo clock that echoes in the hallway.

But there is one city where the war is a constant reminder. In Bastogne, where the Battle of the Bulge raged in December 1944, the citizens have erected a huge historical center and memorial to the American soldiers who took part in the battle. Both of the structures are in the shape of the five-point star used by the U.S. military. The historical center contains a central amphitheater with screens showing photographs of the battle and commentary in six languages.

The open-air memorial is awesome in its simplicity. Each side is dedicated to a different state, and the names and home states of the soldiers who took part are engraved on the pillars. The top of the monument is a walkway with a panoramic view of the Belgian countryside. Leo said the Belgians built the structures to show their appreciation for what the United States did for them during the war. "It's fantastic," he said.

Leo never used to talk about the war. Then, a few years ago, members of the 749th organized their first reunion, and Leo and Jean went to it in Massachusetts. For the first time in forty years, Leo found himself talking about the war with others who had been there, who knew what war was like. It was a kind of therapy for him. But there are some things Leo still can't talk about. He had one bad night during their trip to Belgium. He couldn't sleep. When asked about it by a reporter, he became quiet, and his eyes filled with tears.

"Brought back memories," he said, his voice breaking. He couldn't continue.

"Of Bastogne?" Jean asked gently.

Leo nodded, choked with emotion and shadows of the past.

Battle of the Bulge

Ghost Front

In the bone-chilling winter of 1944, Robert Allen Peck was trying hard to kill and avoid being killed by German soldiers during the Nazi counteroffensive that became known as the Battle of the Bulge. In many ways, the battle was America's finest hour. In the fall of 1944, the Allies had breached Germany's defenses, becoming the first hostile army on German soil since Napoleon's. French troops reached the Rhine River on October 19, and on December 3, the U.S. Ninety-fifth Infantry Division crossed the Saar River.

While American GIs were meeting stiff German resistance in the Huertgen Forest southeast of Aachen, the hills and forests of the Ardennes to the south were eerily quiet. The only Germans to be seen were in low-flying reconnaissance planes, and most Allied soldiers had little to do but watch the snow fall. GIs called the area the Ghost Front. "It was the coldest [winter] in fifty years," said Peck, then a private first class with the Seventy-fifth Infantry Division, Ninth Army, which was posted along the thinly defended eighty-mile front. Three of the six U.S. divisions in the area were made up predominantly of young draftees who had not yet been in combat. But that was fine since nothing was likely to happen in the Ardennes. The front was so lightly patrolled, German soldiers were able to slip through the lines to visit relatives in the occupied zone.

In the face of mounting defeats on both the eastern and western fronts, Hitler concocted an audacious plan. Gathering a patchwork army of twenty-four divisions, he would explode through the Ardennes front, capture much-needed fuel depots and the strategically important port at Antwerp, and in the process, shred Montgomery's armies. Then, with the Allies reeling in the west, he could turn his energies on the Russians.

The attack on the Ghost Front began at 5:30 A.M. December 16 with a massive artillery barrage. The Allied command recognized almost immediately that it signaled a major counteroffensive by the Germans, but snow and fog kept the 8th Air Force grounded in England, and the only available combat reserves were the 82nd and 101st Airborne Divisions, which were still recovering from combat in Holland. They were ordered immediately to the front.

Spearheaded by elite Panzer divisions, the German attack quickly swept through the U.S. forces. In the confusion, many GIs found themselves behind enemy lines and were faced with the prospect of surrendering or holding out against overwhelming odds.

Peck's squad was one of those cut off from its division. It was in the Belgian town of Bastogne. That's also where the 101st Airborne, the Screaming Eagles, was sent to reinforce the 9th and 10th Armored Divisions defending the strategic crossroads. As it turned out, the airborne troops arrived just in time to be surrounded by the enemy. Although cut off from supplies and reinforcements and outnumbered three to one, the GIs fought on. Some of those who surrendered lived just long enough to regret it. Near Malmédy, 140 members of a U.S. field artillery battery were captured by German troops. As they stood unarmed in a snowy field, the Germans mowed them down with machine guns. Afterward, the Germans walked among the bodies and executed the wounded. Unfortunately for the Germans, there were forty-two survivors. As word of the Malmédy massacre spread, the act of taking German prisoners became a rarity. Meanwhile, in Bastogne, the Germans were pouring artillery and tank rounds into the beleaguered garrison. Peck recalls that they even shot the notoriously inaccurate V-1 buzz bombs into the town. "They didn't give a damn where they landed," he said. Although ammunition was precious, the Americans tried to shoot the bombs while they were still in the air with their machine guns and small arms because they packed enough explosives to destroy whole city blocks.

Once, when looking for cover during an artillery attack, Peck found a passageway leading to an underground bomb shelter that had been built during World War I. Hiding in the shelter were two thousand terrified civilians.

The Americans in Bastogne were down to an average of ten rounds per gun when a break in the weather allowed an airdrop of supplies two days before Christmas. Then, on December 26, twenty tanks and a column of halftracks loaded with infantry from Patton's Third Army broke through the German lines and rolled into Bastogne. The siege was over. But the battle wasn't. It had just moved from the ground to the sky. With the clear weather, the Eighth Air Force began attacking the German ground troops. The weather also freed the Luftwaffe, which counterattacked in swarms. Peck said he'd never seen so many planes in the sky at once; there must have been hundreds of them. "One time we saw five planes hit the ground at the same time. We weren't worried about the enemy, we were worried about getting hit by planes."

But one of the strangest stories to come out of the battle was one Peck only heard about. It seems a group of GIs were in a foxhole in Bastogne when eleven unarmed U.S. soldiers marched out of the fog. The GIs had been warned about English-speaking German infiltrators wearing captured American uniforms, so they ordered the soldiers to halt. But the soldiers acted as if they didn't hear them. They simply marched on, and the GIs, inexplicably, let them pass. Peck has an explanation: "They were ghosts marching. They marched right past them and then disappeared into the woods."

Bastogne

When fourteen-year-old LeRoy Dir heard the news in September 1939, that Germany had invaded Poland, he had no idea that five years later he would be fighting for his life, surrounded by Germans, trapped in a garrison in a little town in southern Belgium called Bastogne.

After all, Poland was a long way from Adrian, Missouri, where Dir grew up. "I didn't know the seriousness of it," he said of the beginning of World War II. Dir said he was too young to think that the chaos in a place as remote as Europe would eventually affect him. "Hell no, I never thought about it. Not at the time." That soon changed. He recalls President Roosevelt's radio broadcast announcing Japan's sneak attack on Pearl Harbor. After that, everything was different. "I was wanting to go because it kept getting seriouser and seriouser," he said. "I got the idea that it was for real."

He was eighteen and still in high school when he went to the recruiting station to enlist in May 1943. He tried the navy first, but their quotas were filled, so he settled for the army. He was assigned to the Second Armored Division as an engineer and was trained to build pontoon bridges for river crossings. Then he learned he could earn fifty dollars more a month by joining the paratroopers. He volunteered and was sent to Fort Benning, Georgia, for jump school. When he graduated, he was sent to England to join the 101st Airborne Division—the Screaming Eagles. "They told us we were a suicide outfit," he said, and could expect to have a 96 to 97 percent casualty rate. "But at that age, you didn't think nothing about that. . . . But you found out they were serious."

In England, preparations were being made for the D-Day invasion. Dir said they were never told in advance whether their jumps were practice or the real thing, so they always jumped with their faces blackened and carrying more than one hundred pounds of equipment, including grenades, extra ammunition, and K-rations. During one practice night jump, the planes got lost and dropped Dir's group over a heavily forested region. The night was overcast, he recalled, and there was only inky blackness below. "I hit them damn trees," he said. "I fell right on a damn stump and knocked a bunch of vertebra out of my back." He ended up having a disk removed from his neck and was laid up for weeks. The army was going to discharge him, but he managed to get transferred back to his division before the papers arrived.

He rejoined the 101st just before Market-Garden. On September 17, 1944, he jumped from a low-flying C-47 Dakota, which was trying desperately to avoid heavy flak over the drop zone. He estimated the altitude was about 550 feet. "We no more got out of there [the plane] and you'd hit the ground," he said.

Their initial job was to clear the Germans out of the landing areas to be used by the gliders being towed by the Dakotas. "We jumped into the middle of the damn Germans," he said, but luckily, they were not where the Germans expected them. After landing safely, Dir noticed several holes in his chute. He saw at least eight Allied planes shot down and watched helplessly as several gliders carrying troops and equipment crashed nearby. "God, you could see gliders for miles," he said. "They were landing on each other. It was a mess." After the gliders were on the ground, the 101st was deployed to capture and hold the bridges over the canals near Eindhoven. The Germans, however, were more numerous than expected and slowed the Allied advance.

Although trained as a rifleman, Dir was assigned to a bazooka squad and later was issued an air-cooled, thirty-caliber, tripod-mounted machine gun. He was glad to have the extra firepower, but he was distressed to learn that machine guns tend to draw a lot of enemy fire. "They do about anything they can to knock you out," he said.

Dir went seventy-three days without a bath, and he was still taped like a mummy after his spinal injury. He recalled running across a field trying to avoid being cut in half by a German machine gun nest. "We had seven guys hit just crossing that little old field," he said.

In Holland, Dir's squad had the job of clearing and laying minefields. When things got tight, Dir, by then a T-5 (corporal), used horses to clear troop paths through the mines. "It sounds pretty bad, but I did it," he said. "They will run on three legs. When the second one goes, you have to kill them."

On December 16, 1944, the Germans dashed across the Siegfried line in a blitzkrieg attack on Allied positions in the Ardennes region. The Germans called the plan Operation Autumn Mist, but operation maps showed the German penetration as a huge bulge in the Allied lines. A newspaper correspondent coined the now-famous name: the Battle of the Bulge.

The 11,000 men of the 101st were loaded onto 380 open trucks and sent to Bastogne, a small Belgian town where seven crossroads come together. Their job was to reinforce elements of the 9th and 10th Armored divisions defending the garrison. Soon after they arrived, many of them without adequate winter clothing and low on ammunition, the Germans closed the trap, and the garrison was surrounded and under heavy attack. During the siege, the Germans issued a demand for surrender, to which Brig. Gen. Anthony McAuliffe, commander of the garrison, responded with a written reply: "Nuts!" Hitler's response was no less succinct. "Erase Bastogne," he said.

It was cold and snowy in Bastogne in December 1944. "We lived right out in the damn snow and everything," Dir said. "We about froze to death."

"He's lucky he didn't lose his feet," said Dir's mother, Francis. She soaked his feet constantly when he returned to the States after the war and "big flakes would fall off." Dir said to this day his feet remain sensitive to colored dyes, and he can only wear white socks.

The fighting was terrible. Dir started out on a thirty-caliber machine gun and soon moved up to a fifty-caliber. He said it was like going from a rifle to a howitzer. "You hit a man with that . . . and you tear hunks out of him." His emplacement was a foxhole in the middle of a snowy field looking down into a valley. "I was right out in the wide open," he said. One of his closest calls was when he was caught in the crossfire between three German panzers and a German machine gun and advancing enemy troops. "I shot at least three truckloads of them," he said matter-of-factly. "I killed at least, I don't know, that one morning, 100 or 150." Miraculously, he wasn't wounded, but after the battle, he discovered seven bullet holes through his backpack. "You don't have to go to church to know there's a Jesus Christ," he said. "Me and Him had some awful serious talks. . . . I had a lot of help."

Although a few supplies were airlifted in, troops usually had to make do with whatever was available. Food was a problem, not because it was scarce, but because cooking fires tended to attract German artillery. "I milked cows for three days to keep us going," Dir said. "That warm milk warmed us up a little bit. My country experience paid off."

The casualty rate remained high among paratroopers in Bastogne. Dir was one of only two survivors from his seventeen-man squad. And he had a tough time staying alive. The Germans kept up an almost continuous barrage from tanks, mortars, rockets, and heavy artillery. During one attack, Dir sought shelter in a barn. As soon as he got inside, the barn received a direct hit.

By December 1944, Francis had moved her family to Wichita, Kansas, and gone to work at the Boeing plant. One night in December she had a dream. She saw her son LeRoy standing on a snowy hill. He was trying to tell her something, "but I couldn't hear a word he said." The next morning, she told her other son, "Your brother's in trouble." A few weeks later, she received a telegram saying that LeRoy was missing in action. He was reported missing on the day Francis had her dream. "I was absolutely crushed," she said. "War is a horrible thing."

When Dir came to, he was blind, and the barn was on fire. Led by a wounded soldier, he climbed the ladder into the hayloft and jumped out the window to safety. Dir had shrapnel in his leg, but his companion was riddled with it. "He was in bad shape," Dir said. Dir doctored him as best he could, and then the two of them took stock of their situation. Their position had been overrun, and the Germans were everywhere. Dir was blind and hobbled, and his buddy was seriously wounded. They decided to hide during the day and try to make it back to friendly lines at night. They headed west. Four days later, Dir's eyesight began to return, although it remained blurry for almost two weeks. "It blasted a bunch of dirt and stuff into my eyes," he said of the explosion. The two men eventually made it back to Allied territory as the German assault stalled four miles from the Meuse River. Soon the Germans were in full retreat.

Strictly in terms of losses, Autumn Mist was almost a success. American casualties were 76,890, compared with 81,834 for the Germans, but the U.S. lost almost twice as many tanks and aircraft. What made the battle catastrophic for Germany was that the Allies could replace their lost fighting men and equipment. The Germans couldn't.

After a brief recuperation—his companion also survived his injuries—Dir was sent back into action in early 1945. The 101st was assigned the job of ferrying the lead combat troops over the Rhine River into Germany and then mopping up behind them. But several times his fifty-caliber was called up to knock out enemy machine gun nests when the gunners had Allied troops pinned down. The 101st mopped up at Merchingen, Ulm, Kaufbeuren, and Berchtesgaden, Hitler's Eagle's Nest hideaway and summer Reichschancellory, and hunted SS troops in the Austrian foothills. "Most of them were committing suicide before we could get to them," Dir said.

After the war in Europe ended, Dwight Eisenhower, the Allies' supreme commander, reviewed the 101st and asked if there were any Kansans among the men. Dir got to shake Eisenhower's hand. "He wasn't much of a president," Dir said, "but he was a hell of a general."

Like many combat veterans, Dir had some trouble adjusting to life back in the States. He refused to go hunting, a favorite pastime before the war. "I was so damn used to fast pulling [triggers], I didn't trust anyone," he said. "I didn't trust myself." Francis was just glad to have her son home. She said when he returned safely, "that was the greatest feeling of all."

Years have passed and memories have faded, but the effects of World War II linger for Dir, who draws a 40 percent disability pension because of his wartime injuries. Knowing what he knows now, would he volunteer if he had it to do over again?

Dir just smiles. "Oh, I think so."

War in Europe, Part 2

"Our Real Adventure"

George Rhodes Jr. can still remember lying on a dark mountainside in France, his leg shredded by a German landmine, looking up at tracer bullets flitting overhead like angry, luminous bees. "I was still in high school when the war broke out," Rhodes said. Caught up in the patriotic fervor, Rhodes, like many of his classmates, went to the recruiting center in downtown Kansas City to enlist after graduating from Lee's Summit High School in the summer of 1942. "I was eager to get in, as were most young men my age," he said. However, he was turned down because of poor eyesight. "I even tried the merchant marines. Even they wouldn't take me."

That, he acknowledges, was probably lucky for him because service in the merchant marines was extremely dangerous duty during the early years of World War II. But at the time, he said, it was hard watching his friends leave for boot camp. "I was somewhat downhearted over the whole thing because I wondered if I'd ever get in." He needn't have worried. He enrolled at the University of Missouri–Columbia that fall, and in January 1943, he received his draft notice. Because of his high grades, he was accepted into the army's specialized training program and was sent to an army air corps engineering school.

Meanwhile, the war was heating up. In January 1944, the Allies landed at Anzio and moved toward the fortified Gustav line south of Rome. In the Pacific, Adm. Chester Nimitz's carrier strike force attacked the Marshall Islands on January 31, and within a month U.S. forces had taken Eniwetok and Truk and gained a foothold in the Admiralty Islands.

But the event that would shape Rhodes's future was the massive D-Day invasion of France. The War Department decided it had enough specialists and needed more GIs. Rhodes was assigned to the Forty-second Infantry, the

Rainbow Division, so named because when it was formed during World War I, it was composed of National Guard units from twenty-six states.

Rhodes left New York Harbor on a Liberty ship the day after Thanksgiving and—after spending most of the trip seasick—arrived in Marseilles on Dec. 10. Although the city was in Allied hands, the harbor hadn't been cleared yet, and he remembers passing huge capsized freighters, only their hulls showing above the water. Rhodes and his fellow GIs were dropped off the landing craft in a breakwater nearly a mile from shore and had to wade in carrying nearly one hundred pounds of equipment each.

On December 16, 200,000 German troops counterattacked across the Ardennes front. The Rainbow Division, which still hadn't received its support units from the States, was assigned to Task Force Linden—named for its commander, Brig. Gen. Henning Linden—and thrown into battle on Christmas Eve near Haguenau. "They needed additional manpower to contain the bulge and we were it," Rhodes said. Soon the division was in the northern Alsace-Lorraine region of France near Switzerland. "The joke was, we're only 15 miles from the Swiss border, so if you want to desert, this is the time to do it," Rhodes said.

He remembers his first combat experience as an extended holding action punctuated by occasional forays into enemy territory. Part of the time was spent on the Maginot line, France's legendary defensive perimeter of concrete bunkers along its eastern frontier, which had proved so ineffectual against the German blitzkrieg in 1940. Rhodes said they used the bunkers mostly as observation posts. "We never really fought from them because they were too easily taken."

Friendly fire casualties were common in World War II. Rhodes recalled one such incident, which took place in January 1945. A five-man patrol was sent out one night into no man's land to make contact with the enemy and report back their position. Due to the darkness and risk of enemy infiltration, the soldiers had to repeat a password to reenter the perimeter. The machine gunners on the front lines were instructed to shoot anyone who didn't know the password. The patrol got lost and returned to the lines at a point different from where they had started. As luck would have it, the password there had been changed. The machine gunner opened fire, killing all five soldiers. "I was among the detail that had to go out and bring them in," Rhodes said. "The guy on the machine gun that night was really broken up about it."

One time they were attached to a tank unit that was trying to take the town of Killestett. The Americans had been repulsed several times and had suffered heavy losses. Rhodes's unit, which was being held in reserve, received its call-up orders at 0330. The men were issued extra bandoliers of ammunition and candy bar rations, which usually meant they were expecting a protracted offensive. They were formed up behind a line of stone houses on the outskirts of town and would attack across an open field. Adding to their foreboding, Rhodes said, were seven burned-out U.S. tanks sitting in the field, grim reminders of the previous attempts to take the town. But the attack was called off at the last minute. "The tank commander refused to take his last three tanks back out there," Rhodes said. Instead, the Americans were pulled out, and a seasoned unit of French colonials was sent in. "They tried to take the town and they were thrown out," he said. So, they changed their plan of attack. Instead of a frontal assault, the colonials waited until dark and then infiltrated the German lines, slitting throats as they went. Eventually they were able to capture the town. "They were real night fighters," Rhodes said.

After two months in combat, Rhodes had realized that the life of a U.S. infantryman was often violent and short. Of the forty original platoon members who had arrived in France in December, only fifteen were still around in February. The rest, he said, had been "either killed, wounded, or captured." High casualties were part of being in the infantry. Although they made up only 11 percent of the U.S. armed forces, the infantry suffered 70 percent of the U.S. casualties. Soon Rhodes himself would join the ranks of the wounded.

It began in late February 1945 near the town of Reipertswiller near the Rhine River. By then most of the German forces were still on the west side of the river but were being pushed closer to the river's edge. A battery of 105-millimeter howitzers supported Rhode's regiment, which was strung out on a ridge facing the river. On that cold February day, the Germans had pulled back, and the Americans had lost contact with them. When that happened, the usual course of action was to send out patrols to draw their fire and relocate their positions. Rhodes's eight-man patrol set out at dusk and headed across a valley into some low, tree-covered hills. The snow was gone, he remembers, but the night was cold and damp. Rhodes carried the patrol's voice-activated field telephone and a bale of communication wire so that he could contact the artillery if and when the patrol located the enemy.

They had gone over the first hill and had almost reached the top of the second—Hill 403—when a German machine gun nest opened up on them. "The first scout apparently was killed," Rhodes said, but the second scout crawled back to the now-hunkered-down platoon and told them the location of the machine gun. "I called back and told [the artillery] where they were." By then, enemy rifle fire had joined the machine gun and the patrol was ordered to pull back fifty yards while the howitzers were called in. Rhodes said he dropped the spool of wire and ran, crouched over, straight back through the underbrush, rather than returning by the path he had used before. With the bullets whistling overhead, he went down into a shallow depression. "That was my mistake. I stepped on a shoe mine there," he said. "I just did a flip-flop in the air and landed on my back." The shoe mine was a small wooden box, buried just below the surface, containing half a pound of TNT. The explosion all but severed his left foot. "It didn't take the whole foot off," he said. "It kind of left it hanging by the Achilles tendon."

At the time, there was no pain, Rhodes recalled, just a deadened feeling in his lower leg. He didn't try to move, which was lucky for him; a buddy who came to his aid found three more shoe mines buried around him. "I was lucky I didn't roll when I hit the ground," he said. The Germans tried to flush the two men out with knee mortars. The machine guns continued to fire over their heads. "I remember looking up and seeing those tracers going over me," he said. After his buddy defused the shoe mines, he decided to try and knock out the machine gun, Rhodes said. "He said, 'Cover me,' and as he went forward, I pointed my rifle in the direction he was going." Lying in the shallow depression, with the fifty-caliber machine gun bullets ripping inches above his head, Rhodes didn't dare raise up very high. "I never felt such terror in my life," he said. "[Those bullets would] cut you in two before you'd hit the ground."

Although he was losing blood rapidly, Rhodes decided to take matters into his own hands. He attached a grenade-launching adapter to the barrel of his M-1 rifle. "I'm going to get that sucker," he said to himself. He raised up until he could see the flash of the machine gun and then fired. "I must have hit it because it stopped firing and didn't start up again. I heard someone yell, so I must have hit him." Moments later, the 105-millimeter howitzer rounds began to fall. "They landed right on them [the Germans]," Rhodes said. "There wasn't much firing after that." As someone wrapped a tourniquet around his foot and ankle, he was told that besides the point man being killed, two others had been wounded.

Two uninjured soldiers helped Rhodes back over the ridge and down the mountain to a waiting jeep, which took him to a nearby field hospital. (Rhodes learned later that when the division began its major offensive on March 15, one of the men who had helped him get down the mountain was killed in the first hour of fighting.) At the field hospital, they took one look at Rhodes's leg and said it would have to be amputated. The surgeon was a German POW. "Our people were just overrun by casualties," he said. They ended up removing the leg below the knee. He was given only a spinal injection before the surgery, which deadened his body below the waist. "I could hear that saw," he said. "You're still conscious. I remember hearing that saw, and I passed out after that."

After the surgery, he remembers them bringing in a young paratrooper who had lost his left arm all the way to the shoulder. They did what they could for him, pumping him full of morphine for the pain, but the youth was unable to sleep. Rhodes said he can still see him in his mind's eye, sitting under a bare lightbulb, an army nurse sitting at his side, lighting his cigarettes and talking quietly with him through the night. "Along about five o'clock they took him back to his room and he died," he said.

Rhodes, who received the Bronze Star for his actions, was sent back to the States and ended up in a hospital in Temple, Texas, where he underwent additional surgery. After the war he became a partner in his father's insurance business. He retired in 1986. He still thinks about the war and the way it shaped his life and the lives of millions of young men. "We were overseas, killed or wounded and back home, most of us, before we were twenty-one. Our real adventure. We felt like we were part of a turning point in history and I guess we were."

Big Enough

West of the Rhine, 1945—Cpl. Oscar "Runt" Pruessner opened his mouth and flexed his knees as the order to fire was given. The concussion of the 105-millimeter howitzer kicked the Sherman tank backward several feet. Even with his ears stuffed with "waste," Pruessner's ears rang. The Sherman was shooting at a German train and a nearby salt mine. The last round had fallen short. Corporal Pruessner, the tank's gunner, looked through the scope and shouted new coordinates. The first cannoneer elevated the barrel. Pruessner shouted, "Ready!"

"Set!" said the cannoneer.

"Fire!" said the tank's executive officer.

The tank lurched backward from the force of the blast. The jarring could break a soldier's teeth if he wasn't ready for it. Moments later, a message was radioed to the crew from the forward observers: direct hit. Off to the left was a small German village serviced by a railroad. Antiaircraft guns mounted on flatbed cars protected the village. Pruessner heard the familiar pom-pom of the flak guns being fired, but no planes were overhead. Then he realized the guns were firing at his tank. Pruessner heard the flak rounds whine overhead. A direct hit could blow the tank to pieces. But the crew's orders were to destroy the train and the mine. The tanks in the group stayed in position; the men inside the metal machines prayed.

When the flak started coming in, most of the soldiers accompanying the tank force had dropped to the ground, hoping to avoid the shrapnel whining around them. As Pruessner watched, an antiaircraft shell burst beside one of the soldiers. "The explosion lifted that man's body twenty-five feet in the air. . . . He just took off like a feather," said Pruessner, recalling the incident forty years later. "I didn't really know it was a human body until later." Flak kills two ways—with shrapnel and concussion. "Concussion can break every bone in your body and hardly break the skin," Pruessner said. That was what killed the soldier he saw hit by the flak burst. "You could roll him up like a tarp," he said grimly. On that day, the battle went in the Americans' favor. They destroyed the train and the salt mine, and another tank blew up the flak guns. But Pruessner will never know how the antiaircraft gunner missed his tank at such close range. "That old boy didn't have to miss us that many times," he said. "The good Lord was with us there or we never would have made it."

Pruessner served in the 6th Armored Division of Patton's 3rd Army during World War II. A third-generation German emigrant—his grandfather left Germany as an infant—he joined the 128th National Guard unit in Clinton, Missouri, on February 5, 1940. At the time he was an eighteen-year-old senior in high school. The unit, which drilled once a month, was mostly a social group, he said. "It was kind of like Boy Scouts. We was having a good time until they mobilized us."

That day—November 25, 1940—they went from part-time to full-time soldiers. The unit was sent to Columbia, Missouri, and then to Fort Jackson, South Carolina, for gunnery training. The training gun was a World War I–vintage French seventy-five-millimeter straight-trajectory howitzer with a range of five miles.

At Fort Jackson, which had formerly housed a cavalry unit, the recruits were issued shiny riding boots, but they never rode a horse. "They shore took a lot of polish, 'cause you had to polish 'em to the knees, you know. We used them for parades." They stayed at the camp for fourteen months with no idea where they would be sent or what they'd be doing. "We didn't know where we were going," he said. "We were really a confused bunch of kids."

Finally they received orders to proceed to Fort Blanding, near Jacksonville, Florida; from there they went to Arkansas to join the Sixth Armored. Then it was into the Mohave Desert to train with Patton. "That's where he got his name," Pruessner said. "Old Blood and Guts." He remembers Patton as a "big man [who] generally stood taller than the men under him." Luckily, it was winter when they arrived in the desert. Pruessner was introduced to the Howitzer M-7 tank. The M-7's main cannon was a 105-millimeter howitzer, which fired forty-five-pound high-explosive rounds. It also had a fifty-caliber machine gun turret on top, which could turn in a complete circle. The howitzers had a five-mile range and were especially effective against ground troops. The shells could be set to either explode on impact or detonate as sky bursts. The rounds had a kill radius of twenty-nine feet.

A six-man crew operated the M-7, which had a top speed of thirty miles per hour. There was the gunner, who determined the sighting coordinates; the cannoneer, who elevated the barrel and pulled the lanyard to fire the "piece"; the exec, sometimes a sergeant, who stood behind the gunner and relayed orders from the command post—he had the final say in the tank and issued the firing orders; two ammunition handlers; and the driver.

Pruessner's job was to sight and aim the guns. First he'd establish a base point—a tree, building, rock outcropping—something immobile from which he could determine distance. Then he'd figure out how far the target was from the base point and relay those coordinates to the cannoneer. After the guns were fired, a forward observer would tell the men how far they had over- or undershot the target. The howitzers had a forty-two-inch recoil, so they had to be realigned after each salvo. "It would kick that old tank around," Pruessner said. The tankers plugged their ears with shredded cloth they called "waste" to protect their hearing.

The Sixth Armored trained through the winter and then was sent to San Francisco. "Runt" Pruessner was five feet, seven inches tall. He had been an amateur boxer before the war, and in the army, he rose through the ranks from truck driver and cook to BAR expert and cannoneer. In San Francisco, he made gunner corporal. The Sixth's next stop was New York City, where they boarded the USS *Barnett,* which was part of a convoy heading to England. In late July 1944, forty-nine days after D-Day, the Third Army landed on Omaha Beach. The Normandy beaches and bridgeheads were secured along a fifty-mile front, but U.S. forces were meeting strong German resistance at St. Lô.

On July 25, the U.S. First Army spearheaded the "Cobra" breakout through the Periers-St. Lô front. The Third Army was close behind. It was Pruessner's first taste of combat, and he doesn't remember much about it. He does recall a lot of confusion, a lot of fear. "Everybody just went ape," he said. "We were kind of a little bit berserk." Half the time, he said, they had no idea which way they were going or who they were shooting. They settled down after the first few encounters with the enemy, but they never really got over the fear. "You got used to it. You just got kind of immune to it," Pruessner said. When you went into action, the fear was there, twisting your insides like a washrag. When it was over, you laughed about it.

One time their cannoneer was standing outside, urinating beside the tank, when a stray round landed almost beside him. It was close enough to kick dirt on him, but it didn't explode. The cannoneer unceremoniously clambered back into the tank. "He didn't even take time to pull his pants up," Pruessner said. "We laughed about it. The kid could've been killed. . . . If nobody got hurt, we'd pass it off as a joke."

One night, Pruessner had guard duty, and he was listening to the mortar rounds "flutter" overhead. He heard a round come in. Barely missing him and the ammunition trailer he was standing next to, it landed and exploded in the middle of the hexagon formed by six tanks. Many of the men were sleeping in the enclosed space. Miraculously, no one was killed or even seriously wounded. One soldier felt an intense, burning pain; he ripped off his shirt, expecting to find a gaping wound. Instead, he found a piece of hot metal lying next to his skin, which was beginning to blister. "He was getting branded," Pruessner said. "When it was all over, everybody was standing around grinning about it." Finding something to laugh about in the face of sudden death was necessary to the men's survival, he said. "You'd go nuts if you wasn't."

Somewhere in France, 1944—Corporal Pruessner was waiting. Outside his M-7 tank—nicknamed "Big Enough"—he could hear the muffled rattle of gunfire, mostly from small arms and machine guns, and the heavy thud of exploding artillery rounds. Inside the tank it was momentarily quiet. Pruessner absently poked a wad of waste deeper into his ears.

There were five men in Big Enough. The sixth crewman, a close friend of Pruessner's, was busy cutting down a tree that was in the tank's line of fire. As Pruessner watched, a stray artillery round landed next to his buddy. It had to have been a stray, Pruessner thought, because no one knew he was there. A lucky shot. Unlucky for his friend. A piece of shrapnel sheared off the top of his head. "It just killed him instantly," Pruessner said. "He didn't even know what hit him. Something like that really upsets you," he said, the pain still evident more than four decades later. "We were a family."

After the Normandy breakout, the Third Army drove to Brest then turned and followed a wide northeastern arc through Lorient, Orleans, and Metz. The M-7s avoided the tank battles being waged along the advancing front by the larger tanks and the German panzers. Each M-7 carried five to seven rounds of special armor-piercing shells, but the tanks in which Pruessner served never used them against other tanks. Instead, the crews were ordered to concentrate their fire on enemy infantry, observation posts, and supply lines. "A dead man don't bother us," Pruessner remembers being told once. "Work 'em over good." Most of their targets were in visual range, usually within two miles. They often fired on church steeples, a favorite spot for German observation posts, and German ambulances, which were often used to haul ammunition.

During the Battle of the Bulge, the Third Army was part of the Allied counteroffensive that helped drive the Germans back. Pruessner remembers that it was intensely cold and that it snowed almost constantly. He also remembers a lot of death. During one battle, he saw a German 88 round come through the open door of an American halftrack. He knew it wasn't a mortar shell by the sound. "They [mortars] had a kind of sneaky, silent flutter sound," he said. "Those 88s came in whining." The halftrack driver was killed instantly. During the Battle of the Bulge, Pruessner lost another close friend, Alva French. Alva was a good-natured hulk of a man and well liked by everyone. One day he was standing under a tree when a mortar round burst above him. Pruessner was by his side when he died moments later. "He just coughed a time or two and that was it. He didn't hardly feel the pain."

Later, some friends described to him another heartrending scene. After a battle, the "dead soldier truck" was sent around to gather up the men who had died. The soldiers with that grisly duty would turn a body onto a litter and then flip it into the back of a truck. The other soldiers got used to seeing the truck and the callous handling of the corpses. But it was different if it was someone they knew. Some men from Pruessner's unit saw the soldiers pick up Alva French. They pushed his body onto the litter, carried it to the truck, and with one motion, flicked it into the truck bed "just like a stick of cordwood," Pruessner said. "It just about broke their hearts."

Although the Malmédy Massacre was one of the most infamous atrocities of the World War II, Pruessner said random executions of U.S. prisoners were common, especially during the final months of the war. "If something like that doesn't make you want to fight," he said, "I don't know what will." Once they found seven soldiers huddled together in the snow. All had been shot between the eyes. But the atrocities weren't committed solely by the Germans. Once Pruessner and his crew came upon the body of an American soldier far behind the front lines. His ring finger had recently been severed. "That's an upsetting sort of thing too," he said. "I figured that was his own American boys that done that."

By January 18, the Allies had pushed the Nazis back to the German border. The Third Army swept into Germany and crossed the Rhine River on a U.S.–

built pontoon bridge just south of Mainz on March 22. To the north, the U.S. First Army crossed the Rhine on the Ludendorff Bridge at Remagen.

Pruessner said he has no bitter feelings toward his former enemies. "I've got relatives over there. I figured they were doing what they had to do, just like I was doing what I had to do," he said. "The soldier, as a soldier, is just a servant of the nation he represents." He remembers passing by Buchenwald, which had just been liberated. Outside was a group of Australian POWs who were holding guns on some scared German guards. The guards had given up without a fight. When the Americans reached the group, one of the Aussies turned to the GIs. "Don't harm these guards," he said, his accent thick. "They've been bloody good to us."

On V-E Day, May 8, 1945, Pruessner was in Narsdorf, Germany. The Allied command had agreed to allow the Russians to invade Berlin. In Pruessner's opinion, that was a mistake. "Patton's Third Army could have taken Berlin easily," he said. "We should've gone ahead and took it and then we wouldn't have the trouble with the Russians we have now."

Pruessner acknowledges that he was lucky to escape injury during his tour of duty, especially considering the amount of combat he saw. "We didn't know how many times we escaped death," he said. "The potential was there. I just never was hurt."

He returned to the States on a troop ship, this time without a navy escort. When the ship arrived in Boston Harbor, all the other ships and trains in the area were blowing their horns. "It was something to listen to," he said. He went back to Clinton and worked at a dairy before moving to Kansas City to work at Sealright Paper Company, from which he retired in 1984.

He remembers Europe was beautiful, even during the war, but he's never been back. "I still prefer my Ozark hills for loafin' places," he said. "The southern part of Missouri is the most beautiful place in the world."

Real True Heroes

Outside Kassel, Germany, February 8, 1945—The seven-man squad moved quietly through the forest. The men slowed as they neared a break in the tree line. Through the branches they could see the pillbox. They split into two groups. Four would attack from one direction; the other three, all former members of a tank crew serving temporarily as combat infantry, would attack from the other. They hoped someone would get through.

They all had plastic explosive putty in their packs. If one of them could get close enough to stick it on the pillbox, they could detonate it with a carefully placed shot. Of course, getting close enough was the problem. The pillbox was a circular concrete bunker with walls two feet thick. Not even a tank round could penetrate it. The ugly snout of a fifty-caliber machine gun protruded from one view slot. German sharpshooters manned the others. The Americans would have to cross open ground to reach the pillbox. The ground was littered with the torn bodies of American soldiers who had tried and failed to destroy the bunker. But there was nothing else to do. The pillbox stood in the way of the American advance and had to be eliminated.

The group of four GIs attacked first and were picked off one by one. The tank crewmen didn't even get that far. The wooded area was strung with piano wire attached to explosives hidden in the trees. Someone stepped on a wire. The tank commander, a young lieutenant, took the brunt of the blast; his head was blown off and blood geysered from the open carotid artery in his throat. The tank driver also went down, a quarter of his buttocks blasted away. The tank gunner, Dean Stringer, was partially shielded by the lieutenant's body, which flopped back on him. When Stringer tried to get up, he found he couldn't move his leg. "I got it in the leg," said Stringer, sixty-six, recalling the incident forty-seven years later. "Got four inches of my bone blown away."

The Germans, hearing the explosion, raked the trees with machine gun and small arms fire. Stringer knew he was going into shock, so he fumbled for his pack and jabbed himself with morphine. He went through the lieutenant's pack, found his morphine and took that, too. Then came the hard part. The Germans would be coming out soon to make sure everyone was dead. Stringer gripped his rifle and waited.

Stringer had graduated from high school early and joined the navy in mid-1943 at the age of seventeen. He wanted to be a pilot and was accepted for naval air training. Three weeks later he washed out; he was color blind. Because he wasn't eighteen, he had to wait for the draft to get back into the service.

In the meantime, he auditioned for and was hired by bandleader Lionel Hampton. A saxophone player, Stringer was one of only three whites in the group, which played the Big Band music popular during the era. It was an eye-opening experience for a seventeen-year-old white kid from rural Jackson County, Missouri. "I became a black musician. I [just happened to be] white," he said. The band played at many of the big shows, including Bob Hope's wartime USO production. The experience also allowed Stringer to see the underside of American society in the 1940s—the racial inequality and hatred that was prevalent across the country, not just the Deep South. He remembers being refused hotel rooms and restaurant service and even being beaten up once while traveling with the group. "I was ashamed of my race at the time," he said. But the experience of playing with "Pop" Hampton far outweighed the bigotry they had to endure, he said. Unlike some members of his own race, the black members of the band accepted him into their fraternity and came to respect his musical skills. One night, after he had finished a particularly good solo, one of his black bandmates grinned and whispered, "You must have a little nigger in you."

"That's a first time I heard it as a term of endearment," Stringer said. "I felt good about that."

Stringer finally received his draft notice in 1944. The army rushed him through basic training and sent him to gunnery school in Fort Hood, Texas. "They needed gunners," he said. "I was in combat shooting people less than three months after I was drafted." He was sent to France. When he arrived in Le Havre, he was assigned to a Sherman tank nicknamed "Maggie" and became a member of the Sixth Armored Division, Third Army. He remembers seeing General Patton several times. Often he would be standing in the middle of a crossroads, Stringer said, directing traffic and shouting at the tanks to hurry up. "He was a tough son of a bitch," Stringer said.

Stringer manned the fifty-caliber machine gun mounted on the tank, which meant he usually rode with his head outside, in the open. "I was frightened the whole time," he said. The tanks were spearheading the offensive into Nazi Germany, with the infantry bringing up the rear. He saw his first combat near Luxembourg. Shooting people was an unsettling experience for the eighteen-year-old, who only weeks before had been playing the sax for couples gliding over the dance floor. But he became hardened to it out of necessity. "It was a funny thing in those days, we used to brag about killing people," he said. And the crew of a Sherman tank could dispense death in large quantities. "Sometimes you'd get fifty, sixty guys [in one battle]." After a while, he said, he stopped thinking of the enemy as human beings. It was more like shooting rabbits. "You really are in a state of shock when you're in combat. You really don't know what you're doing," he said. "It was just a sick, sick, sick time for everyone."

Stringer remembers the Battle of the Bulge well. "The Bulge was ugly. You couldn't move forty feet. I saw the same terrain for three days." Since the tank wasn't moving, and since a tank tends to draw enemy fire, only one man was left inside while the others dug foxholes nearby. Once Stringer was in his foxhole, and a German 88 round landed inside it. Somehow he survived, but he was stunned by the concussion. Twenty years later a minor operation would correct the hearing impairment caused by the explosion.

During the fighting, the men lived on Spam and stew, which they usually ate cold. The temperature ranged from twenty degrees to two below zero. "A lot of guys lost their toes and fingers to frostbite," he said. Eventually the weather, which had grounded the Allied air forces for two weeks, cleared up, and the German advance was stopped. Stringer said as the Americans moved forward, they hit the first paved roads they'd seen in two months. The GIs thought it was a good omen. "We knew we were coming home," he said.

Nothing had gone right for the seven-man squad assigned to knock out the pillbox. First, half the group had been forced to watch as the rest were picked off one by one. "They were all killed by small arms fire," Stringer said. Then the tree mine had taken care of most of the tank crewmen. Finally, there were just two men left alive. And the Germans would be out soon with their bayonets. Eventually, Stringer and his wounded companion heard something moving toward them. The Germans were coming. There were three of them. The two wounded crewmen held their breath as the enemy soldiers approached. Stringer was on his stomach, clutching his rifle, when a pair of jackboots stopped beside him. There was no time to stop and think. Only react. "One guy was standing on top of me when I turned over and got him," Stringer said. As the soldier toppled, Stringer swung around and shot another German. His buddy killed the third. "We got even," Stringer said. "We got three of them."

Despite having had a part of his buttocks blown off, his buddy was able to walk, and he headed back toward the American lines to get help. Stringer never saw him again. A day passed and another night. The next day, lying among the dead, he heard a voice calling, "Missouri, Missouri. . . ." It belonged to a friend he knew only as Nevada. The two had met a few days before. "We were sitting on a bunch of [frozen] dead bodies eating C-rations," Stringer said, when the subject of hometowns came up. It turned out that both were from Missouri—one from rural Jackson County and the other from Nevada. Stringer said when you're eighteen and seven thousand miles from home, anyone from your home state is your friend. As it turned out, Nevada carried Missouri off the hill to an aid station.

Stringer, weak from loss of blood, was taken to Kassel, where the wounded were being loaded onto trucks and transported back to field hospitals in France. He remembers lying on a stretcher out on a street with two hundred other wounded GIs and seeing a woman for the first time in four mouths. She was dressed in black, and he couldn't tell her age, but he watched, mesmerized, as she moved between the rows of stretchers, bending over the wounded men as if searching for someone. "You get hungry to see the opposite sex," he said. But as he was watching, he said, "somebody shot her. Somebody just blew her away." He was first shocked and then outraged, but someone filled him in. "I found out later she was going down the rows stabbing people," he said. She managed to kill twenty wounded soldiers before someone killed her.

Stringer was taken to an amputee ward housed in an airplane hangar in Paris. There must have been fifteen hundred men in the hangar, he said, some screaming, some weeping quietly, others remaining stoically silent. Stringer had his own demons to battle. He'd been married only a few months—and, though he didn't know it at the time, his son was born two days after he was wounded—and he wondered what his young wife would think about having a husband with only one leg. Although heavily drugged, he was awake during the operation. "I remember them splitting it [my leg] open like a watermelon." But when the operation was over, he still had two legs. Instead of discarding the bone fragments, the surgeon had taped them back to his leg, hoping the pieces would regenerate, then left the wound open so the healing process could be monitored.

Casualty rates were high, and large numbers of doctors were being drafted and shipped overseas. However, many weren't trained for the duties they were given. Surgeons were in especially short supply. Stringer got to know one of the doctors in the amputee ward. "He was a dermatologist and he was amputating out of a book." Many limbs that a qualified surgeon could have saved were lost.

Stringer was sent to England, where he underwent a bone-splicing procedure. Eventually, a round metal tube was implanted inside his leg bone and secured with metal pins, and he was in a body cast for nine months. He was sent back to the States, and the army awarded him the Silver Star for valor and two Purple Hearts. Actress Shirley Temple visited him and other wounded GIs in the hospital in Denver. "We were treated like kings," Stringer said. "Real true heroes. They really cared."

While Stringer was lying wounded in the German forest, he had promised himself that if he survived, he would go to Fort Smith, Arkansas, and find his commanding officer's young wife. He would tell her how the lieutenant had died bravely and give her his medals. When he was released from the hospital after eighteen months, he made the trip, but it didn't turn out the way he had expected. "She'd remarried and had some kids and she didn't give a shit," he said. "She had a new life and she didn't want to hear any of my stories. So I gave her the medals and left."

Stringer returned to the music business. He was still in a leg cast when Lawrence Welk hired him. It was a shock, he said, because he had been receiving about $20 a week from the government. "Mr. Welk paid me $250 a week. I was rich," he said. "[But I] couldn't understand a word he said." Stringer worked full time as a musician for five years, but he found it too difficult to travel and raise a family at the same time. Eventually, he returned to the safety equipment business he had started with his father in 1943.

In the midsixties, with his children grown, he decided to get back into music. He moved to California and got a job on the *Tennessee Ernie Ford Show* in San Francisco, and later he taught music at San Jose and Stanford universities. At Stanford, they had a program where you could talk to psychiatric interns for five dollars per session. Stringer, who had never been able to talk about his experiences during the war and had recurring nightmares about them, decided to give it a try. It was a cathartic experience. The memories of the dead and dying, the friends lost, the horror he had seen and inflicted came flooding out. "That was the first time I could remember feeling bad about [the men I killed]," he said.

He told his therapist of his biggest fear while he was in combat:, that he would die on the battlefield and his body would be left there, ravaged by animals and the elements. Then, if he was lucky, someone would find what was left, collect his dogtags, and eventually a bulldozer would plow him under the cold earth, unmourned and forgotten. He talked of the horrors he had witnessed—like the crossroads he had passed where more than fifty U.S. soldiers had been executed and then stripped naked. The Germans had used rifle butts to knock out the soldiers' teeth to get the gold fillings and snapped off frozen fingers to get rings. There was the death camp you could smell from two miles away and the poor GI who had had the misfortune of dying in the middle of the road in front of a column of tanks. "I bet forty tanks ran over him," Stringer said.

Today (1992), Stringer walks without a limp, although he still carries a metal tube in his leg, which sets off metal detectors at airports. And he can talk about the war. He remembers the time he saw a line of about one hundred German POWs coming down a road. Bringing up the rear was one MP with a holstered sidearm. "Those Germans wanted to go home," he said. And he recalls how his crew used to paint X's on the sides of their tank to show the number of enemy tanks they'd destroyed—that is, until they found out the Germans were executing the crews of captured tanks that had X's on them. They decided to paint over the X's.

Yet, even when he couldn't talk about the war, Stringer was proud of the part he played in it. It was a different time, a different war. It was a war where patriotism had more meaning, he said, and the soldiers "were willing to give their lives if they had to." They were fighting for something concrete: the lives and freedom of their loved ones. There was no gray moral area when it came to whose was the righteous cause. "It was the last war of its kind," Stringer said.

The Bridge at Remagen

REMAGEN, GERMANY, MARCH 1945—Despite Hitler's threat to execute any officer who failed to destroy a Rhine River bridge before it fell to the enemy, the U.S. Ninth Armored Division managed to prevent the destruction of the Ludendorff railway bridge at Remagen. Intact, it would give the Allies a direct route to the heart of Nazi Germany. But the Germans weren't ready to give up the bridge.

Tank commander Kenny Winburn was waiting for orders. He was on the west bank of the Rhine with the company's kitchen unit when a massive artillery barrage began. The Germans, trying to destroy the bridge, were overshooting their target, and the 88 rounds were falling all around the Americans. There was nothing to do, Winburn said, except to wait out the attack, which lasted about twenty minutes and killed one soldier.

The capture of the bridge at Remagen, which was the site of the first permanent Allied bridgehead over the Rhine River, was one of the important events Winburn was involved in during the war, but it wasn't the only one. Winburn, who commanded a light M-5 tank in Company D, Fourteenth Tank Battalion of the Ninth Armored Division, also took part in the Battle of the Bulge and won a Bronze Star for knocking out a German tank. He never got a chance to cross the Remagen Bridge, which was captured on March 7, 1945. Weakened by German attempts to destroy it, it was closed on March 12 for repairs, and all traffic across the river was shifted to two Allied-built pontoon bridges nearby.

After crossing to the east side of the Rhine, Winburn and a friend returned to the riverbank on March 17 to take a picture of the now-famous bridge. But they were too late. "That thing had just fallen in," he said. "They [the Germans] hit it pretty hard with their artillery, so it was weakened." When it collapsed, twenty-eight U.S. engineers, who were doing repair work on the bridge, were drowned in the swift-running Rhine.

Winburn (seventy-two in 1991) had joined the army in January 1941. "There was a [draft] lottery, and I happened to have a low number," he said. "I always said that was the only thing I won in my life." He had signed up for the Coast Guard, but he was sent to the Second Cavalry Division in the

Arizona desert. It was an actual horse cavalry, he said, and he was assigned to a machine gun unit. The thirty-caliber, water-cooled, tripod-mounted guns were carried on packhorses. "They were a potent outfit. I believe we were the toughest outfit in the army because we had to be on the go all the time," he said. He was only supposed to be in the army a year, but then the Japanese bombed Pearl Harbor. "I only had five or six weeks to go," he said, "but they got me for four [years]."

Later he was transferred to the 9th Armored, and he traded his horse for a M-5 tank. The 15-ton "light" tanks were propelled by 250-horsepower air-cooled aviation engines and could reach speeds of nearly 70 miles per hour. The armament included a 37-millimeter gun, a coaxle machine gun mounted beside it, and a .30-caliber machine gun on top. Winburn started as a member of the maintenance crew, but by the time he reached Europe in September 1944, he was a tank commander. "They had this 19th tank, so they gave it to me," he said. "I was the last tank and always lost." Winburn's crew included a driver, an assistant driver, and a gunner, who sat in the turret. The commander controlled the tank by standing on the bucket seat with his head sticking outside.

One evening his company was bivouacked in an open field about fifty yards from a wooded area somewhere in the Ardennes. Winburn's commander told him to take his position on lookout while he went to dinner. Later, Winburn heard what sounded like a motor coming from the woods. When he reported the noise to his commander, he was told to stay on the alert. Minutes later a German light tank rumbled out of the trees and headed toward the encampment. Winburn shouted over the radio, "It's one of those Nazi bastards!" He ordered his gunner to fire a shot canister—a shell filled with steel ball bearings—at the tank to knock out its telescopic sight. He still had his mike open and his commander said calmly, "Give him some APC [armor piercing core]." The APC round had a corrosive core that burned through steel. "It can go through quite a bit of armor," Winburn said. "I don't know why I didn't think of giving them that the first time." The gunner fired the shell and destroyed the tank before it could get off a shot. "They gave me a Bronze Star for it. I never did think I really deserved it," Winburn said. "There were other guys that did a lot more."

When the Battle of the Bulge began, Winburn's company was already heading toward the front, having moved out the day before, December 15. At first, he said, the men thought it was a local attack on a much smaller scale. "We didn't know that they had massed there with their big armies." But even more memorable than the fighting was the ferocious Belgian winter. The tanks were unheated, and the aviation engines sucked the frigid air in through the open hatch. The driver and his assistant, in the belly of the tank, were somewhat buffered from the extreme cold, but the commander and the turret gunner were at the mercy of the elements. "I used to think I had to button my collar real tight or [the wind] would suck my clothes right off," Winburn said.

The leading elements of the Ninth Armored Division arrived at Remagen on March 7 and were shocked to find the Ludendorff Bridge still intact; German troops were streaming across it to the east bank of the Rhine. The bridge, which connected the towns of Remagen and Erpel, had been built during World War I to improve Germany's troop-movement capacity. The medieval-looking bridge had two turrets on either end. On the east bank the railroad plunged into a twelve hundred-foot tunnel hewn through Erpeler Ley, a six hundred-foot basalt cliff. German machine gunners and sharpshooters were positioned in the stone towers on the east end and at the mouth of the railway tunnel to cover the retreat.

As the U.S. forces prepared to attack, they received an intelligence report that the Germans were planning to blow up the bridge at 4 P.M.—which was less than two hours away. The Germans, who had set charges on the bridge, detonated a large explosion on the central span before the attack could be mounted, but the bridge proved sounder than expected and remained standing. U.S. infantrymen charged across the battered bridge, accompanied by combat engineers who searched for and disarmed the explosive charges under withering fire from German machine guns and small arms. U.S. tanks lined up on the west riverbank to provide cover fire.

After the bridge was captured, the Luftwaffe made several attempts to destroy it, even using its new Messerschmitt 262 jet fighter. Winburn said it was the first time he'd ever seen a jet, and he remembers them roaring down the river channel, moving so fast that the U.S. flak exploded in the jets' contrails. In a last-ditch effort, Hitler ordered that his newest terror weapon, V-2 rockets, be fired at the bridge. Launched from sites in Holland, none of them hit the target.

Though the bridge eventually collapsed, the bridgehead allowed the Allies to get eight thousand troops across the Rhine in the first forty-eight hours. Within a week, the Allies had twenty-five thousand across the river. They were there to stay.

As expected, Hitler court-martialed four high-ranking officers responsible for the bridge. The officers were shot in the back of the neck and their bodies buried in shallow graves—a grim warning to others of the swift retribution in store for those who failed to carry out the Führer's orders.

With the war winding down, Winburn's company received new tanks. Although still considered a light model, the M-7 had a 75-millimeter turret gun. "I was glad to get it," he said. "It had a lot of room in it. A lot more than the little M-5." One night near the end of the war, when the tanks were deep in Germany, some German infiltrators slipped into the Americans' camp and killed several soldiers in their sleep. The next morning, their commander ordered the tanks to fire on farmhouses in the area, where he suspected German soldiers were hiding. Winburn said they chose highly flammable phosphorus rounds. "That was the first time I got to fire those seventy-fives," he said. "We burnt down a few houses." Later, they were fired on from a nearby town, he said, so they promptly "shot the heck out of it. The next few days we just saw white flags everywhere," he said. "Those Krauts learned their lessons pretty quick."

The Secret War

Commando

In the 1960s Marvel Comics published a comic book called *Sgt. Fury and the Howling Commandos.* The brainchild of writer Stan Lee and artist Jack Kirby, the comic book was about a handpicked team of soldiers who performed top-secret commando missions during World War II. Led by cigar-chomping Sgt. Nick Fury, the "Howlers" spent more than a decade—in comic book time, that is—creating havoc and causing destruction behind enemy lines. But there's often a grain of truth in fiction, even in the comic-book variety. Sometimes more than a few grains. Just ask Russell "Woozy" May.

May, a former star halfback for Lee's Summit High School, quit school in midterm 1944 to join the air cadets, washed out and became a gunner on a B-24 flying patrol off the coast of Florida. That was his official job. Unofficially, May was a member of a secret commando unit organized by the Office of Strategic Services (OSS). The unit was sent to Europe on classified missions during the waning months of the war. More than forty years after the war ended, information about the unit's existence remains classified by the U.S. government, and May could talk about it only in the most general terms. "We weren't just under the penalty of court-martial," May said from his home in Alexandria, Virginia, in 1990. "We were under the penalty of death."

May considers himself a success story—a poor kid whose father died when he was twelve; a budding juvenile delinquent who skipped school and raised hell until his high school teachers straightened him out; he joined the military, served honorably, and retired as a colonel. Now living on a comfortable government pension, he wants to thank the people who made it all possible.

"Somebody had to start my foundation out right," he said. "Put the credit where the credit's due—with the teachers."

His family arrived in Lee's Summit in the late 1800s, and his father and uncles started a nursery business, selling fruit trees from the back of a wagon. Eventually they opened the May Brothers Nursery, which survived seventy years before closing in the early 1950s. Growing up, May had no interest in following in his father's footsteps. After his father died, he was like a rudderless ship, going whichever way the wind blew him, looking for direction. In school he was a below-average student but not for lack of brains. He remembers playing hooky regularly and getting into minor scrapes.

Thelma Higgins, the former Thelma Dozier, who taught mathematics in Lee's Summit for thirty-nine years, recalls May. "I don't remember him being such a bad boy," said Higgins. "I do know he exaggerated a lot. . . . He was a smart boy, but he didn't apply himself." Charlie Dick, Lee's Summit High School's principal until 1943, has only a vague memory of Woozie May, but Dick made a lasting impression on the teenager. "I was about as close to being a juvenile delinquent as you could get," May said. "Charlie always had faith in me. . . . I owe a helluva lot to him. He helped me when I needed direction," he said. "Old Charlie was a hard case, but he was fair."

May had always had athletic ability. His strength and speed helped him to excel in football, and he lettered all four years. But near the end of his high school career, he also began to achieve scholastic success, slowly raising his C's and D's to B's and A's.

May left school in December 1944 to join the army air corps. He wanted to be a pilot but ended up as a gunner on a B-24 based in Florida. The B-24s looked for enemy submarines getting too close to the U.S. coast. During one flight, they located what they thought was an enemy sub and dropped their bombs. When they returned to base, the crew was told to report to their commanding officer. "We all thought we were going to get a medal," May said. Instead, the CO said, "Congratulations, you bombed a whale."

But May's military career wasn't as quiet as it appeared. Every so often, he had to take emergency leave from his regular duty. For one leave the story was that he had to fly home because his mother was dying. May's mother, Bertha, alive and well at the time, would have been surprised to learn of the sudden decline in her health. In reality, the OSS flew May to a secret site in England, where he and the rest of his squad, usually numbering about ten, were briefed on their assignment. Typically they were flown to their target and then dropped by parachute behind enemy lines to knock out a German munitions dump, fuel depot, or communications center. "It was a quick surgery-type thing," said May, who, like his fellow commandos, was young and fearless. "I wasn't afraid of dying or anything like that," he said. "It was like we were playing a big game."

Each member of the squad, chosen from a pool of hundreds of soldiers, sailors, marines, and airmen, had a specific area of expertise, ranging from demolitions and communications to weapons and hand-to-hand combat. "I was an excellent shot, so my job was more or less a protector role," May said. When a mission was over, the squad would go to a prearranged rendezvous point where it would be picked up and flown back to England for debriefing. Eventually, the men would return to their units, often with healing wounds they would have to somehow explain. One time May had to come up with an explanation for a gunshot wound he received when a German shot a bayonet out of his hand. "You just had to put lie upon lie," he said. "You almost had to have a catalogue to keep them straight."

In a sense, the lies have had to continue long after the war. Much of the information about the secret commando teams used during World War II and the Korean War remains classified, which means, as far as the government is concerned, the commandos didn't exist. It also means that veterans like May can't get credit for combat wounds and citations that supposedly exist in their still-secret files. May said he was awarded several medals for valor and "more than one" Purple Heart for wounds he sustained, but the government hasn't declassified information on those.

After the war, May left the service for a few years and then rejoined as a second lieutenant during the Korean War. Later he became a troubleshooter for the Strategic Air Command, inspecting U.S. air bases for illegal appointments and discrimination. He retired as a colonel in 1975.

He's come a long way for a high school dropout, but the lessons he learned have stuck with him—like the one about success. "Don't worry about success. Success will take care of itself," he said. Besides, he added, success really doesn't mean anything. "Achievement, now that's something they can't take away from you."

Jedburgh

Partisan resistance fighters paid a high price for each success during World War II. For every rail line blown up, every telephone wire severed, every Nazi official assassinated, there was payback. This was especially true in war-torn France, where the German SS, Hitler's elite killers, played a brutal game of cat and mouse with the outnumbered but highly organized French Resistance.

Such was the case in late 1944 when the Germans had been overwhelmed by the Allied onslaught and were retreating toward the Rhine. The French Resistance had ambushed a German patrol the day before, and the SS decided to retaliate by wiping the French village of Liminil-Mitry off the face of the earth.

Bob Lucas, a former U.S. paratrooper attached to the OSS, was part of a covert unit working in the area when he received word that the Nazis were preparing to attack Liminil-Mitry. He and the other agents joined about three hundred Free French Resistance fighters who had learned of the impending attack and were preparing to defend the town. Lucas said the Germans opened the attack with machine guns and mortars at about 9:00 A.M.. Two hours later, the Free French commander was wounded, and the Americans, who were fighting alongside the French, were asked to assume command. Lucas said they decided to stay on the defensive rather than counterattack and risk getting more of their French allies killed. Within a few hours, the battle was a stalemate. "There was a lot of wild shooting," Lucas said, speaking of the incident forty-nine years later, "but no one was taking the initiative, no one was advancing." At 5 P.M., the Germans broke off the attack and withdrew. Lucas said their decision no doubt was influenced by the proximity of the U.S. Third Army, as well as the defense the Americans and the French Resistance had put up. "We lost about twenty men during the day," he said. "We didn't beat them, but they didn't beat us either."

Lucas, who lives in Roeland Park, Kansas, was part of the OSS's Jedburgh Operation. Named for a town in Scotland, the top-secret operation sent multinational teams of three men each behind enemy lines in France, Holland, and Norway shortly after D-Day. The "Jed" teams gathered intelligence, trained resistance fighters, blew up bridges and supply lines, cut communications, and generally harassed the Germans.

Lucas said that in France it wasn't always easy to stay in front of the rapidly advancing armored columns. "We were overrun by the Third Army three times. We couldn't stay ahead of them." He noted that many people think the OSS was mostly about spying. However, only a small number of OSS operatives were actually involved in traditional espionage. The vast majority of the intelligence gathering, he said, took place in the public domain using sources like newspapers and libraries. Because of the language barrier, he said, spies in France were most likely to be native Frenchmen and -women.

Among the OSS branches were Secret Intelligence (SI); Special Operations (SO), which worked closely with resistance forces; Operation Groups (OG), which were specially trained commando units that conducted hit-and-run operations behind enemy lines; and Moral Operations (MO), which handled propaganda.

Another member of the Jed team was Bill Thompson of Leavenworth, Kansas. Thompson was trained in England and sent to North Africa as part of the invasion force. Recruited from the Signal Corps, Thompson had first been sent to Washington, D.C., where he was told to keep the address of the OSS office a secret. When an OSS recruit took a cab to work, he or she gave the driver directions to a nearby corner, got out there, and walked the rest of the way to the building. But they found that when they told the cabbies at which corner to let them off, they would say, "Oh, you're some of the OSS guys." So much for security. When Thompson's team was sent to France as part of Operation Jedburgh, it was mostly involved in sabotage, working with the French underground to determine which targets to attack. He later received a Bronze Star for his efforts.

As the war in Europe came to a close, both Thompson and May were sent to China to continue the war against the Japanese. Among Thompson's jobs were radioing Japanese targets to the Allied air forces and training the Chinese in underwater demolition. He said the Chinese recruits were adept at swimming underwater and attaching the magnetic explosives to the bottoms of Japanese ships. But they liked to stand on shore afterward and watch the vessels explode. "We had more agents get killed that way," he said.

Luzon

Behind the Front

Luzon Island, the Philippines, February 1945—The amphibious truck bounced and lurched across the beach and plowed into the rolling surf. Tech Sgt. Harold J. Meyer disengaged the wheels and turned on the prop as he steered the "duck" toward the row of supply ships anchored in the South China Sea. The vehicle was kept afloat by four suction-type water pumps and had a top speed of six knots. It could haul five tons of cargo when the water was calm, three tons when it wasn't. Meyer and the other members of the 466th Amphibious Truck Company were working back-to-back twelve-hour shifts, transporting ammunition to the troops on land.

It was mid-February of the last year of World War II. A month before, the U.S. 6th Army, commanded by Gen. Walter Krueger, had invaded Luzon, the capital island of the Philippines. Luzon, about the size of Great Britain, was the largest Japanese-held island between New Guinea and Tokyo. The Japanese had invaded the island in early 1942, and three years later it was defended by 250,000 troops of the Japanese 14th Area Army commanded by Lt. Gen. Tomoyuki Yamashita, the "Tiger of Malaya."

Following a three-day bombardment, General Krueger's 200,000-man attack force landed on Luzon on January 9. On February 4, U.S. forces began their assault on Manila, the capital of the Philippines. More than 17,000 naval troops under the command of Rear Adm. Sanji Iwabuchi were determined to hold the city to the last man. The assault on Manila was considered the only urban battle of the Pacific War. The attack was led by the 37th Infantry and the 1st Cavalry and later reinforced by the 11th Airborne. By February 12, many of the Japanese troops had been forced back into Intramuros, the old walled inner city of Manila; the bloodiest street fighting took place there.

One hundred miles to the north, Meyer thought he could hear the distant thunder of the artillery laying waste to the Filipino capital. "We imagined we could hear the 155s," he said. "We never really knew if we were hearing it or it was just imagination." That was as close as Meyer got to combat during his tour overseas. "We were never in action," he said forty years later. "And fortunately we weren't. For a sidearm they gave us a carbine. Can you imagine driving a duck and having to use a carbine?"

Harold Meyer, sixty-nine, and his wife, Nadine, sixty-five (also a World War II veteran), were interviewed at their Gladstone, Missouri, home in 1985.

Nadine Rankin grew up on a farm in Stet, Missouri. Harold's father died when he was ten months old, and he was raised in Cole Camp. "My mother did about anything a widow woman could do in a small town to make an honest dollar," he said. Harold was an only child. He was drafted in July 1943 at the age of twenty-seven. He had been working as a stockman at the Firestone store in North Kansas City. After his induction at Fort Leavenworth, he was sent to New Orleans for basic training and then to Virginia, where he worked in a military auto pool as a parts clerk. Later he returned to New Orleans for a refresher course in basic training and then headed to California to prepare for his trip overseas.

In 1942, Nadine was working in Washington, D.C., as a secretary in the Navy Department's "Big Gun" section. When the marines began accepting women into their ranks, she decided to enlist. But since she was working in a classified navy department, she had to request clearance to leave. She had to wait several months for clearance to be granted. She enlisted in the marines in April 1943. After her enlistment, she was sent to Indiana University to take a bookkeeping course. The sole purpose was to kill time until the women's barracks were completed amid the sand dunes of Cherry Point, North Carolina. "During World War II," she said, "they took in an awful lot of people they didn't know what to do with." Later she was assigned to the Marine Corps' officer training school in Quantico, Virginia, where she became secretary to the base commander. She would have preferred working as an air traffic controller at the air base, she said, but secretaries were in short supply, and her requests for transfer were turned down. Like her future husband, she rose to the rank of technical sergeant.

Harold Meyer arrived in Luzon shortly after the January 9 invasion. The motor pool was located in a rice paddy because it was one of the few level spots in the area. During the rainy season, he said, they couldn't haul enough gravel to keep the ducks running. "They go in water pretty good," he said, "but not mud."

He soon discovered the one difference between the wet and dry seasons in the Philippines. During the dry season, it only rained at night. The wet season ended with a prolonged monsoon that made work all but impossible. Despite the tropical dampness, the soldiers had few problems with mosquitoes and the accompanying malaria. That was because much of the vegetation in the area had been leveled by the air and sea bombardment, and low-flying planes regularly sprayed the island with pesticide. During the month-long siege of Manila, the duck drivers worked twelve-hour shifts—either noon to midnight or midnight to noon—hauling ammunition and supplies for the combat troops. They brought them to the beach, then the supplies were shipped to Manila by way of a narrow-gauge train.

By February 24, U.S. forces occupied most of Manila, although there were still isolated pockets of resistance. The city wasn't completely secured until March 3. The battle for Manila exacted a heavy toll. The once-beautiful city lay in ruins. The Japanese had refused to evacuate noncombatants, and nearly 100,000 civilians perished. On the American side, more than 1,000 were killed and 1,500 wounded. The Japanese kept their promise and died almost to a man. After Manila fell, the battle for the Philippines continued at Corregidor, Ipo Dam, and Bambang. The men of the 466th stayed busy. When they weren't on duty, they attended USO shows and watched a lot of movies. Unlike most of the servicemen on the island, the 466th had its own transportation and could go wherever the movies were being shown. Meyer saw Bogart and Bacall in *To Have or Have Not* at least two dozen times. Luzon was finally secured near the end of June. Nearly 8,000 Americans were killed and 30,000 wounded. An estimated 190,000 Japanese died during the campaign.

When Meyer's rotation number came up, he returned to the States. "I came home on rotation," he said. "I didn't have enough battle stars or anything. I came back on time." He was discharged on January 27, 1946, and went back to his job at Firestone. Nadine was discharged a month later. "I enjoyed being in the service," she said, "but I was glad to get out." She continued working for the navy for a while; assigned to Kansas City, she handled the discharge of area naval officers. Eventually she went to work at the Firestone store in North Kansas City, where she met Harold. They were married in June 1949. Harold retired from Firestone in 1977 after thirty-five years of service.

He shares a feeling common to many World War II veterans. "Everyone I've talked to said they wouldn't want to do it again," he said, "but they wouldn't have missed it either."

A Whole New World

Off Luzon Island, the Philippines, near dusk, January 4, 1945—A kamikaze flew out of the sun toward the escort carrier *Ommaney Bay.* The Japanese plane, a twin-engine "Frances" loaded with high explosives, clipped the carrier's island and pinwheeled into her starboard side. The impact of one bomb tore through the flight deck and touched off a series of fiery explosions among the fully fueled aircraft parked on the carrier's hangar deck. When the second bomb went off, it ruptured the ship's fire mains.

A thousand yards from *Ommaney Bay*'s flaming starboard side, the destroyer escort *Ulvert M. Moore* (DE-442) was casting off from a mail delivery to the heavy cruiser *Minneapolis.* Radio technician first class Ken Morton was on deck and happened to be watching the *Ommaney Bay* when the kamikaze hit. "I was actually looking that way when it happened," Morton, a retired electrical engineer, recalled fifty-two years later. "All that fuel and everything, it all went up."

The *Moore* finished casting off and immediately headed for the stricken escort carrier. By now the *Ommaney Bay* was engulfed. Soon lookouts on the *Moore* spotted four men in the water. They were pulled from the sea. One of the men died before he could be brought aboard; the others were suffering from flash burns and shock.

Intense heat and cooking off ammunition from the doomed carrier forced other ships in the area to stand off and rescue survivors from the water. Not all the casualties were from the explosions and fire. "There were sharks in the water," Morton said, "so it was really tough." Eventually, a destroyer was ordered to sink the still-flaming wreck with a torpedo. Ninety-five sailors died in the attack.

But the *Ulvert M. Moore* participated in three major invasions (in which kamikaze and submarine attacks were a constant threat) and emerged from World War II virtually unscathed. Its captain, Franklin D. Roosevelt Jr., son of the president, was awarded the navy's Legion of Merit for sinking a Japanese sub during the Philippines campaign.

Morton grew up in Omaha, Nebraska. "I had never seen an ocean when I joined the navy," he said. A friend's father had been a sailor, and his experiences were common topics of discussion while Morton was growing up. "That influenced me to join the navy," he said.

In January 1943 he was nineteen, working two jobs and going to night school. He wanted to get into the electronics field. "Electronics had been my hobby for years and years," he said. On a whim, he went down to the naval recruiting station one afternoon and enlisted. Four hours later, after saying a hasty goodbye to his parents and his girlfriend, he was on a train headed to California, "which, looking back on it, was probably not the best way to handle it," he admits. He was sent to Treasure Island and later to the University of Houston for advanced electronics training. He graduated in the top 10 percent of his class and became an instructor at the navy's electronics school. It was a cushy job, Morton said, but he hadn't joined the navy to be a teacher.

"I requested sea duty, which they couldn't believe," he said. He was assigned to the *Ulvert M. Moore*, a brand-new destroyer escort that was being outfitted in the Brooklyn Naval Yard.

The ship was named for a twenty-four-year-old pilot who had been stationed on the aircraft carrier *Hornet* during the Battle of Midway. Ulvert Moore, taking part in his first combat mission, was a member of "Torpedo 8," a group of fifteen Devastator torpedo bombers, which, despite overwhelming odds, attacked the Japanese aircraft carrier *Akagi*, which was part of the Midway-bound strike force. All fifteen Devastators were shot down, and only one pilot survived. But their sacrifice wasn't in vain because their attack drew off the strike force's air screen and left the skies open to U.S. dive-bombers, who soon sank three enemy carriers.

The *Ulvert M. Moore* was commissioned on July 18, 1944. Among the dignitaries at the ceremony was the captain's mother, Eleanor Roosevelt, whom Morton met and chatted with briefly while she was being given a below-decks tour. "She came across to me as a very warm and likeable person," he said. He also has good memories of Captain Roosevelt. "He was a good captain. He was very knowledgeable. I think he was fair. . . . He was stable under some very trying conditions."

Morton's job was maintenance and repair of the ship's electronics. "I was the only radio technician on the ship," he said. "I took care of the radio, radar . . . pretty much all of the electronics aboard the ship." The *Moore* was fitted with both air-search and surface-search radar as well as sonar for hunting submarines. Her armament included two five-inch guns, twin forty-millimeter Bofors, ten twenty-millimeter antiaircraft guns, three torpedo tubes, and stacks of depth charges. "We would screen against submarines and aircraft," Morton said.

The ship spent most of her time in the Pacific. She was part of the destroyer screen for the Philippines invasion in January 1945, where she was credited with shooting down three enemy planes in three days. At the end of the month, while on antisubmarine patrol, she sank a Japanese sub near Mindoro Island.

The *Moore* also took part in the invasion of Iwo Jima in February, and on March 21, in preparation for the invasion of Okinawa, she began a grueling period in which she didn't turn off her engines for seventy-eight straight days, steaming an amazing twenty-seven thousand nautical miles. During that time the crew had to contend with everything from kamikazes to typhoons. "That was a rough time," Morton said.

At only 306 feet long and weighing just more than 1,300 tons, the *Moore* was not considered a smooth-riding ship. In rough seas she bounced around like a cork. The South China Sea was especially bad, Morton recalled. Much of the time it was so rough they couldn't cook. "We'd just make sandwiches," he said. During really bad storms, the ship's list (side-to-side roll) would reach 65 percent; it felt like the ship was turning over. Luckily, Morton was never seasick. He gained a healthy respect for the ocean. "Man is puny. You realize that if you've ever been in one of those storms," he said.

More than fifty years later, he still has strong memories about those months at sea. "We were under attack so many times," he said. "You dreaded dawn and dusk because that's when the planes would come out of the sun." He remembers once when a kamikaze hit a destroyer in their group. "We heard the call for help," he said, but there was little they could do. The ship sank in a matter of minutes. "I remember that terrible sound of general quarters at all hours of the night," he said. "Most of the time we didn't even take our clothes off to sleep. . . . We'd take our shoes off and that was it."

But he has good memories, too, like when the *Moore*'s crew would return downed pilots to their carriers and come away with gallons of ice cream from thankful shipmates. "We never had any of that, so that was a treat," Morton said. His best memories are of the men he served with. "We had a good crew. The guys worked together and did the things they were supposed to and did them well."

After the war, the *Moore* was placed in reserve. She returned to active duty during the Korean War. She was officially decommissioned in 1965 and became a vessel in the navy's target fleet. On July 13, 1966, the carrier *Coral Sea* sank the *Ulvert M. Moore* off San Nicholas Isle, California. After the war, Morton returned to school, got married, and graduated with a degree in electrical engineering. Eventually he went to work at the Western Electric plant in Lee's Summit, where he became manager of the engineering department. He retired in 1984.

He admits he still thinks about the war. "It was a challenge," he said, but "when you're twenty, twenty-one, you kind of like those challenges." And although he settled in the nation's Heartland, thousands of miles from the nearest ocean, he admits that the sea still has a hold on him. "It's a whole new world, living at sea for several months," he said. "I think I could handle it even today."

Back Alive in '45

LINGAYEN GULF, OFF LUZON ISLAND, THE PHILIPPINES, JANUARY 9, 1945—The LVTs of the 727th Amphibious Tractor Battalion carried the U.S. 6th Army to the beaches of Luzon in five waves. The first troops stormed ashore just minutes after the beach had been swept by naval batteries and the tractors' own machine guns. Initial Japanese resistance was confined to sniper fire and strafing by planes. Soon the tractors had carried the troops five miles inland. Offshore, kamikazes were inflicting heavy damage on the 7th Fleet, which lost 17 ships and saw another 50 heavily damaged.

LVT Crew Commander Stayton Parr made his first trip to the island on January 11 and spent much of his time carrying ammunition, food, and medical supplies to the front-line troops. A month later, the 11th Airborne Division attacked the island of Corregidor, and hundreds of Japanese soldiers tried to escape by swimming to Bataan, south of Subic Bay. Units of the 727th were sent to pick up the swimmers before they reached the island and escaped into the jungle. So that they could not get aboard with hidden weapons, the Japanese were told to strip down before they were taken onto the tractors. Anyone who refused or tried to escape was immediately shot in the water. It had been less than three years since the infamous Bataan Death March, in which an estimated 10,000 Allied POWs died during a 55-mile forced march to a prison camp in San Fernando, and there were few complaints about excessive brutality.

In April, the 727th arrived at Moluccas Straits and began training with Australian forces for what would be the invasion of Borneo. On May 1, American troops assisted in the Aussies' invasion of Tarakan Island, a tiny spit of land off the northeastern coast of Borneo, and later, they moved on to the Borneo mainland. "It was hot and sultry," Parr recalled in 1991. Once during the campaign he was told to knock out a Japanese pillbox. "It turned out to be uninhabited, thank goodness."

Parr said while the Australian ships were reloading the tractors, the Aussie sailors would give the American crews cold drinks and the occasional cold beer. "We didn't have ice or anything. That was unheard of for us," he said. "I always remembered those guys. They shared with us."

On July 1, the Americans took the Australians to Balikpapan, east of Borneo. Still held by the Japanese, it was the largest oil refinery in the Far East. "They'd been bombing that thing for several days," Parr said, but he remembers one explosion in particular when an Australian plane made a direct hit on a storage tank. "Oh man," he said, "the fire and the black smoke and the flames and those huge pieces of metal—they were up in the air even before we heard the sound. It was an explosion. . . . I'm glad the Australians were on our side. They were tough, you bet. They were good soldiers."

Later, General MacArthur came ashore and walked within fifteen feet of Parr's tractor. A sniper hidden among the trees fired at the general. He missed, and MacArthur calmly pointed to where the shot had come from. "Somebody got him," Parr said.

In mid-July, the battalion reformed at Aparri on the northern tip of Luzon to begin preparing for what every soldier dreaded—the invasion of the Japanese home islands, code-named Operations Olympic and Coronet. There was already talk of a million Allied casualties. "We'd a been right in the middle of the thing right off the bat," Parr said. Up to that point, he doesn't remember being too worried about not making it home. "I guess I was too young and dumb," he said. "But that going to Japan—it weighed on my mind. . . . Our casualties would have been terrible. . . . You used up a chance here, you used up a chance there. How many do you get?" Then, in August, they heard a rumor that the Japanese were surrendering, that a U.S. bomber had dropped a single bomb that destroyed an entire city. Parr said they were skeptical until they heard the official announcement. "We didn't celebrate until it was official," he said. "Well, there was a celebration, I'm telling you."

He returned to the States in late 1945, his skin dark orange from the Atabrine tablets the men had taken to combat malaria. He arrived home on December 22. Back alive in '45.

The war has stuck with Parr. Nearly fifty years after its end, he still thinks about the men who died—seven from his battalion—and how lucky he was to make it back. "The good Lord watched over us. We lost some, and one is too many, but it sure could have been a lot worse." One of the lasting imprints of the war was of how close the men became—not unusual when you gather a group of young men from diverse backgrounds and send them on a dangerous adventure thousands of miles from home. "I'll never forget, as long as I have any sense at all, I'll never forget those guys," he said. "You have a special feeling for those people." And like many who fought in the Pacific, he retains lasting bitterness toward the Japanese. Parr's philosophy is simple. "I don't buy Japanese products," he said. "I guess I'm not very good at forgiving."

Iwo Jima

Human Butcher Shop

GREEN BEACH, IWO JIMA, FEBRUARY 19, 1945—It was a cool, sunny morning when the first waves of U.S. Marines arrived on the killing ground. They leaped from the amphibious landing craft into the black, calf-deep volcanic sand and labored up the slope to the first beach terrace. The enemy, hidden in camouflaged pillboxes and buried blockhouses and steel- and concrete-reinforced caves that honeycombed the face of Mount Suribachi, overlooking the invasion beach, held their fire. The marines warily moved up the first terraces and across the open sand.

Those first marines on Iwo Jima had a few precious minutes to wonder if the most intense preinvasion bombardment in naval history had done its job. Some began to think the Japanese garrison was so battered that all they'd have to do was a little mopping up. Or maybe the Japanese had secretly withdrawn from the island during the night.

Sgt. Paul Ceynowa, a young forward observer for an 81mm mortar battery, First Battalion, Twenty-eighth Marine Regiment, Fifth Marine Division, harbored no such illusions. By the time he reached the beachhead in the second wave, small arms fire had begun, and mortars were landing among the forward troops with sickening accuracy.

The Japanese defenders had spent months preparing for this day. Machine guns, their fields of fire precalculated, crisscrossed the beaches with a deadly blanket of lead. Sharpshooters on Suribachi's craggy slopes picked off the marines at will. Mortar units, hidden among the island's rubble and craters, sent shell after shell into the sandy plain, filling the cordite-scented breeze with black sand, body parts and blood.

Ceynowa had never seen anything like it. Although he'd gotten in on the last action on Saipan, it hadn't prepared him for this. This was wholesale slaughter. "I didn't think I'd ever make it. I really didn't think I'd make it through there," he said when interviewed in 1993. "It was a human butcher shop."

Lt. Gen. Tadamichi Kuribayashi, commander of the Japanese garrison on Iwo Jima, had devised what was for the Japanese an unusual defense of the island. Unlike previous island invasions, there would be no attempt to prevent the marines from landing on the beaches. According to Kuribayashi's plan, the first wave of invaders would be allowed to advance inland 500 yards, at which time automatic weapons and artillery would cut them to pieces.

Iwo Jima, which means Sulfur Island, is not quite five miles long and only two and a half miles wide at its broadest point. Shaped like a pork chop, it is only 760 miles south of Tokyo, making it a perfect emergency-landing site for B-29s returning from missions to the Japanese home islands.

Although Suribachi, a 550-foot extinct volcano, was a key defensive position, bristling with automatic weapons and artillery, Kuribayashi's main defensive forces were to the north in caves, pillboxes, and concrete blockhouses with walls five feet thick. Where the southern end of the island was mostly soft volcanic sand terraces, to the north were rocky caves and canyons ideal for a protracted war of attrition.

Planning for the invasion of Iwo Jima—code-named Operation Detachment—began in October 1944. Three marine divisions would take part in the operation—the Fourth and Fifth would make up the initial invasion force and the Third Division would be kept in reserve offshore until the southern portion of the island was taken. The Third Marines would be sent in as the campaign moved north.

Sixty thousand marines, commanded by Lt. Gen. Holland M. "Howling Mad" Smith, would land on the island's eastern beaches, which were divided into color-coded sectors—blue, yellow, red and green. The Fourth Division was assigned to blue and yellow beaches and the Fifth would land on red and green.

The American commanders were convinced the Japanese would put up a strong defense at the beaches. They had been through the bloody beach defenses on Tarawa, Saipan and Peleliu, and thought they knew what to expect. They were wrong.

One of the first things Ceynowa noticed when he jumped out of the landing craft onto Iwo Jima was the sand. "It was like running in a . . . granary full of corn or wheat," he said. "You just couldn't hardly make any headway." With mortar rounds exploding around him, he paused for a moment at the top of the first sand terrace. The air was hazy from the smoke, but he could see some brush 150 yards away. In between there was just open sand. "I just took off," he said. He didn't try to dodge; he just ran as fast as the loose black sand would allow. "By running fast, you make yourself a difficult target."

It was like that for most of the day, he said—looking ahead for cover, spotting something and then making a dash for it. Every once in a while bullets would chew at the sand near him. "Machine gun fire was going all the time," he said. It was a bloody morning for the marines. Gunnery Sgt. John Basilone, the hero of Guadalcanal who was the first enlisted marine to win the Congressional Medal of Honor during World War II, was leading a machine gun platoon when a mortar round landed at his feet. The explosion killed Basilone and four of his men. "They made big use out of the mortars," said Ceynowa, who was a mortar specialist. "The bad part of those mortars is you don't hear them coming." A good mortar crew could put five rounds in the air before the first one hits. "When they start, you better jump to cover immediately because the next shell is right behind it."

By midafternoon of the first day, the Fifth Marines had crossed the isthmus, a distance of less than one thousand yards. By nightfall, nearly thirty thousand men and thousands of tons of equipment were crammed into the tiny beachhead. There was little sleep that first night, what with the constant pounding of the artillery and the harsh, daylight-bright star shells fired from offshore destroyers to prevent Japanese infiltrators from attacking the exhausted troops. The enemy mortar and artillery rounds continued to fall among the closely packed marines and casualties mounted. By morning, nearly six hundred Americans were dead and almost two thousand were wounded. And it was just the beginning. It took the Fifth Marines four days to take Suribachi. During the mop-up, the Twenty-eighth Regiment counted more than six hundred dead Japanese. Grenades and satchel charges were used to permanently entomb hundreds more in the volcano.

By February 25—D-Day plus six—the marines had captured the southern airfield and were approaching the core of Kuribayashi's central defense perimeter built into the island's highlands. By the end of the day, one-third of the island was in American hands, but at a terrible cost—sixteen hundred marines dead and fifty-five hundred wounded. The Fifth Division alone had twenty-five of its officers killed that first week. Casualties also were high among the enlisted men. Ceynowa said he was one of only ten marines of his original company that landed on D-Day, to walk off the island under their own power. "Every three days we'd need replacements," he said.

Snipers were everywhere. As a forward observer, Ceynowa was constantly under fire, but was never wounded. Although he thinks luck was involved, he also did what he could to minimize his risks. For instance, although he always carried binoculars, he used them sparingly because they tended to draw sniper fire. "I never used my binoculars unless they were absolutely necessary," he said. When he wasn't using them, he kept them in a pouch on the back of his belt. He never could understand the officers who walked around with binoculars around their necks. "That's unnecessarily identifying yourself," he said. He also never stood up in the open if there was any chance snipers were in the area. "They were good shots," he said. "If you're hit by a sniper, 90 percent of the time you're dead."

One of the most terrible and effective weapons of the campaign was the flamethrower. Ceynowa said it was the only way to knock out the hundreds of bunkers and caves on Iwo Jima. In addition to the handheld model, nearly a quarter of the tanks were equipped with flamethrowers, which could shoot a jet of napalm fifty yards. Ceynowa said he's still haunted by the memory of burning men. "When you hear those guys come out screaming with that stuff, burning alive . . . It was horrible to hear."

Twenty-two marines won the Medal of Honor on Iwo Jima, the most of any marine battle. One of those heroes was Cpl. Tony Stein. Stein, a towering twenty-four-year-old toolmaker from North Dayton, Ohio, had invented a handheld machine gun from a thirty-caliber wing gun from a wrecked navy fighter. He called the weapon his "stinger." Ceynowa remembers seeing Stein—both were members of the Twenty-eighth Regiment—running along the front lines spraying Japanese pillboxes with his huge machine gun. "I tell you, he raised hell with them," Ceynowa said. "It was almost like committing suicide. But he got a Congressional Medal of Honor for it."

Witnesses said Stein killed at least twenty Japanese soldiers leading his company off the beach. Twice he had his stinger shot out of his hands and was wounded by shrapnel in the shoulder. But a few days later he was back at the front. By March 1, the Twenty-eighth was back in action. That morning the First and Second Battalions swept to the top of Hill 362A—a famed battlefield of Japan's civil war back in 1877—only to face an eighty-foot cliff that plunged into a sniper-infested ravine. The only way in was around the rocky shoulders. Stein was one of twenty marines who volunteered to clear the snipers from the ridge. Only seven men came back. Stein wasn't one of them. His body was finally returned to North Dayton in December 1945 and buried in Calvary Cemetery.

One evening, Ceynowa's company took a ridge. But as night was falling, the men discovered a large number of Japanese troops less than fifty yards from their position. That presented a problem because the Japanese were particularly fond of night attacks. "That close, we could have been in real trouble that night," Ceynowa said. His company commander called him over and gave him the job of knocking out the enemy troops. Ceynowa found a high spot where he had a good view of the enemy. He had been assigned four mortars and instructed the gunners to fire five rounds each. He knew what was at stake. With only fifty yards between the camps, there was no margin of error. One short round and a handful of marines would be maimed or dead. He called in the coordinates over the field telephone. The barrage wiped out the Japanese position. And there were no friendly fire casualties. Ceynowa was awarded the Bronze Star with a "V" for valor. "The gunners did a helluva job," he said. "They didn't make one mistake."

By the time the fighting ended on March 26, nearly seven thousand marines were dead and seventeen thousand were wounded. Iwo Jima remains the costliest battle in Marine Corps history. For the Japanese, it was much worse. Of their estimated twenty-two thousand men, only about two hundred survived the battle. General Kuribayashi reportedly committed suicide, but his body was never found.

After Iwo Jima, Ceynowa's outfit was sent to Hawaii to begin training for its next mission: the invasion of Kyushu, the southernmost of the Japanese home islands. The atomic bomb changed all that. Ceynowa has no ambivalence about the decision to use the bomb. Japan, with its hills and mountains, was ideally suited for a long defensive campaign that might have cost a million American lives. "If you don't think Harry Truman didn't do the right thing, you ought to go over there and look at that terrain," he said. "That old atomic bomb saved our necks."

Into Hell

IWO JIMA, FEBRUARY 19, 1945—Pvt. Jim Bennett, Twenty-seventh Marines, rode the landing craft to shore in the tenth wave. When he jumped into the sand, it was like jumping into hell. "The beaches were so heated from this volcanic ash that I had hemorrhoids come down on me from laying on this beach. The beach was so hot you had to put a poncho down to lay on it. I was laying on the beach and the oddest thing I ever did see during the war was a Japanese with a Nambu machine gun trying to sink a battlewagon. You could see the tracers from this machine gun. I don't know what he thought, but I sat there and laughed a thousand times," he said laughing.

Bennett remembers being pinned down a while on the beach and then moving fairly quickly to more solid ground. His 81-millimeter mortar team was kept busy. "The mortar weighed 136 pounds and broke down into three pieces. You had your loader and your observers. Your mortar would fire up to two miles. . . . You pulled the safety pin, drop 'er down. A shotgun shell explodes in the bottom of the tube is what throws your shell out.

"The observers would call in the firing orders and you wouldn't even see the target. You'd be down in the hole . . . the navy had bombed and shelled this island so much, we'd get in the holes the navy had already dug out. The Japanese was always trying to get in on the mortars. We'd have to set barbed wire up at night to protect our guns. One night, I was on the side of the gun and we had barbed wire up and the Japanese broke through. And I'm out here by myself all night [laughs]. The Japanese hit this trip flare and it lit up and one of the guys in the hole shot and he [the Japanese] dropped down. But I'm out here on the side right by him all night wonderin' [laughs] if they got 'em."

Bennett said one of the things that helped them on Iwo Jima was the number of combat veterans present. "The invasion on Iwo, I believe you had more veterans that knew what they was doing. The squad leader I had, had four campaigns in, two years of college and was a corporal [laughs]. That's what always amazed me, the ratings in the Marine Corps. The ratings were so different from the other services. I made pfc out of parachute school. Thirty-two months later I made corporal [laughs].

"This squad leader I had, I'd go to hell with him 'cause he wasn't afraid of the devil hisself. He was really somethin' else." The squad leader was an ex-raider from Winona, Minnesota, named Lloyd D. Luke. "Here's a little something I'll tell you about him. I woke up with him bout thirty-some days [in a row] in a foxhole. One morning we was facing each other, and my eyes opened, and he looked at me, and I looked at him. He says, 'You know what?' I said, 'What?' He says, 'You're the ugliest man I ever did see' [laughs]."

"I went up to Winona a few years back. I called him up, I didn't know exactly where he lived. I said, 'Luke? You know who this is?' 'No.' I said, 'Who's the ugliest man in the Marine Corps?' 'Jim Bennett!' [laughs].

"He was a real good man in combat. He'd take care of his crew. We lost one man out of the mortar section. We was on the gun and was out on the flanks and the man came in, didn't stay in position, and one of our own guys shot him. But that's the only man we lost . . . The 27th Marines was 963 men that went in of the 3rd Battalion. Seven hundred and ninety-five was either wounded or killed." Bennett was one of the few who made it through the battle unscathed. "The only wound I got was right here." He noted a scar on his right arm. "I done that in the Solomon Islands. We was on a work detail and I had a K-bar, my knife, and I was opening a can of peaches and slipped [laughs]. I was very fortunate."

The enemy had a wide variety of weapons in their defensive arsenal, Bennett said. "The Japanese had a rocket launcher they would pull out of a cave and had a [barrel] about this high [two feet], like a carbide can. They would fire that and it would go like this [making pinwheel motions with his arms], just turn round and round and you better get in a hole because the concussion from that thing would knock you for a loop. I hated to see a weasel [an amphibious tractor used to carry supplies] bring up mortar shells because every time anything mechanical [showed up], tank or anything, they would fire this mortar, this rocket, and you'd have to dig in. Finally our artillery observers sealed 'em up in the caves, which was a great relief [laughs]."

Not all the wounds suffered by marines on Iwo Jima were physical. "We came by an outfit one time. There was five or six fellows gathered in this hole that had combat fatigue. It's the most pitiful sight that a man can see . . . They were just sitting there crying. Just more or less frozen."

The combat-weary Fifth Marine Division left Iwo Jima in late March 1945. "We got on a merchant marine ship, which we thought was heaven because we could sit down and eat at a table. And we also could lay in our bunks in the holds and watch a movie [laughs]." The marines were shipped back to Hawaii, and after a long rest, they began training for the invasion of Japan. All that became academic when atomic bombs were dropped on Hiroshima and Nagasaki that August. Within a few days the war was over. The Fifth Marines were sent to Sasebo, Japan, as part of the occupation forces. After seeing Japan for himself, Bennett became convinced the atomic bomb saved his life. "I do believe if they hadn't used the atomic bomb that we'd have been blowed out of the water during the invasion of Japan," he said. "The Japanese were ready for an invasion. . . . If we hadn't used the atomic bomb, there would have been a lot of dead marines. A lot of children who wouldn't be here." Bennett said they had few problems with the Japanese during their time there. "The people wasn't too friendly at first. We started giving candy to the children and they finally would come out."

After his outfit left Japan, he had fifteen months remaining on his four-year tour of duty and was transferred to the Second Marine Division. He was discharged sixty days early. "I came back to Kansas City and my wife and I got married and I went back to Burlington Northern Railroad to work for thirty-seven years." He retired in the early 1980s.

Bennett remembers a lot of racism during the war. "There wasn't many blacks. They had all the blacks together. They took the firing pins out of their rifles. They was used as stevedores to unload ships and stuff like that."

In a lot of ways, he said, World War II was a different war. "I feel in World War II you had to do it. But the way they do the Marine Corps now, like in Beirut and Lebanon. . . . The marines are not trained to set in one place all the time. Like in Vietnam, take a hill and give it back the next day. That's not war, that's politics." His own son was old enough to be drafted for Vietnam, but received a medical deferment due to hearing loss. Bennett said he was relieved. "The kind of war they was fighting . . . I felt sorry for the servicemen 'cause they was playing politics in war [laughs]. I don't believe in that."

Seabee

Iwo Jima, February 19, 1945—It was a scene out of some nightmare vision of hell: geysering explosions, torn bodies bobbing in the oily surf; a black, smoking moonscape of shell craters and whining shrapnel; a butcher's assortment of blown-off arms and legs, torsos without heads, dead men frozen in the sand, at rest for eternity; the maimed screaming for a corpsman or lying silently, waiting, perhaps even thankful they don't have to go any farther into the hazy killing ground of bullets and choking volcanic ash; a nightmare world of tears and curses, unimaginable pain and violent death.

That was the hell that engulfed Harvey Wilson. A platoon chief with the 133rd Naval Construction Battalion—the Seabees—Wilson arrived on Iwo Jima on the heels of the first assault waves of marines—some battle-hardened veterans of Guadalcanal and Saipan, others seeing combat for the first time. Their goal: to wrest control of the speck of rock and sand from more than 20,000 entrenched and fanatical Japanese soldiers. "A person just can't imagine," said Wilson, a retired lineman for Independence Power and Light. "That island was only 8 square miles. . . . You [can't] imagine what a mess that was."

The Seabees weren't Wilson's first choice. "Ever since I was a kid, I wanted to get into the navy," said Wilson (eighty-four in 1992). But when he tried to enlist in the regular navy in 1943, he was already in his midthirties. "They wouldn't have me. I was too old." He was working as an electrician, being shuffled between defense plants in Missouri and Illinois. "They put us where they wanted us to go," he said. He was married and the constant moving was hard on his wife, Billie. So, he decided to join the Seabees. And what did Billie think of that?

"She understood the situation. It was getting to a point where she was tired of running around on different defense jobs." Besides, he said, neither of them thought the Seabees would be particularly dangerous work. Wilson figured it was just another job. And Billie had doubts that her husband would get in at all. "She didn't think I'd get any farther than boot camp," he said. "She had no idea we were going into combat. And I didn't have any idea either."

Wilson was sent to Honolulu. "Our [main] job was to build B-29 airstrips," he said. "We had never heard of a B-29, which was the biggest [bomber] they had at the time." He spent a year in Hawaii stationed at Hickam Field where the Seabees were expanding the landing strips. Wilson said building an airfield during World War II was a rather uncomplicated job. In Hawaii, they simply dredged coral from the sea to use as a base and then covered it with asphalt. "Just like building a road, only bigger," he said. He described his job with the Seabees with characteristic self-deprecation. "I was more or less a handyman, screwing in light bulbs and so forth," he said. In reality, because of his age and experience, he was put in charge of the work crews and eventually made platoon chief.

All in all, things were going fairly well for Wilson. The work wasn't hard and the weather in Hawaii was nice. The war, which had been going on for nearly three years, seemed very distant. "To me, the war was going to be over before we got anywhere near," he said. The first sign that that might not be the case came when the 133rd was attached to the 4th Marine Division, which had recently fought at Saipan. But one of Wilson's marine friends reassured him. When you're tagging along with the marines, he said, you've got nothing to worry about. At Iwo Jima, Wilson said, "I found out they were lying."

Although dominated by Mount Suribachi, Iwo Jima's most impressive feature was hidden from view. Virtually the entire island was a labyrinth of tunnels, troop quarters, and command centers for its garrison of over twenty-two thousand men. In some areas the tunnels went seven levels deep and included several fully outfitted field hospitals complete with bunks, medical supplies, doctors, and nurses.

Lieutenant General Kuribayashi had no illusions about the outcome, but he was determined to make the conquest as costly as possible for the Americans. "Every man will resist until the end," he told his troops, "making his position his tomb. Every man will do his best to kill ten enemy soldiers." And before the onslaught, he wrote his children: " . . . from now on you must reconcile yourselves to living without a father."

Wilson and his platoon of Seabees reached Iwo Jima a few hours after H-hour. "We hit the beach at 11 o'clock. Bodies were scattered all around," he said. He remembers the sound of bullets whizzing by his head and the ground-shaking thump of artillery. "They were firing from every direction."

Although the black sand was hard to run through, it was easy to burrow into, which suited Wilson, who got busy scooping out a foxhole with his entrenching tool. Near misses would launch the sand over the marines in blinding, choking waves, becoming embedded in wounds and complicating treatment. But for shrapnel, the sand was a lifesaver. Those jagged pieces of hot metal would come spinning out of explosions and hit the sand, their momentum immediately absorbed. "If it had been hard ground," Wilson said, "we'd have never taken that island."

Like the marines, the Seabees were issued M-1 rifles, but rarely used them. There was no use. "The Japs, you didn't see 'em because they were back in their caves firing," he said. "You didn't know what you were firing back at." Wilson said there were so many American dead on the beach that the Seabees were ordered to dig a mass grave. Wilson was watching a bulldozer driver cover the bodies with sand when a mine exploded, blowing off one of the treads and knocking the driver out of his seat. He wasn't seriously injured. As soon as they could get a ship in close enough, the Seabees went to work unloading equipment as the bullets and shells rained down on them. "You didn't watch out for 'em, you just hoped they weren't [meant for you]. They were firing on us up to the end."

Was he scared?

"You were numb," Wilson said. "You knew there were certain things you had to do, your duties, and you did them the best you could. "It just kept you busy trying to keep things organized. It was disorganized," he said. "As soon as you were done with what you were doing, you hit the foxhole and tried to get some sleep."

February 23, 1945, was a memorable day for Wilson. That was the day he saw the flag go up on Suribachi. It also was the day he came within an inch of dying. There were two flag raisings on Suribachi. The first flag was just barely visible from the beachhead, so Col. Chandler Johnson ordered a larger flag sent up. Associated Press photographer Joe Rosenthal arrived just in time to take the famous flag-raising photo. Wilson isn't sure which flag he saw raised, but said it was clearly visible from his position on the beach. "We were unloading a ship and I was on the beach when I saw [it] go up," he said.

Wilson's brush with eternity came later that day while digging a foxhole. He had stopped a moment to say something to his squad when he felt something hit his helmet. At first he thought the man digging next to him had hit his helmet with his shovel. "I said, 'What'd you hit me for?' " Then he looked at his helmet. On the outside he could see the end of a Japanese twenty-five-caliber bullet. When he looked inside, he saw that the nose of the bullet projected a half-inch through the helmet liner, not quite grazing his hair. "Man, I dug a foxhole right quick then."

When it was all over, nearly seven thousand Americans would be dead. Twenty-six marines and navy medics would be awarded the Medal of Honor, seven of them for throwing themselves on grenades. Few Japanese would survive to be taken prisoner. "Those Japs just didn't give up. They were trained from little kids on to defend their country," Wilson said. "Theoretically, you didn't blame them because that's all they knew." The number of Japanese casualties is only an estimate because thousands remained underground in the island's cave network. Wilson said the demolition teams would stand at the cave entrances and try to talk the soldiers out. If that didn't work, a water and gasoline mixture was pumped into the caves and then ignited. In the mid-1950s, thousands of bodies, many of them preserved by the island's sulphur beds, were discovered in several sealed-off caves. In one cave they found six hundred bodies. Incredibly, the last two Japanese defenders on the island surrendered in 1951, six years after the war ended.

As the marines moved inland, the Seabees went to work on the damaged airfields, which had to be completely rebuilt to handle the massive B-29 Superforts. On March 4, a B-29 that was almost out of fuel made an emergency landing on the island as marines nearby fought the Japanese with bayonets and flamethrowers. It would be the first of 2,251 bombers to make emergency landings on the island during the war.

Wilson was still on Iwo Jima when he heard about a new type of "super bomb" that was dropped on Hiroshima. Later he found out his wife's cousin, Maj. Dutch Van Kirk, was the navigator on the Enola Gay, the plane that dropped the bomb.

"It's bad that we had to drop that bomb, but on the other hand, we were packed up and ready to go to Japan," he said. "We realized that we was going to a slaughter sure enough. . . . It was more or less a trade-off. That bomb sent us home."

The Trench

Iwo Jima, February 19, 1945—Wayne McMeins remembers the day he landed on Iwo Jima like it was yesterday.

He remembers the wind and the noise of the engines, the awesome spectacle of the landing craft of the first attack waves heading toward the black volcanic sand beaches.

He remembers feeling pretty good because no one was shooting at them. "It was just a big joy ride because there was nothing going on," McMeins said.

The three-day naval and air bombardment that preceded the invasion had been impressive, but the marines still expected a fight from the entrenched Japanese defenders. Now, as the first amphibious tractors hit the beaches and still no shots were fired, some began to wonder: Could it really be this easy?

McMeins was a member of a military police company attached to the Twenty-eighth Regiment, Fifth Marine Division. The Twenty-eighth was assigned to land on Green Beach, the stretch of sand closest to Mount Suribachi, which crouched over the invasion beaches like a sleeping prehistoric monster. The question was, would it stay asleep?

As the tractor carrying McMeins's company neared the beach, he could see the marines already ashore laboring up the ascending sand terraces. The beach was clogged with men and bogged-down vehicles. If the Japanese were waiting to spring a trap, he thought, the Americans would be sitting ducks. When McMeins's tractor hit the sand, two things happened almost simultaneously: The landing ramp went down and all hell broke loose. Preregistered artillery began crashing among the tightly packed marines on the beach, and the landing craft disgorging troops at the shoreline. "They hit a boat to the right of us with a mortar," McMeins said. "Blew it out of the water."

Heavy machine guns from bunkers hidden in the sand dunes began spraying the beach in a murderous crossfire. "Hell, they were just sweeping it," McMeins said. "Man, they slaughtered them." There was no place to hide. The sand was so loose you couldn't dig into it very deep without the sides collapsing. Running in it was like running through deep snow. McMeins said the beach was so crowded you had to struggle just to find a place to lie down. "It was just solid men," he said. And it was every man for himself. "There wasn't anybody leading you," he said. "You were on your own." The only thing to do was move forward. Get the hell off the beach. As men died around him, McMeins took off across the sand. "I went across that thing like a scalded dog," he said. "Buddy, I wasn't on that beach five minutes."

McMeins grew up on a farm in Bates County, Missouri, near Drexel. One of nine children, he said they never had a lot, but they always had enough. "We always had plenty of food and never owed anybody," he said. His father was an old-time farmer who didn't put much stock in machines. "He didn't believe in tractors," McMeins said. "He was wrong about that."

McMeins attended Merwin High School where he played basketball. Like other boys of his generation, he couldn't wait to go to war. He enlisted in the Marine Corps in 1944 at age seventeen. His father, who was sixty-nine at the time, had to sign for him. After boot camp, McMeins was sent to Camp Pendleton, where the Fifth Division was being organized. He was trained as a combat MP, which meant his primary responsibility was to provide security for frontline command posts. In reality, however, the MPs were used for everything from stretcher-bearers to combat patrols. They also received heavy weapons training. "We could handle anything but artillery and mortars," he said. He was assigned to the Third Platoon, Second Battalion, commanded by Col. Chandler Johnson. Col. Harry Liversedge was the regimental commander.

The Fifth Marines left San Diego Harbor on November 19, 1944, stopped in Hawaii for some advanced amphibious training, and in January boarded troop ships for what would be a forty-day journey to their destination, then known only as "Island X." Two days out of Pearl Harbor, they were told they were going to Iwo Jima. Few had ever heard of the island—a wasteland of volcanic ash that stank of sulfur.

Aboard the troop ship *Talladega*, McMeins's MP company was given its orders: As soon as they landed, they were to wheel left toward the ominous bulk of Mount Suribachi. They would help take the mountain. When the troop ships arrived offshore, the navy was pounding the island with artillery and dive-bombers. McMeins said the bombers usually went on bombing runs in threes, one after the other. The Japanese knew that and often had their range by the time the third plane came diving in. He remembers seeing one group of bombers swoop over the island. The third plane was hit by an antiaircraft round, which sheared off a wing. The plane crashed into the ocean, but he heard later that a passing ship had rescued the pilot. "They said he survived it," he said. "Glad he did."

As soon as McMeins cleared the first sand terrace, he saw something that's bothered him ever since. It was a large trench dug into the sand off to his right. At the edge were two dead marines. At the bottom of the trench were about 30 bodies—all Orientals and all with their legs bound together.

McMeins thinks the men were Korean slave laborers brought in to build the island's fortifications and then put there by the Japanese as a diversion. Apparently when the marines came upon them, they thought they were Japanese soldiers and slaughtered them. Of all the terrible things he saw on Iwo Jima that really got to him. "That always bothered me," he said. "Those poor sons of bitches."

Past the trench, McMeins saw a large shell crater and dove into it with 10 or 12 other marines. A Japanese machine gun on Suribachi was aimed at the crater and kept them pinned down so no one could get out. Then, to make matters worse, mortar rounds began bracketing the crater. As the explosions walked toward the marines, they realized the Japanese were trying to get their range and drop a shell in their midst.

Finally McMeins had had enough and decided to take his chances with the machine gun. At almost the same instant, there was a huge explosion on Suribachi. "That whole mountain shook," he said. As he took off running, he noticed that both the machine gun and the mortars had stopped. Later he learned that several rocket launchers had been aimed at the mountain and fired at once, apparently wiping out both the machine gun nest and the mortars. McMeins said it came at an opportune time. "The only reason I'm still alive is because of those rockets," he said.

Eventually McMeins got out of the sand and into the rocky brush near the base of the volcano. As they set up Colonel Liversedge's command post, the marines were sent on sweeps to root out snipers and infiltrators in the area. McMeins said the Japanese were likely to pop out of a hidden cave almost anywhere. "They'd infiltrate and sneak out and throw grenades." When they found a cave or tunnel entrance, they'd pin the enemy down with fire from rifles or BARs and then bring up a flamethrower to finish the job. "That erased the problem and we sealed it up," McMeins said. That first night, they established a perimeter around the command post. "Anything that moved in there died," he said.

Like many on Iwo Jima, McMeins saw the flag-raising. He said he knows it was the first one. On the morning of February 23, a forty-man patrol was sent up the volcano. Before they left, Colonel Johnson gave the patrol's leader, Lt. George Schrier, an American flag. "If you get to the top," Colonel Johnson told Schrier, "put it up." McMeins said everyone in the area was watching the mountain that morning to see the flag go up. "We knew they were getting ready to do that," he said. Everyone was told to hold their fire while the patrol snaked its way up the steep face of the volcano. The flag finally went up at about 10:20 A.M. A spontaneous roar went up from the marines watching from below. “That first one kind of gave us a big thrill,” McMeins said. The second flag-raising, immortalized by Joe Rosenthal, occurred later that day, but by then no one was paying much attention.

There is a misconception about the battle for Iwo Jima that once Suribachi was taken, the rest of the island fell quickly. Nothing could be further from the truth. It would be another month before the island was secured.

McMeins had already had his share of close calls, but more were in store. The Japanese would send out nighttime suicide squads made up of men carrying bottles of nitroglycerin strapped to their bodies. One night, McMeins was asleep in his foxhole when he was awakened by the sound of gunfire. “I heard a machine gun open up and this guy blew up,” he said. The “guy” turned out to be a Japanese infiltrator, who had crept into his foxhole. At the last moment, his buddy saw him and gave him a burst from his Thompson machine gun, which detonated the nitro. “All I remember of that guy was his ribcage,” McMeins said. “It was all laid open and I could see some rice inside . . .”

The MPs were kept busy. “They used us wherever they needed people,” he said. “We did a lot of mopping up and the bastards didn’t like to be mopped up.” On one occasion, he and two other marines trapped a group of Japanese at the bottom of a cliff. The marines were at the top, firing down on the Japanese and rolling grenades down on them. Whenever a grenade would land near them, the Japanese would try to throw one of their dead comrades on it to smother the blast. As McMeins took aim at one of the Japanese, he noticed the Japanese was aiming at him as well. “I saw the bastard aiming at me just as the bullet hit,” he said. It struck the rocks six inches below McMeins’s face and “that made me mad.”

Another thing that made McMeins mad was what the Japanese did to the marines they captured. Often, he said, small groups of Japanese would emerge from a hidden cave and drag an unsuspecting marine inside. There they would proceed to torture him to death. “They did everything in the book to him, including castrated him,” he said. “We didn’t like them very well.” In early March, near Motoyama Field, McMeins had a chance to exact some revenge. He was on patrol when he came upon two Japanese soldiers. One was wounded in the arm and leg. McMeins’s first inclination was to shoot them but held his fire because it seemed like that’s what they wanted him to do. He spoke a little Japanese, and he told them to surrender and neither of them would be hurt. “Probably didn’t believe me,” he said. One of the Japanese pulled out a grenade, but instead of throwing it, he held it to his body and let it explode. “Just put it right in his stomach,” McMeins said. The other Japanese—the wounded one—eventually agreed to surrender. After he was taken to the stockade, it was determined that he was a battalion commander named Maj. Mitsuake Hara. Years later McMeins tried to contact Hara in Japan, but he was told by a family member that Hara declined because he still felt shame for allowing himself to be captured.

McMeins's company finally left Iwo Jima in late March and returned to Hawaii to begin training for the invasion of Japan. He volunteered to become trained on a BAR, a portable machine gun that could fire 360 rounds per minute. If he was going to invade Japan, he wanted to have as much firepower as he could get.

In August 1945, they were in the middle of a live ammunition drill when it was suddenly halted. "They said, 'Shoot up your ammo, you won't need it.' " The war was over. His company was sent to Sasebo, Japan, north of Nagasaki, on the southern island of Kyushu. When the marines landed on the home island, they didn't know what to expect. "We set up a perimeter. We figured they'd hit us. We were combat ready," he said. But nothing happened. They soon realized the Japanese had no interest in continuing the bloodshed. "The civilians were great," he said. "They were scared to death of us at first."

McMeins returned to the States in March 1946. He went through some rough times in those postwar years. Stricken with recurring nightmares and other symptoms that today would be diagnosed as post-traumatic stress disorder, he drifted through a number of jobs before finally joining the Kansas City Police Department in 1953. He retired from the department twenty-six years later. Twenty of those years he spent as a detective.

He no longer has nightmares, but sometimes he still thinks about the war and the guys who didn't make it. "What I remember is those other marines," he said. "You sure hated it when your buddy got it. But you were sure glad it wasn't you." He never went back to Iwo Jima after the war. "I started to a couple times," he said, but eventually decided against it. He thinks he still may have some repressed memories he would prefer not to dredge up. "I don't think it's a good idea," he said.

Code Talker

During World War II, 540 Navaho Indians served in the U.S. Marine Corps. Nearly 400 of them volunteered to serve in a top-secret communication program, which used their native language as code to transmit messages during the marines' island-hopping campaign in the Pacific. The so-called code talkers were used in every marine invasion of the war, from Guadalcanal in 1942 to Okinawa in 1945. When the code talkers were operating, Japanese intelligence reported they overheard "strange language, gurgling" transmissions when they listened to American communications. The Japanese were unable to break the code.

Because the code talkers' mission was secret, few were aware of their contribution to the war effort. In fact, it wasn't until 1969, during a reunion of the Fourth Marine Division in Chicago, that the code talkers finally received national recognition and were presented with a medallion specially minted to commemorate their service. Still, the story of the code talkers is largely unknown to Americans. Thomas Begay wants to change that. Begay, who was a code talker during the invasion of Iwo Jima in February 1945, spoke to a roomful of marines at the Ninth Marine Corps Division headquarters at Richards-Gebauer air base in Kansas City, Missouri, in May 2000. The seventy-three-year-old Arizonan was brought to Kansas City as part of the Marine Corps Association's visiting scholar program.

Of the thousands of languages in the world, Navaho is one of the hardest for a nonnative speaker to master. It consists of numerous dialects and has no written alphabet or symbols. For those reasons, American cryptologists considered it the perfect code. Begay was one of nearly four hundred Navahos who volunteered to become code talkers. But it wasn't his first choice.

Born in the tiny Navaho community of Chilchitah, south of Gallup, New Mexico, he grew up speaking Navaho and didn't learn English until his parents sent him to boarding school at Fort Defiance, Arizona, when he was thirteen. In 1943, at age sixteen, he drove with a group of relatives to a nearby town, where an ammunition depot was hiring local workers. Although his relatives were hired, he was passed over because he looked too young. That made him angry. "I said, 'I'll show you.' I went and joined the marines." He enlisted that September despite his age. He said that wasn't unusual; most Navahos at that time were born at home, and few had birth certificates.

Begay's lifestyle change was dramatic. His trip to the West Coast for boot camp was his first time on a train. As a volunteer, he was assigned a sleeping berth, but he didn't use it. "I sat up all night. No one told me I was supposed to sleep," he said. But his upbringing, which had conditioned him to hard labor and hunger, had prepared him for the rigors of marine training. "The obstacle course was nothing," he said. "The way our life was at home, we had a very harsh life," he said. "I felt the marines was a good way of life. Three meals a day."

When Begay joined the marines, he wanted to be an aerial gunner. However, they eventually convinced him to join the code talkers program, which already had been used successfully in several campaigns in the Pacific. Taught to use a variety of communications equipment, the code talkers translated classified messages into Navaho and sent them or (if they were receivers) translated messages from Navaho into English. Certain words in Navaho were given specific meanings in English. For instance, *cha,* which in Navaho means beaver, signified minesweeper. *Ca-lo*—shark in Navaho—meant destroyer. *Na-sey*—ahead in Navaho—meant advance. The Navaho word for frog—*chal*—stood for amphibious. "We made a code within a code," Begay said. Other marines called all the code talkers "chief," but the Navahos didn't consider it a derogatory term. "We were real pleased because we were called chief," he said. "We're the chiefs of the United States Marines." Begay and thirty-two other code talkers were assigned to the Radio Section of H&S Company, Twenty-seventh Marine Regiment, Fifth Marines. They were loaded onto troop ships and headed into the Pacific, bound for Iwo Jima.

Early on the morning of February 19, 1945, Lance Corporal Begay and his fellow marines were roused from their racks for their traditional preinvasion "last meal" of steak and eggs. He'll never forget his landing on the island's black volcanic sand. "I was scared like hell. I hit the beach and my body was numb. No feeling at all. . . . Things blowing up. . . . It was real sad to see, but the main thing was to maintain communication," he said. "You're an important person. . . . What the enemy is looking for is to knock out communication." Begay went to work almost immediately. When one of the code talkers was killed on the beach, Begay was ordered to take his place. Although he was never wounded, he said he had numerous close calls. "The mortars was flying," he said. "If that's your day, that's it, [but] you always have in your mind that you're going to be safe." Begay spent more than a month in combat on Iwo Jima and transmitted hundreds of messages, ranging from reporting enemy troop movements to directing naval gunfire. The island was honeycombed with caves and tunnels, and the threat of enemy counterattack was constant. "You didn't expect someone to come out of the cave," he said. "They'd come up either to surrender or they'd come out shooting." One of his most vivid memories is of seeing the flag raised on Mount Suribachi. "I felt ten feet tall when I saw that flying," he said. He added that people today don't respect the flag like they used to. "I don't know what's going on today," he said. "We had very high respect for America's colors. . . . Navahos were very patriotic people."

Begay remained on Iwo Jima until the mop-up operations were completed in late March. He said in the Fifth Marine Division, the code talkers suffered five casualties. "Two Navahos were killed, three wounded," he said. "We lost two men on the beach on February 19th. . . . The rest of us made it back."

Maj. Howard M. Conner, a signal officer for the Fifth Marine Division on Iwo Jima, praised the contributions of the code talkers: "During the first forty-eight hours," he said, "while we were landing and consolidating our shore positions, I had six Navaho radio networks operating around the clock. In that period alone, they sent and received over eight hundred messages without an error . . . were it not for the Navahos, the marines would never have taken Iwo Jima."

Being a code talker was one of the most hazardous duties of World War II. Of the four hundred who served, only one hundred survived the war.

After his honorable discharge from the marines in 1946, Begay enlisted in the U.S. Army as a paratrooper. "The only reason I joined the army was because of they paid fifty dollars extra," he said. But he still considers himself a marine. "Once you're a marine, you're always a marine," he said. Begay was part of the occupation forces in Japan when the Korean War began in 1950, and he took part in the invasion of Inchon and later, during the Chinese counterattack, fought alongside the marines during the heroic breakout from Chosin Reservoir. Begay said to his knowledge, the code talkers were never used after World War II. Now he and his wife, Nina, have taken it upon themselves to do what they can to preserve the legacy of the code talkers. They also want to keep their native tongue alive, but Begay isn't optimistic. "I doubt very much that they use the language again. The language is dying off," he said. "I think it's going to be lost someday, but we're trying to hold on."

War in the Pacific, Part 4

Lost at Sea

Early on the morning of March 19, 1945, a U.S. B-29 nicknamed "Jack Pot" roared seven thousand feet above Nagoya Bay and flew directly into the searchlights of the harbor's antiaircraft batteries. The plane, which was on a low-level night-bombing mission, immediately began taking heavy flak. As the bombardier prepared to release the load of incendiary bombs, a forty-millimeter round knocked out the plane's number three engine. "Bombs away," he shouted. A moment later, the plane's number two engine was hit and caught fire. Another shell blew a hole in the left fuselage near the navigator's position and shattered some of the Plexiglas panels in the plane's nose. The crew didn't know it at the time, but the radio also was damaged.

Although their number two engine was shut down, it continued to flame. Knowing he had to do something quickly, the twenty-three-year-old pilot, Lt. Warren C. Shipp, opened the cowl flaps and put the huge airplane into a diving turn, which blew out the fire. Fortunately for the crew, the searchlights and antiaircraft guns had pulled away from them and were now directed toward other incoming planes. The Jack Pot limped back out to sea into a pea soup fog, hoping to reach Iwo Jima, 750 miles away, on its two remaining engines.

But that was not to be. A few hours later, the plane was five thousand feet above the heaving North Pacific when a third engine began sputtering. It had been damaged and was rapidly losing oil. Now there was no question. They were going down.

Finis J. Saunders was a nineteen-year-old radar operator aboard the crippled Jack Pot that morning. "I had my parachute on, I was thinking we would have to [bail out]," said Saunders (in 2001). "Things looked pretty bleak." Later, Shipp admitted he considered giving the order to bail out, but he knew there was little chance the crew would land anywhere near each other in the rough water, which he felt would significantly lessen the chances of their all being rescued.

What Shipp didn't know was that their damaged radio, although it couldn't receive messages, was allowing them to transmit their SOS call. A rescue mission was already being organized. In the meantime, the transmitting station advised the Jack Pot crew to bail out because the ocean was considered too rough for ditching. But the men never got that message, which may have been a blessing. If they'd bailed out, Saunders said, "they'd never have found us." The alternative also was worrisome. The waves were cresting at forty feet, but Shipp was convinced he could get the plane down safely. The crew was ordered to assume ditching positions and prepare for impact. Shipp turned the Superfortress into a crosswind and aimed for a trough in the black ocean. Saunders was hunched with his head clamped between his knees when the plane hit the water. The impact knocked him backward, and his head crashed into the bulkhead. He lost consciousness.

Saunders was born in Macomb, Oklahoma—Dust Bowl country—in 1925. When he was five, his family pulled up stakes and headed northeast. "Most of the Okies went to California. We somehow came to Missouri," he said. They moved to a farm near Warrensburg in 1931. His father, a former sharecropper, took care of a local farmer's livestock and helped out on his farm. Saunders, the youngest of four children, grew up doing farm chores, and in his free time he hunted rabbits and squirrels. The family's farm was near a creek, so he also spent a good deal of time fishing and trapping muskrat. "We spent a lot of time on [the creek] or around it," he said.

He remembers hearing the radio reports about the attack on Pearl Harbor. He was sixteen. "We didn't know where Pearl Harbor was. Had no idea where Hawaii was." By the time he graduated from high school in 1943, he knew he would eventually be drafted. Everyone his age was going into the service unless they failed the physical. "It was just an accepted fact that you would go when you were old enough to go," he said. "Everybody was quite patriotic back then." Saunders registered for the draft in October, when he turned eighteen, was called for a physical in December, and was inducted into the army air corps at Fort Leavenworth, Kansas, in January 1944. He went through basic training at Jefferson Barracks in St. Louis and then was sent to Laredo, Texas, for aerial gunnery school.

Originally he was to have been trained as a tail gunner for a B-24, but he was switched to the brand-new B-29 Superfortress. He ended up at Clovis, New Mexico, in B-29 gunnery school. The B-29s were the newest and most technically advanced high-altitude bomber of their day and in 1944 were "in very short supply," Saunders said. "In fact, we didn't even fly in gunnery school. We just learned the principles."

The B-29 had an 11-man crew, a maximum bomb capacity of 20,000 pounds, and a top speed of 290 miles per hour, although to conserve fuel they usually flew at 215 miles per hour. The plane was armed with 10 remote-controlled machine guns and a rapid-fire 20-millimeter cannon. The cabin was kept pressurized to enable the crew to bomb from 30,000 feet. The only time it was depressurized was when the crew opened the bomb bay doors over the target. Then the crew had to don oxygen masks. The crew was made up of two pilots (the airplane commander and copilot), a navigator, bombardier, flight engineer, radio operator, radar operator, the CFC (central fire control) gunner, two blister gunners, and the tail gunner.

Saunders was sent to the army air corps base at Harvard, Nebraska, where the airmen were formed into crews and continued their training. Since there still weren't enough B-29s to go around, the men did much of their in-flight training on B-17s. Saunders also went to school to learn the radar system, then an innovation on airplanes.

He was assigned to the 484th Bomber Squadron, 505th Bombardment Group, 313th Bomber Wing, 21st Bomber Command, 20th Air Force. At Kearney, Nebraska, his crew received a brand-new B-29, which they nicknamed "Jack Pot." "We somehow thought that would make it harder to hit," he said. "Didn't work." In late December 1944, while the Battle of the Bulge was raging in Europe, Jack Pot headed to the North Pacific. It was payback time.

The Jack Pot ended up at the huge U.S. airdrome on the island of Tinian in early 1945. Soon after the crew arrived, a Seabee artist painted a voluptuous half-naked beauty on the Jack Pot's nose. Toward the end of the war, the often risqué "nose art" on planes was discouraged after a general's wife complained about it to her husband.

Bomber crews in the Pacific were required to fly thirty-five missions to fulfill their tour of duty. By early 1945, most of those missions were to the Japanese home islands, a three thousand-mile round trip from Tinian, almost all of it over ocean. Saunders said that was both good and bad. It was good because they weren't shot at the whole way. But it was bad because there are few landmarks on the ocean. "Nothing but water. It looks all the same," he said. Saunders recalled, "I was just a nineteen-year-old kid. Very dedicated. Very scared most of the time."

His first two combat missions were to Iwo Jima, which was being softened up for the February 19 invasion. Iwo was about halfway between Tinian and Japan, which made it an ideal emergency landing site. The Iwo Jima missions were high-level bombing raids. "We had antiaircraft guns shooting at us," Saunders said, "but it wasn't like when we went to the [Japanese] homeland." His third mission was to Nagoya, Japan. It was a daylight raid, and the crew's target was the city's Mitsubishi aircraft engine plant. They would be precision bombing from twenty-seven thousand feet. The mission began badly. "We got into some really bad weather. We all got separated," Saunders said. When the planes reached Nagoya Bay, they ran into heavy flak and were attacked by enemy fighter planes. But the Jack Pot and most of the other bombers made it back.

Saunders had his share of close calls. The runways on Tinian were made of crushed coral, which generated a lot of dust. When too much dust got into the planes' engines, they would suddenly fail just before takeoff. The pilot would then have to abort and try to stop the speeding bomber before it ran out of runway. That happened once as Saunders's crew was heading out on a mission in a borrowed plane. Their pilot, Lieutenant Shipp, burned out the brakes, but the plane, fully loaded with bombs, still crashed off the end of the runway. Saunders said when they came to a stop, everyone jumped out and ran for cover. The plane didn't explode.

Saunders took part in the historic March 9 bombing mission to Tokyo, which went down as one of the most destructive raids of World War II. During the low-level nighttime incendiary raid, more than one hundred thousand people were killed in the initial bombing and the ensuing firestorms that consumed half the city. "[That raid] killed more people than the atomic bomb," Saunders said. During the raid, the planes flew individually—not in formation—and without lights at seven thousand feet. The Japanese fighters weren't equipped with radar, so if the crews could avoid the searchlights, they were usually not spotted. The only problem was, if the Japanese couldn't see them, neither could their own planes. "We lost quite a few B-29s because they ran into one another," he said. Saunders couldn't see much from his radar position, but has been told the fires were visible from two hundred miles away. "It must have been a sight to behold," he said.

Jack Pot's ninth mission—Saunder's tenth, because he flew as a replacement on the Tokyo raid—was a March 19 raid on Nagoya. Jack Pot was designated as the pathfinder. That meant its crew would locate the target by radar, reach it first, and drop the incendiary bombs. The other crews, following close behind, would then use the fires caused by the first explosions to target their own bombs. However, Saunders said as soon as they reached Nagoya Bay, they were caught in the searchlights sweeping the night sky. The lights, he said, lit up the inside of the plane. "You can't imagine how intense those [lights] are," he said.

The plane immediately started taking flak hits. "You could hear it hitting [the plane]."

By the time they reached the target, some of the planes had beaten them to it and had already dropped their bombs. The Jack Pot, shuddering from the flak hits, with two engines knocked out, dove away from the lights. Soon it was back over the ocean. Iwo Jima was somewhere in the distance. Although the island wasn't secured, the airfields were in American hands and could be used for an emergency landing. The crew got no response from their SOS, but continued transmitting their situation and location. As it turned out, Saunders said, "they were hearing us. We [just] couldn't receive."

There was another problem. The flak had jammed the rear bomb bay doors open. If the plane was to ditch into the ocean, the crew would have to close those doors somehow. The bombardier and another crewman ended up holding Ernie Fairweather, the CFC gunner, by the ankles while he leaned out over the open bomb bay and hooked the doors with the bomb winch cable, pulling the doors closed. "Our pilot said if that hadn't been done," Saunders said, "we wouldn't have survived the ditching."

After flying for three or four hours, the plane's third engine went out, and Shipp prepared to ditch. Saunders said when he saw the huge swells, he didn't like the look of things. "It was bad. It was terribly rough," he said. Shipp seemed to be the only one who wasn't worried. He turned the plane into the wind and dropped the bomber into a trough between waves. Later he said he'd made harder landings on solid ground.

For Saunders the landing was plenty hard. Thrown backward by the impact, he struck his head on the bulkhead, and everything went black. He woke up underwater. Luckily, when he raised his head, he was above the water, which was waist deep in the cabin. He remembers the shrieking of the wind and the pounding of the waves hitting the plane and the terrible grating sound of the metal fuselage tearing apart. The Jack Pot was breaking in two.

The two five-man rafts were quickly inflated, and all the crewmembers reached them safely. Saunders said the tail section sank first. Then the nose section tipped forward, dragged by the weight of the engines, and for a moment the plane stood upright. "It looked like a ship that was sinking. It hesitated a minute and then went down. It was an awful sight," he said. "What a helpless, hopeless feeling it is when the last of your plane disappears." The whole thing had taken only a few minutes. Of the 180 planes that took part in the raid on March 18 and 19, the Jack Pot was the only one lost.

It was about 6 o'clock on a dreary morning in the stormy North Pacific about 160 miles northwest of Iwo Jima. The rubber rafts rode like rollercoaster cars over the huge ocean swells. The men tried tying the rafts together, but the waves kept snapping the ropes. They spent the day bailing water; and by nightfall they were exhausted, soaking wet, and chilled to the bone.

The next day was sunny, which raised their spirits some. Then, at about 3 P.M., they spotted a navy PBY Catalina seaplane coming from the east. When they fired a flare, the PBY turned toward them. The water was still too rough for the PBY to land, but it made several passes over them and dropped sea marker dye and supplies. They couldn't reach the supplies, but finally the plane dropped a peanut can with a long white streamer, which they were able to retrieve. In it was a note that said a rescue ship was on the way and gave the score of a ballgame that had been played back in the States earlier that day. The PBY stayed with them until it began to get dark, and as it left, another PBY took its place. Throughout the night, the seaplane dropped floating flares to keep them in sight.

Saunders said he dozed off for a while, and when he woke up there was a huge ship bearing down on them. "We thought it was going to hit us," he said. Lieutenant Shipp grabbed the flare gun and shot off a flare. He intended to shoot it straight up, but the rough sea caused him to fire the flare at an angle through the ship's rigging. Immediately a voice boomed over the ship's PA system. "Cease fire! Cease fire!" The ship was the USS *Gatling*. The destroyer had been pulled away from shelling Iwo Jima and sailed 160 miles through enemy waters to rescue them.

Getting aboard the destroyer proved difficult in the rough seas, but eventually all the men were pulled from the rafts. Saunders remembers being grabbed by a sailor, who walked him through the darkness to an officer's quarters. "That was the best feeling," he said. When the men awoke the next morning, their uniforms had been laundered and pressed. That morning they were put ashore on Iwo Jima. "As we walked onto the beach, there was a newsreel camera taking our picture. Being all starched and pressed, I'm sure no one would have believed we had spent two days lost on a very rough ocean," he said.

After an extended rest in Hawaii, Saunders and his fellow crewmen returned to Tinian. There they got a new plane—they decided not to name it—and flew eighteen more missions before the war ended in August. By then Saunders was still only nineteen, a staff sergeant with twenty-eight combat missions to his credit.

He returned to the States in October and was discharged in November. Back home in Warrensburg, he worked at his brother's filling station for a while before heading to college on the GI Bill in early 1946. During his junior year in 1948, he went to work as a draftsman for Missouri Public Service. He ended up working there for thirty-seven years and retired in 1985.

Saunders said, compared to the other military branches, the army air corps didn't have it too bad. "We had good food, a good place to sleep," he said. "The being-shot-at-time wasn't too long. But I don't want to belittle it either," he said. "The likelihood of completing 35 missions was pretty bad." During World War II, the 505th lost a total of 25 planes and 170 airmen. Saunders is just glad he was young back then. "Kids can cope. They are scared, but they don't talk about it. They never lose hope."

Okinawa

War Diary

March 21, 1945. We left Ulithi today for the invasion of Okinawa. As we pulled out of the harbor, I saw the longest line of battleships I'll probably ever see. All the ships, battlewagons, cruisers, heavy and light, and destroyers all in a single line as far as I can see. I went to the highest place I could to watch the spectacle. This is my first day as turret electrician by myself.

Those words were written by Raymond Johnson, who served as an electrician aboard the heavy cruiser USS *San Francisco* (CA-38) during World War II. Johnson kept a brief diary of his experiences during the war. That was against navy rules, but many sailors did it anyway.

March 24. We arrived at the Ryukyu Islands of which Okinawa is the largest. We lay off the smaller islands. We are preparing to fire bombardment.

Johnson and his wife, Rhoda, were married in Kansas City, Kansas, in 1938. Shortly after that, the couple moved to California, where Raymond got a job at the "World's Largest Service Station" in Hollywood. The 10-acre facility featured 16 gasoline pumps, a huge repair garage, and an "endless chain" wash rack that could handle 350 cars a day. Raymond worked as a uniformed motorcycle deliveryman for the station.

In the 1940s, the Johnsons moved back to the Kansas City area. Raymond worked at one of the metro area's first drive-in theaters near Rosedale and at the Kansas City stockyards before landing a job at the Lake City Ammunition plant, which was running full bore for the war effort. There he rode a motorcycle around the sprawling plant, picking up and delivering messages. After a while, Rhoda went to work there as well.

Then, in 1944, at the age of twenty-seven, Raymond decided he wanted to get more personally involved in the war effort. He talked it over with Rhoda.

"I asked her if she minded if I enlisted," he said. Rhoda wasn't surprised by his decision. "I had been thinking about it too," she admitted. Raymond decided to join the navy. Years earlier, he said, his uncle had told him that the navy was the best branch of service to be in when there was a war. "You get better food and a clean place to sleep," his uncle told him.

Raymond soon found himself in Farragut, Idaho, for basic training. He was asked what kind of work he wanted to do in the navy. Raymond said he was best suited to be some sort of clerk. "That was the only thing I really knew how to do," he said. So the navy, in its wisdom, sent him to St. Paul, Minnesota, to train to be an electrician. In the navy's accelerated training program, he received the equivalent of a four-year electrical engineering degree in eight weeks.

After graduation, he headed to the West Coast to join the crew of the heavy cruiser USS *San Francisco,* just returned from combat duty in the Pacific and undergoing a major overhaul at the San Francisco shipyards. There would be no safe stateside duty for Raymond. Before the year was out, the *Frisco* would be heading back to the Pacific, where Raymond would soon learn the meaning of words like Iwo Jima, Okinawa, and kamikaze.

Completed in 1933 for $11.3 million and commissioned on February 10, 1934, the *San Francisco* was a 588-foot New Orleans-class cruiser with a maximum speed of 32.75 knots. In 1944, she carried a crew of 128 officers and 1,054 enlisted men. Her armament consisted of 3 triple 8-inch turrets (9 guns), 8 5-inch guns, and 24 40-millimeter and 26 20-millimeter antiaircraft guns. She also carried four Curtiss Seagull seaplanes, which were launched by catapult. The *Frisco* was in the war from the beginning. She was being overhauled in Pearl Harbor when the Japanese attacked in 1941, but she escaped damage. Serving in the Pacific during the early months of the war, she took part in the invasion of Guadalcanal in 1942 and remained as part of the island's covering force to prevent the Japanese from landing reinforcements. On October 10 and 11, she took part in the Battle of Cape Esperance–Second Savo just north of Guadalcanal in which U.S. warships repelled a large Japanese naval force. As the flagship of the newly formed Task Force 67.4, the *Frisco* sailed with troop transports headed to Guadalcanal that November. On November 12 and 13, the *Frisco* was in the Battle of Guadalcanal–Third Savo. During the battle, an enemy torpedo plane crashed into the *Frisco*'s conning station and at least 45 enemy shells hit the ship. Casualties totaled 83 killed and 104 wounded. After extensive repairs and overhaul in the States, she returned to duty in February 1943 and helped recapture Kiska in the Aleutians and Wake Island. In early to mid-1944, she supported U.S. landings on New Guinea,

Tinian, Saipan, and Guam. In August, the *Frisco* returned to the U.S. for her last major overhaul of the war. On October 31, she left San Francisco bound for Ulithi in the Caroline Islands. On board was a twenty-eight-year-old motorcycle deliveryman turned electrician. Raymond Johnson was about to get his first taste of war.

On December 14 and 15, 1944, the *San Francisco* took part in the invasion of Luzon in the Philippines. The cruiser's main duty was to launch her seaplanes, which were used for antisubmarine patrol and air rescue. On December 16, as the *Frisco*'s group was rendezvousing with another task force, the ships were caught in a typhoon. Johnson said the storm was worse than anything he had ever imagined. Waves were crashing ten feet above the *Frisco*'s decks, and any man going out on deck had to be tethered to something immovable. The waves were so powerful they could rip loose the steel gun mounts. "The storm would pretty much clear the deck even if it was welded down," he said. "You talk about war, but there isn't anything worse than wind like that."

All the ships in the task force were having a hard time. Several of the small destroyers were running low on fuel, which could be disastrous in a typhoon. Ships had to steer into the wind and wait out the storm, and if a ship ran out of fuel, she would be at the mercy of the wind and waves.

So, several of the larger ships, like the *Frisco,* tried to share their fuel with the smaller ones. In gale-force winds, the transfer of fuel was a particularly dangerous undertaking, and two of the *Frisco*'s crewmen lost their lives. Johnson recalled that the fuel line was a huge, steel-reinforced tube. "It took several men to hold it still." As the *Frisco* tried to refuel one of the destroyers, the tube got away from the sailors and crushed two crewmen. "They were mashed against the ship," Johnson said. Three destroyers capsized in the typhoon. After the storm, the *Frisco* searched in vain for survivors, but there were none. "It was just too rough," he said.

Johnson quickly learned that, unless there was a typhoon, he wanted to be on deck. The electricians' quarters were located in the bowels of the ship. Not only were they hot and stuffy, but it took a lot of time to get from them up to his battle station on turret number one when the general quarters alarm sounded. So, he began sleeping in the gun turret.

"I wanted to be where I was supposed to be when they wanted me there," he said. Also, he added, "I liked it better up there where there was air and I could see."

On February 21, 1945, the *Frisco* launched dozens of eight-inch shells into Iwo Jima in support of the marines who had landed two days before. Johnson said he happened to be looking through the turret's periscope at Mount Suribachi when the U.S. flag was raised. "I don't know if it was the first or the second," he said. "I never will forget that I saw them do that." Around that time, Johnson was seriously injured when he was nearly impaled on a trapdoor lever in the gun turret. The injury left him with three broken ribs, which bothered him for weeks afterward.

On March 21, the *Frisco* departed Ulithi to take part in Operation Iceberg—the invasion of Okinawa. It was during the Okinawa campaign that Johnson kept a brief diary.

March 26. So far have fired about 12 rounds of 8-inch. No 5-inch yet. I have spent 14 hours in the turret today besides the 8 to 12 on the board. We have been sailing around the small group of islands west of Okinawa about 7 miles. We covered landings made today and the minesweepers. We were just missed by a suicide plane this a.m. early. I didn't see it as I was asleep in the turret.

Kamikazes weren't the only enemy the sailors had to worry about off the coast of Okinawa. There also were suicide boats packed with high explosives and suicide swimmers who swam out to sea towing explosives on wooden rafts. Johnson said a contingent of marine sharpshooters aboard the *Frisco* would shoot the swimmers, and the rafts, as they tried to get near the ships. "I saw them blow up a lot of them," he said.

March 27 (Tuesday). Dawn alert at 0500, we are now closer to Okinawa. 5 Jap planes attacked our force. I saw 3 go down. The Nevada, a battlewagon, was hit by a zootsuiter [kamikaze]. I saw it hit, it really threw plenty of fire. A Jap 3-motored plane made a bomb run ahead of us and hit a couple of cans [destroyers]. We helped to bring it down. I was sure glad to see him hit the water and not us. I watched the other ships bombard the island. A can got hit from Jap shore guns, but not too bad as far as I know. There are Jap subs all around us so we breath very lightly and I stay topside as much as I can.

March 28. Dawn alert and soon after GQ for the whole day. In the early a.m. just after dawn our force brought down 3 Jap planes. We fired 84 rounds of 8-inch at Okinawa today. Boy when a plane is spotted such a barrage of antiaircraft fire goes up it's too hard for me to tell who actually brings him down.

March 29. Dawn alert started about 0430 and lasted until 0700. We pulled into an island harbor somewhere west of Okinawa. This harbor is called Suicide Gulch, and for good reason, if we were hit in here it would be goodbye Frisco.

We are taking on ammunition. These islands are really beautiful, lots of vegetation, but I can't see any other life. We shelled Okinawa this afternoon for a couple of hours. Day before yesterday one of our pilots [Gable] was out on a spotting mission and went down close to the beach to rescue a pilot from the carrier

Yorktown, but our plane was shot up, he couldn't take off again, he taxied out a ways and a minesweeper picked them up. Both pilots are OK.

March 30. We picked up some more ammunition today and our turret crew was plenty busy. I felt good so I helped to load and put it below. The island of Okinawa is 60 miles long. The landings of our troops on Okinawa is still a few days off. We have not had any casualties so far this trip. We fired a few rounds of 8-inch at the island but not from turret 1. No trouble yet today.

April 1 (Easter Sunday). Well Easter is here. I am up at 0330 but not to hunt eggs, but to relieve the watch on the generators . . . H-hour is 830 so only God knows what will happen next. We're to get in close enough to strafe the beach with 20 & 40mm. Things are going to get hot I'm thinking.

Well not much of an Easter Day, the invasion went as planned, we spent all day in the turret only out long enough to eat. I slept here all night. We are firing star shells tonight. No opposition on the island so we're told.

April 6. Boy what a day, we refueled and received mail and then about 1600 the Japs started an air attack. Our force just off the island was their objective. They hit 7 of our ships. But not us yet. Thank God. I saw a LST [landing ship tank] hit by a zootsuiter and it sank later, then a destroyer was hit twice. During the battle we were credited with 2½ planes. I was in the booth on the periscope saw it all, boy what a night this is. I hope to God I never see another one. I won't be the only one to pray for those men on the LST and cans this night.

I received a letter from Rhoda dated March 13. Boy but these letters sure help a fellow out.

"I wrote a letter every day," Rhoda recalled. "I did too," Johnson said. "I was homesick as hell."

April 7. Well a routine day until about 1830 a suicide plane got in and hit the Maryland [a battleship] but did little damage. The fire was soon out. I saw it all.

Johnson said the kamikazes usually tried to come in low, often straight out of the sun. When that happened, the big guns could be used as antiaircraft weapons. "The kamikazes flew right over the top of the water," he said. "We found out we could shoot into the water and it would bring up enough water to get into their propellers and bring them down."

April 11. Nothing new just same old stuff bombardment, we're tearing up a lot of ground for the farmers. They won't have to plow this year.

April 14. Well today we turned loose 80 rounds of 8-inch, pulled out and back at 11:30 p.m. for 4 more hours.

I saw a shark in the water beside our ship today. A darn mean-looking thing too. His fins spread about 7 feet.

News says a can was hit by a robot bomb and two others were checked at 800 mph and another at 440 mph. Wow what next. I can't run or swim that fast so here's to luck.

By the time the *San Francisco* was relieved and headed back to Ulithi, she had been credited with shooting down four kamikazes and destroying one suicide boat. The cruiser returned to Okinawa in May and remained there until the island was secured. She was anchored in San Pedro Bay, Leyte, on August 11 when the crew received word that the Japanese had surrendered.

The cruiser returned to San Francisco on December 17. Johnson was sent to a naval hospital in Chicago, where he was treated for pneumonia. He was mustered out of service in January 1946. He returned home, and he and Rhoda purchased 285 acres outside Kingsville, Missouri, with money Rhoda had saved from working at the ammunition plant. "We kept that farm forty-seven years," Johnson said.

Not surprisingly, he still thinks about the war and what might have been. "I was just awful lucky," he said, "because a lot of them didn't come home."

Picket Duty

Off the northern coast of Okinawa, the Ryukyus, May 11, 1945—On this bloody morning, 2 American destroyers and a swarm of marine Corsairs took on 150 Japanese fighter planes. An hour and 45 minutes later, the gun crews on the destroyers had shot down 38 enemy planes. The Corsair fighter-bombers had destroyed another 50. The remaining Japanese planes scattered. The USS *Evans,* which sustained 4 kamikaze hits, was credited with 15 confirmed kills and 4 assists. The USS *Hadley,* hit by 3 suicide planes and a bomb, received credit for destroying 23 enemy planes, a new record for destroyers. Later the ship's crew received citations signed by President Harry Truman.

Back in 1945, Tudie Brisciano (sixty-five in 1985), a bo'sun's mate on the *Hadley,* manned one of the ship's five-inch guns. "I went in August the sixth of '42," he said. "Truthfully, I wanted to find out what the hell our country needed and what I could do for 'em. We had training up at Great Lakes, Illinois. That was a little over two weeks. That was all we had. Then up to New York and picked up a ship and it took us down to the Panama Canal. . . . It was one of them old ships. It shoulda been sunk a long time ago. It came from World War I. They captured it from the Germans.

"They [the Navy] wanted to put me as a storekeeper, because I have—I don't want to brag—but I have beautiful handwriting. . . . We kept the records of everything that came in and out, to the last article that came in for the naval depot mostly."

The weeks turned into months. Eventually Brisciano complained to his commanding officer that he didn't enlist to spend the war counting bars of soap in Central America. "The next thing I knew, they said you're going back to the States. . . . They took me back to Miami and in Miami we had gunnery training. Then they put me in sound school and that stuff just about drove me nuts."

In sound school, he said, he learned how to operate navy sonar. Sonar sends out sound waves, which make different sounds when they hit different objects. "If you don't hit anything, it just goes piiiiing," he said, mimicking the sound, "and it dies out. When you hit something, it says ping ponk and you know you've hit something. . . . Then you had to study whether it was a sunken ship there or a school of fish. Or there is a submarine. Sometimes, even a big school of fish could fool you. Fool you bad.

"They started trainin' us to tell the difference in sound. You was supposed to be able to learn the sound of one of our submarines. Whether it was a German, a U.S., Jap, English, whatever it was. . . . That just about drove me nuts."

Brisciano was assigned to the USS *Raby*, a destroyer. "When I got aboard ship, they found out that I did study store keeping, so they put me into that. Well, that was a good, easy job. It really was. All except the chief I had to work under." Eventually, he asked to be moved to deck duty, which suited him fine. "I was on gun one. The five-inch guns. Twin fives."

The *Raby* left Miami and headed for the North Atlantic. "Where I couldn't tell ya," he said. "All I can tell ya, it was cold and really cold. In fact, we had so much ice on the ship when we was coming back later into Boston, we had to break ice off the mooring lines to tie the ship up. Normally [the lines] was about four-inch diameter. When we got into Boston, it was about ten or eleven inch in diameter with all that ice on it.

"The waves had hit the ship so bad that it took the shields on the twenty millimeter and just bent them tight against the guns. They wouldn't fire."

The *Raby* was ordered to proceed to the South Pacific. There, the destroyer was immediately assigned to antisubmarine duty. According to Brisciano, it was pretty easy work. "We'd find a submarine, sink 'em, change course and go over to here and sink 'em," he said.

Brisciano, now a coxswain, was reassigned to the newly commissioned USS *Hugh W. Hadley* in November 1944. The *Hadley* was a 2,200-ton destroyer whose armament included 6 5-inch guns—4 in the front, 2 in the back—4

40-millimeter guns, 6 20-millimeter guns, 10 torpedoes, and numerous depth charges.

"A destroyer is designed to fight any battle," he said. "Antiaircraft guns, we had them. Your star shells, that's for invasions. We done bombarding. Then the armor piercing. That's supposed to have a soft nose on it so when that hits a ship, it won't glance off. It will hold it till the other part goes right through."

In late March 1945, the crew found themselves off the coast of an island only 340 miles from the Japanese home island of Kyushu. The island was Okinawa. "We didn't know ourselves if we was going to hit Okinawa," he said. "Sometimes they would shell some islands that they're never gonna touch. We didn't really think anything was gonna happen, but when we stayed up there about two, two and a half days and kept bombarding, we knew something then. Then the whole invasion force came up. Good God, it looks like you could look sixteen miles in any direction and see ships."

Operation Iceberg began on the morning of April 1, 1945, as the first wave of the 182,000-man American invasion force landed on the beaches of Okinawa. The torturous 3-month campaign eventually claimed 12,500 American and 109,000 Japanese lives. An estimated 100,000 Okinawan civilians also died in the battle. Almost half of the American casualties—nearly 5,000—were seamen, many of whom were killed in mass kamikaze attacks. The U.S. planned to use the island as a jumping-off point for its invasion of the Japanese homeland.

In addition to the kamikaze fighter planes, the Japanese used manned jet-propelled rocket-bombs, which were carried by bombers. After a bomb was released, the suicide pilot would steer it to its target. The Japanese called the rocket-bombs *okas*—cherry blossoms. The Americans called them "baka bombs." In Japanese, *baka* means idiot.

"Their suicide stuff that they had, it was really bad," Brisciano said. "They would take a fast boat [filled with explosives] and try to catch the best ship they'd like it to hit. The bigger the better. And hit 'em and destroy them and themselves. They was good at that.

"We were told, if you go out in a boat and it gets dark, don't come back to the ship. We sink anything that moves. . . . The suicide swimmers would climb up the anchor chain and kill the men on guard and they'd get down in the ammunition room, pull a hand grenade and that's it."

After bombarding Okinawa for several days, the *Hadley* was deployed into a "picket line" surrounding the island to protect the vitally important supply ships.

Like Iwo Jima, Okinawa had thousands of natural and manmade caves, which made ideal fortresses for the embattled Japanese. "I'd like to have seen some of those caves that those Japs dug," Brisciano said. "They said the way they was dug, good God, you could fire a shell and have a direct hit on it, but then maybe it [the cave] goes four feet this way, then down, then that way and this way. I think the only way to really get 'em out was when they come with those [flamethrowers]."

The *Hadley* was teamed with the destroyer *Evans* and together the two ships patrolled a section of the East China Sea. On May 8, V-E Day, the war in Europe ended. "We really thought when the war ended in Europe, we thought probably in about two days we'd hear that Japan surrendered too. It didn't work out," he said with a laugh. The first indication that a large Japanese attack force was heading to Okinawa came on May 10. "The night before [the May 11 attack], Washing Machine Charlie spotted us, and he was out of gun range and we couldn't bring him down. We knew it was coming, but we didn't know when."

Waves of kamikazes attacked early the next morning. Brisciano was on the bow in the turret of a five-inch gun. "There would be forty-three shells a minute come out of those turrets. When those planes attacked us there north of Okinawa, we ran out of ammunition, so we was firing some star shells. And boy they came down over the speaker and said, 'What the hell is wrong with you guys, firing star shells.' And we said we used all the antiaircraft, we burned up the armor piercing and all we have left is star shells and that one that shoots phosphorus over the troops, you know. It comes down and falls on 'em and burns the hell out of 'em."

Generally, he said, the star shells were only used at night. "If it was at night and the troops were making a push, they needed light ahead of them to see where the enemy was. We'd be offshore and we would fire star shells to light up that area for 'em. Shoot 'em way over their heads so the lights would be on the enemy and they'd have a beautiful view shootin' him."

Brisciano said he didn't know how many planes he helped shoot down on May 11. "Truthfully, you can't tell because there are so many guns firin,' usually in the same direction. . . . They always tried to send up a bunch of 'em at the stern because they had less guns firing at 'em. Then, before you knew it, here they came in just the opposite on you. [We] just fired and that was it, you know what I mean? They went down.

"You really can tell on the quads who got [a plane] because every fourth shell was a tracer. You could tell when you were shootin' under 'em or over 'em or leadin' too much. So they did know which [gun] got 'em. . . . But in the turret there's two guns going off at the same time and when you see one come down, good."

In addition to the gunners on the *Hadley* and the *Evans,* a squadron of marine Corsairs cut a swath through the enemy fighters. "After it was over, they figured the total amount was eighty-eight planes hit the water," Brisciano said. However, both destroyers sustained major damage. The *Evans,* hit by four kamikazes, was out of action by 9 A.M. Her casualties were thirty dead and twenty-nine wounded.

At 9:05, a baka bomb hit the *Hadley* squarely amidships. Several bomb and kamikaze strikes later, the order was given to abandon ship. Twenty-eight sailors on the *Hadley* died during the attack. Brisciano was one of sixty-seven who were wounded. "When I came out of the gun turret," he said, "I don't know what hit me but down I went and then the next thing I knew I was on a hospital ship." His injuries included two three-inch gashes, one in his stomach and one on his back, probably caused by shrapnel from the ship's exploding ammunition magazine. He has no memory of being evacuated from the *Hadley.*

Miraculously, the destroyer didn't sink. She was towed to Ie Shima, just west of Okinawa, and patched up well enough that she could sail back to the States. "They said that the ship cost thirteen million dollars to build it and after we got hit, they estimated the damage at eleven and a half million. That's why they was bringin' it back to the States. To find out why it didn't sink."

Brisciano was able to rejoin the *Hadley* for her trip home. "I could see where it was patched," he said. "It was no longer in any fighting condition, except for the smaller guns, the quads and the twin twenties. When we got into San Francisco, oh God, they had those harbor ships and they was shootin' water in the air, you know, congratulating us."

After his discharge, he returned to Kansas City. He retired in the early 1970s due to debilitating arthritis in his hands. He still considers himself patriotic. "I just can't see the people letting this country go to pot," he said. "It is really a shame, in my honest opinion, and I think any veteran will tell ya the same thing. The people buyin' all this Jap stuff, they're just hurtin' the Americans so bad it's unbelievable. I don't own a damn thing that comes from Japan," he said laughing.

"I was in three years, two months and four days. You don't think much of it then, but later, as you're getting older, every month, day behind you that was lost . . . it wasn't lost for a good cause. I really look at it [the war] worse now than I did then. 'Cause then we done it for a good cause. Now, I begin to wonder really what the cause was. I just hope America wakes up. I really do."

Handguns and Hand Grenades

After Peleliu, the 1st Marine Division returned to the Solomons to rest and refit. Soon, however, the men began amphibious training in the now-tranquil waters off Guadalcanal, Guam, and Tinian. On April 1, 1945, more than 1,200 ships carrying 180,000 Marines and soldiers converged on a 60-mile-long banana-shaped island named Okinawa in the Ryukyus.

The Japanese Thirty-second Army, commanded by Lt. Gen. Mitsuru Ushijima, had only seventy thousand troops, which wasn't enough to defend the island's beaches or even the important airfields at Kadena and Yontan. Instead, Ushijima established a system of concentric defensive positions around the ancient castle town of Shuri, in the south-central sector of the island.

Like other islands in the Pacific campaign, Okinawa was shielded from attack by natural and manmade caves. On this island they riddled the mountains around Shuri. The caves were interconnected, and hidden inside were machine gun nests, antitank guns, and seventy-millimeter howitzers. The Japanese defenders also were armed with grenade launchers and mortars. From those all but impregnable positions, the Japanese hoped to maintain control of the southern half of the island with its airfields, the port town of Naha, and Nakagusuku Bay, which the Americans planned to use as a fleet anchorage.

When the invasion force landed along a seven-mile front on the Hagushi beaches, it met only light opposition. Jack Young, a marine specialist with the Thirty-ninth Demolition Platoon, was to have been in one of the first waves on the beach, but a gunner was needed for the fifty-caliber machine gun in one of the landing craft, and he volunteered. That first day, Young made six trips from the troop ship to the beach and back and never fired a shot. By evening, fifty thousand troops were ashore.

Young spent the next seven days ferrying supplies to the beach. On the eighth day, he was sent to the front lines to blow up some limestone caves harboring Japanese snipers. Two days later he was back on the beach for more demolition supplies. While waiting to be resupplied, he went into one of the makeshift huts built of sandbags and slats salvaged from supply crates, which the marines used to get out of the North Pacific sun. It was dark and cool inside, and Young took a nap. When he woke up, he started to crawl out of the hut then stopped when he realized he'd forgotten his cigarettes. As he turned back for the pack, the hut suddenly filled with light; then everything went black.

Young found out later that a mortar round had landed in the doorway of the hut, where he had been on his knees only seconds before. The sandbags had saved his life, but the concussion fractured his shoulder, and he was flown to a hospital in Guam.

Meanwhile, the invasion force was making steady progress. In three weeks the U.S. had captured four-fifths of the island. The first major resistance had been encountered on Kakazu Ridge, which was the outermost and strongest ring of defenses around Shuri Castle. It took the U.S. Ninety-sixth Division two weeks to batter through the perimeter. As the Americans moved toward the inner defensive lines, the First Marines were brought in to relieve the battle-weary Twenty-seventh. At about that time, the Japanese launched a counterattack. It began with small amphibious units, which tried to get behind U.S. lines. The amphibious attack failed, but it was quickly followed by a massive artillery barrage, air attacks, and a frontal assault by three experienced Japanese regiments. The attack was repulsed. The Japanese lost upward of six thousand men; the Americans, about seven hundred.

While the soldiers and marines fought their way through the gorges and ridges toward Shuri, the navy ships offshore were being harried by masses of kamikazes. Young watched as the suicide pilots dove out of the sun or skimmed above the waves, trying to breach the navy picket line. Most of them were shot down, but those that got through did considerable damage. During one attack in early May, six ships on picket duty were sunk, including two destroyers. The kamikaze planes were light, maneuverable, and fast, and each carried a full payload of bombs. "You hit them in the nose," Young said, "and they were gone."

He was kept busy trying to flush out enemy snipers and knock out gun emplacements in the fortified ridges and caves. Many of the caves had several entrances and exits and were no wider than a man's shoulders. "They were a bear," Young said. "They took some time." When possible, interpreters tried to convince the Japanese to surrender. "We tried to talk them out," he said, "and they wouldn't come." So the Americans did the only thing they could: "We sealed the caves," Young said. "They were more like burial tombs."

Young remembers Hand Grenade Hill. "It was too close to fight with rifles, so we were using hand grenades. We were just damn near overrun by them," he said. "It was handguns and hand grenades. We lost a lot of men there." The M-1 rifle had armor-piercing bullets, he said, so if you shot one of the enemy, "you may kill one of your own men down the line." The grenades, which disintegrated into shards of flying shrapnel, were more effective when the enemy was bunched up. "You needed to get three or four of them running together," he said. Young doesn't know how long the battle lasted. It was over, he said, when the last Japanese soldier was dead. "To me it lasted about five hours," he said. "They just kept coming. It was like sitting on a beach and the waves just kept coming."

Snipers were a continual threat. One who was hidden in a cave and shooting through a twelve-inch opening in the rock was a particular problem. It took them a long time to find him because the gun barrel never stuck outside the cave. "He was making four hundred-yard shots and didn't miss," Young said. The sniper had shot six men by the time Young arrived. "Not all of them were killed," he said. "The object of war is to wound because you need five or six guys to take care of him." The marines finally killed the sniper; he was a slight man with glasses, and they found him lying next to a thirty-caliber rifle with a scope.

Young never reached Shuri Castle. His five-man squad was inside one of the inner defensive perimeters trying to rescue some troops pinned down by a machine gunner. Young was running alongside a rice paddy. "The next thing I know, I was laying in the rice paddy. Consequently, I never got to Shuri Castle." He had been shot in the left leg. Luckily, he said, it was only a flesh wound. "Any shot is painful. You know you've been hit," he said. "It's the worst damn bee sting you've ever had."

On June 22, General Ushijima and his staff committed suicide as American troops approached their cave complex. Although most of the organized resistance on Okinawa had ended, the mopping up continued through the summer. After Young returned to duty, his squad was assigned the task of searching the Okinawan villages for hiding Japanese soldiers and then, just to be sure, burning the villages to the ground. One of the grass huts he searched had two levels and several rooms. As Young walked through a doorway, he heard movement behind him and racketing gunfire. He turned in time to see a marine from his squad finish off a Japanese soldier who had been about to behead Young with a samurai sword. "If my buddy hadn't shot, I wouldn't be here," he said. The sword turned out to be 120 years old. "That was the only souvenir I brought home."

Slowly the campaign wound down, but the worst was yet to come. Many of the remaining Japanese refused to surrender and committed suicide. But it wasn't just the soldiers. Many Okinawan civilians, brainwashed by the Japanese about American atrocities, also committed suicide by jumping off the cliffs into the ocean hundreds of feet below.

Young said the interpreters pleaded with them, usually to no avail. "It was like you were talking to a wall. You feel so helpless. . . . It was the civilians, the women and children . . ." he said, his voice trailing off.

Young was still on Okinawa when the atomic bombs were dropped on Hiroshima and Nagasaki, ending the war and plans for the long-dreaded invasion of Japan. "We didn't have to go to Tokyo, thank God," he said. "I couldn't imagine what that would be like in my wildest dreams."

After the war, Young joined the reserves and served at the air naval station in Olathe, Kansas. When the Korean War began, he joined the marines' covert reconnaissance unit as a parachute, demolitions, and long-range sniping specialist. He declined to discuss his covert work except to say he came out of Korea somewhat disillusioned. "We really weren't too happy with Korea. We couldn't win the war. It was like fighting a boxer with one hand tied behind you."

Young was injured in Korea during a parachute jump—"Thank God for snow banks"—and left the marines in 1957 to begin a twenty-five-year career in law enforcement. His philosophy on war is simple. "I hope we never have another one," he said. "Technically, that's why I enlisted. I had a son at the time. So he wouldn't have to fight."

Scars

Operation Iceberg—the invasion of Okinawa—was the last of three major offensives in the Pacific and was designed to stretch Japanese resources to their limits. Luzon, in the Philippines, had been invaded in January 1945. Iwo Jima had been invaded in February. On April 1, it was Okinawa's turn.

The U.S. 10th Army, under Gen. Simon Bolivar Buckner, was formed especially for the invasion. The force consisted of seven component units: the 7th, 27th, 77th, and 96th Infantry and the 1st, 2nd, and 6th Marines. A six-day naval and air bombardment preceded the invasion, and by evening, 50,000 U.S. troops were ashore. The 2nd Marines didn't see action the first day because they were deployed in a diversionary attack on the other side of the island. Eight waves of landing boats moved toward the beach simultaneously as the real invasion took place at Hagushi. At the last minute, the diversionary force turned back to the fleet. The marines repeated the performance on the morning of April 2 before eventually landing on the established beachhead.

Cpl. Robert Barackman, a marine with the Second Division, remembers the day—June 18, 1945—General Buckner was killed. Barackman was the battalion radio operator in the advancing front line, and Japanese mortars had everyone hugging the ground. He was crouched in a shell crater when General Buckner and his entourage arrived at the front. Barackman stared in amazement as the general, dressed immaculately in his starched khakis, mounted a knoll and began scanning the terrain with binoculars. "I just couldn't believe anyone would stand on that knoll," he said. "[He] looked like Moses standing up there."

Barackman also remembers thinking to himself that there must be a reason for the general's apparent lack of concern for his own safety. "I guess generals don't get shot at," he decided. But he was wrong. Moments later, an incoming mortar round exploded nearby and Buckner, son of a Civil War Confederate general, was felled by a piece of shrapnel. He died minutes later.

Barackman turns serious and reflective when asked about the men he killed during the war. It's not something he's proud of, nor is he ashamed. "I was fighting for my life," he said. "You don't think twice . . . it's either me or them and I wanted to live." He doesn't know how many men he killed. "I shot at a lot of them. It wasn't a matter of keeping count," he said, "[but] you knew you got somebody 'cause you couldn't miss. . . . I was just scared." He knows, however, that he killed at least four men—two on Tarawa, one on Saipan, and one on Okinawa. He especially remembers the one on Okinawa.

It was just after General Buckner was killed, a day or two before organized resistance on the island ended. The main Japanese force had been driven from their mountain strongholds and were cornered in a large open field. With the ocean cutting off any further retreat, they were making their final stand.

Barackman's company was advancing through a low cane field. The marines were fanned out, about fifteen yards from one another, when thirty or forty Japanese, who had been hiding in a nearby ditch, suddenly charged them. A Japanese soldier carrying an obsolete bolt-action rifle was running directly toward Barackman. Unlike the automatic and semiautomatic weaponry used by the Americans, most of the Japanese rifles could not be fired repeatedly in quick succession because a new bullet had to be manually chambered after each shot. Barackman had a semiautomatic carbine fed by a fifteen-bullet clip. He could fire all fifteen bullets as fast as he could pull the trigger. Barackman immediately dropped to the ground. The Japanese soldier fired. Barackman fired his carbine and continued firing until his clip was empty. The Japanese soldier went down. "He got one off and I got fifteen off," he said. "The funny thing was, he kept coming. I hit him about four times before he went down."

Looking back over nearly four decades, Barackman is convinced the atomic bombs dropped on Hiroshima and Nagasaki saved his life. At the time, the

Second Marines were preparing for the invasion of Japan. Operation Olympic was scheduled for November 1, 1945, and called for the Second, Third, and Fifth Marines to invade the southwestern shore of the island of Kyushu. Having survived three amphibious invasions, Barackman had the feeling his luck was about to run out. "There was no doubt in my mind that I'd never last through four," he said.

The Japanese had already demonstrated their willingness to fight to the death, even in the face of hopeless odds. Barackman still had fresh memories of Japanese soldiers, their ammunition expended, tying their bayonets to bamboo poles and rushing headlong toward fortified U.S. positions in human waves. "And you had to kill 'em to stop 'em," he said. "I thank Harry Truman every day of my life," he said. "He saved millions of lives."

After the war, Barackman left the service and moved to Kansas City. He ran a restaurant for a while and eventually got into the wholesale meat business; arthritic knees forced him to retire in 1981. Now he walks with the aid of crutches. Forty years after World War II, he still struggles with his feelings toward the Japanese. For Barackman, the old hatreds die hard. "Oh, I'm old now. I've mellowed," he said. "I don't have the resentment I had then. The hatred. I probably still have a few . . . oh, I don't know," he said. "I don't have any Japanese friends, if that's what you mean. Nor do I want any." Over the years, the wounds have healed, but the scars remain.

War in Europe, Part 3

Volunteer

GERMANY, APRIL 10, 1945—The B-17 had just dropped its payload of thousand-pound bombs on an underground war factory in Oranienburg and was banking left to head back to its base in England when a bogie hurtled out of the clouds at five o'clock. Bob Sommer saw it—a strange-looking aircraft with swept-back wings—but from his position in the bomber's waist, he couldn't get his fifty-caliber machine gun around far enough to shoot at it. The wingman saw it too and snapped a picture of the plane seconds before it opened up with its thirty-millimeter cannons.

Things happen very fast in combat. One moment Sommer was standing at his waist gun. The next, he was lying on the floor of the plane. "The lights went out. I came to with my head on the ball turret," he recalled. The ball-shaped Plexiglas gun turret, which protruded from the belly of the bomber, was turning, "and my head was bouncing off the rivets." A lot of things went through the nineteen-year-old's mind—like wishing he were back at his air base, which he would have been if he hadn't volunteered for this mission. On an earlier run, he had caught a piece of flak in the face, and he had been forced to skip a mission with his normal crew. Bomber crews in Europe had to fly thirty-five missions before they were rotated home, and Sommer had only thirty-two missions to his regular crew's thirty-three. "I volunteered because I wanted to finish up with my crew," he said. At the time it had seemed like a good idea. But as the crippled Flying Fortress tilted toward the German countryside, he began to have serious doubts.

Sommer had been drafted into the army air corps in early 1944. "I was going to be a great pilot," he said. But his plans got sidetracked one day when his whole training squadron was called into the gymnasium for an announcement. "You are all washed out at the convenience of the government," they were told. Some of the aspiring pilots were reassigned to the infantry. Others, like Sommer, were sent to gunnery school. "Gosh, I don't know how it happened. They just made me a tail gunner. They didn't ask," he said. He thought that it probably had something to do with his size. "I was pretty small then. I weighed about 130 or 140 pounds dripping wet." In the cramped quarters of a B-17, particularly the claustrophobic tail section, which you could only enter on your knees, small stature was a requirement. (Sommer had a chance to get inside a B-17 at an air show long after the war, and when he looked through the crawl space into the tiny tail compartment, "I wondered how the hell I'd done it back in those days," he said. "It looked a lot smaller than I remembered.")

After gunnery school, Sommer was assigned to the 379th Bomber Group, 8th Air Force at Drew Field in Tampa, Florida, where the B-17 crews were assembled for additional training. There, in the Florida swamps, they practiced low-altitude strafing and bombing using ten-pound flour sacks filled with sand.

In December 1944, Sommer's crew took the train to Savannah, Georgia. "We picked up a brand new B-17 and flew it to England," he said. Upon arrival, they were immediately put into combat rotation as a replacement crew. "Somebody finished up or got shot down, one or the other," he said. Sommer still remembers the speech the base commander gave them shortly after their arrival. He said it was strikingly similar to the one new crews received in the movie *Twelve O'Clock High*. You don't have to be a mathematician to figure out your odds of getting through the war alive, the commander told them. The army air corps' attrition rate per mission was 3 percent. So, if you had to fly 35 missions to get home. . . . "Not all of you are going to get home," the commander said. "Forget about going home. Just forget about it. Just consider yourself already dead. With that attitude, it'll be a lot easier."

Sommer's first aerial combat was during the Battle of the Bulge. Before the planes could bomb, the weather had to clear. Finally, as the 101st Airborne stubbornly defended the crossroads town of Bastogne, the snow and fog lifted. "One day it cleared up and we bombed the front lines. That day and the next two. We clobbered 'em." Unlike most subsequent missions, which usually were high-altitude bombing raids with five hundred- or thousand-pound incendiaries, the missions into the Ardennes were low-altitude runs with "twenty-five-pound frag bombs, 'cause we were bombing people. . . . It doesn't really make a difference what you're bombing. It's a target."

Combat is a hard thing to explain to anyone who hasn't been in it. Sommer said the fear you felt before a mission was mostly forgotten during the heat of battle. Mostly. "Every day was different, but yeah, everybody was scared," Sommer said. "In my estimation, if anybody said they weren't, they were a damn liar." Sommer had numerous close calls on his thirty-three missions. Often the plane took direct hits, lost engines—the B-17s had four—and were smoking, riddled hulks when they limped back to England. "Sometimes we got back and there were holes in that airplane you wouldn't believe," he said.

During one mission over Munich, Sommer spotted three fighter planes coming toward his B-17 from below. "I told the pilot, 'There's three bogies coming in at 6 o'clock. And they're coming in fast.' " The pilot asked him what he was going to do about it. Sommer fired a burst from his fifty-calibers and the three U.S. P-51 Mustangs quickly peeled off. "They should have known better than that," he said.

Fliers, like sailors, are a superstitious lot. It's partly because they're at the mercy of elements they can't control. Sommer was no exception. During the war he had a St. Christopher's medal that a girlfriend had given him. He wore it on every mission. Once he accidentally left it in the barracks. He discovered it was missing when he reached the mess hall, and he borrowed a bike and rode all the way back to the barracks because "I wasn't going to go without it," he said.

Sommer said his ill-fated thirty-third mission seemed doomed from the start. The signs were all there, beginning that morning. By the time he'd dressed and was ready to leave, the members of his regular crew had gotten up to shake hands with him as if they might not be seeing him again. "I didn't feel good about it," he said. He was replacing another B-17's gunner, who was sick. The crew had completed fifteen missions, and he noticed that it was a looser, more boisterous group than his own no-nonsense crew. "They sounded like a cheerleading squad," Sommer said.

There were other bad omens. When he arrived at the bomber, the tail gunner offered to let Sommer take his place for the mission, but he changed his mind at the last minute, so Sommer manned one of the waist guns. Then, after takeoff, the panic-stricken ball turret gunner discovered that he'd forgotten his parachute harness. Usually the bombers carried a spare, but there wasn't one on the plane. The men had to tie his chute to him with parachute line. After that, things went normally until the bogie showed up at five o'clock. (Decades later, at a reunion of the 379th in New Orleans, the B-17's wingman gave Sommer a photograph of the aircraft that shot them down—a Messerschmitt 262.

The Luftwaffe's secret weapon, it was the first jet fighter widely used in combat and could fly rings around any other aircraft in the world. Unfortunately for the Germans, it was produced too late and in too few numbers to have a significant impact on the war.)

When Sommer woke up, the bomber's lights and radio were out, and there were holes in the floor and fuselage big enough for a man to fall through. "We were going down like a bucket of bolts," he said. He was in a lot of pain. His right arm was shattered, and shrapnel had torn a four-inch hole in his back, exposing his spine. Another member of the crew gave him two shots of morphine, put his parachute on him upside down so he could pull his ripcord with his left hand and shoved him out into the cold, rushing sky.

Although dazed by the pain, blood loss, and morphine, Sommer knew enough not to pull the ripcord too soon. He was still thousands of feet up, he didn't have an oxygen mask, and he didn't want to die a slow, agonizing death from asphyxiation. So, he free-fell for a while, plunging through a cloud layer that "looked like concrete." Then the countryside seemed to rush toward him—a pastoral setting of scattered timber, rolling hills and pine trees—and he pulled the cord and gently floated to earth. It was midmorning on a beautiful spring day. Sommer hit the ground, rolled, and found he couldn't get up. The tail gunner landed nearby, and he untangled Sommer from his parachute and laid him on it. The two men weren't alone for long. "There was some rifle fire and there's the Germans," Sommer said. "We landed right in the middle of the German army."

The Americans surrendered. Using the parachute as a stretcher, the Germans carried Sommer to a truck and later transferred him to a Red Cross ambulance that took him to a hospital in a nearby town. The rest of the crew, all of whom had escaped serious injury, were taken to a local jail. (As it turned out, they'd made a small error when they tied the parachute on the ball turret gunner. When the chute opened, it flipped him upside down and he descended headfirst. "He was upside down, swinging like a pendulum," Sommer said. "It's a good thing that sucker landed in a tree.")

Sommer was in the German hospital twenty days. It wasn't much of a hospital—there were no painkillers or antibiotics. "If the British hadn't come when they did," he said, "I'd have been a piece of dead meat." The hospital was liberated without a shot being fired. Sommer remembers looking out a window and seeing groups of German soldiers throw down their guns and run off. Later, he was evacuated to an army field hospital in England, and eventually, he was flown back to a hospital in the States. He was released from the army hospital nine months and five surgeries later and still has an ugly crater-shaped scar on his back.

The irony of being shot down and wounded less than a month before the war in Europe ended isn't lost on Sommer. "I'm the only one that got hit," he said. "Does that tell you something? Don't volunteer."

Holocaust

Joe Crouch gets angry when people say the Holocaust never happened. He was there. He saw it with his own eyes. And sometimes he wishes to God he could forget it. "I don't regret the experience I had," he said. "Without the terrible incidents of war, I would have enjoyed it. But the sights burned into my memory cells I'll never wash away." Many of those sights came from Gunskirchen Lager, a Nazi concentration camp about eleven miles north of Lambach, Austria. The camp was liberated in early May 1945.

The camp, which was run by German SS troops, was located in dense pinewoods at the bottom of a valley. The still valley air hung over Gunskirchen Lager like a death fog. Eyewitnesses described the stench as a sickening stew of human excretion, body odor, smoldering trash fires, and German tobacco. Crouch (sixty-four in 1988) was a medic with the Seventy-first Division, Fourteenth Infantry medical detachment of Patton's Third Army. He was one of the first Americans inside the camp and said the horror of the scene was almost indescribable. "Human feces everywhere and dead people everywhere," he said. "It was one of the worst days of [my] life."

An estimated eighteen thousand prisoners, most of them Hungarian Jews of the intellectual class—doctors, lawyers, skilled craftsmen—had originally been housed at the camp. The SS and most of the German guards were gone by the time the Americans arrived, and thousands of prisoners had already fled. Of the thousands more left behind, many were too weak to even walk. All were suffering from advanced malnutrition. A typical meal for each prisoner had been a bowl of thin soup; every other day a loaf of black bread was shared among five people. When liberated, most of the prisoners had gone five days without food or water. "I gave one of them a cigarette," Crouch said. "He didn't smoke it, he ate it."

The camp was surrounded by an electrified, barbed wire fence; there were guard towers every fifty feet. Railroad tracks ran through the front gates. It was just inside the gates that prisoners were unloaded, and some were herded into large "showers" that were really gas chambers. Afterward, the bodies were thrown onto a roller conveyer and pushed through an opening in the wall into an adjacent room. There, a prisoner put the head of each corpse on a meat block and extracted any gold fillings. When Crouch walked into the room, there was a bowl next to the meat block half full of gold.

The last stop was the furnace. An English-speaking Jewish prisoner told Crouch the bodies were cremated individually and the ashes compressed into small cakes resembling bars of soap. With typical Nazi efficiency, each inmate's number was stamped on a cake, and all the cakes were buried in a mass grave. Crouch said he can still visualize the pit, which was as wide as a house and about twelve feet deep. It was nearly filled with thousands of the ash cakes. "That's all you could see," he said. "Looked like shaving soap with a number across them."

On the hillside overlooking the camp were cabins where the SS and the guards lived. Crouch said the camp commandant, a woman, also lived there. According to the prisoners, she would spare certain male prisoners, who would accompany her to her cabin and then never reappear. When the Allied troops arrived, the prisoners took them to her cabin; there they found dozens of human skulls and lampshades made of human skin.

The people of Lambach and other nearby towns denied any knowledge of the death camp. Crouch found it hard to believe they were ignorant considering the camp's proximity and the ever-present pall from the crematorium. "They couldn't help but know [about] it," he said.

The prisoners spared from the gas chamber were jammed into low, one-story hovels with dirt floors. Each building, built to house three hundred, was home to more than three thousand. People often had to sleep three deep, one atop another, and when someone died, sometimes the body would remain where it lay until it putrefied. When U.S. troops entered the camp, the prisoners shuffled around the soldiers, some cheering weakly, some weeping, others merely shrieking with emotion. Some of them crawled to the Americans and died on the spot. "When they laid their hands on you," Crouch said, "that was the end of their life." In contrast, the German guards who were rounded up were well fed, their uniforms neatly pressed. "Some of those guards didn't make it out of there. They didn't leave fast enough. Some of them slowly got their throats cut." And worse. "I've tried to forget some of this stuff," he said quietly. "I'd just rather not talk about it 'cause it's a sight most people wouldn't believe anyway."

Crouch, who was a combat medic, spent most of his time inoculating the prisoners and treating their wounds. Some of his patients were starving infants born in the camp. He saw lice an inch long and cases of gangrene that could only be treated with amputation. "It does work on you. It was good for me," he said and then added, trying to express his contradictory feelings, "If it had ended before [I] experienced the worse, it would have been good for me."

About 292,000 Americans died in battle during World War II. More than 670,000 survived their wounds, thanks to combat medics, who spent the war rescuing injured men under fire, probing wounds for bullets and shrapnel, and suturing ripped flesh. "I took a man's leg off one time [in the field]," said Crouch, who was a sergeant. "He just was interested in getting some relief. He didn't care if he had a leg or not. . . . We elected to take it off. We let it lay out there." On another occasion, Crouch treated a first lieutenant whose forehead had been sliced open by flying glass when the building he was in was hit by a bazooka round. "It [the skin] was pulled down over his eyes. You couldn't even see his eyes," he said. "You don't count the stitches. You just put in enough 'cause you don't have that kind of time."

Like many combat medics, Crouch had only the medical training that could be crammed into thirteen harried weeks. Doctors showed them how to give each other shots, and the men practiced their suturing on oranges. Others taught them how to make rescues on the battlefield. "There wasn't no failing it," Crouch said. "You learned it." After that, the men received six weeks of infantry training and then a slow boat ride overseas.

The Seventy-first Division landed at Le Havre, France, on February 6, 1945. Crouch remembers one of the first things the medics were told on arrival was that under the terms of the Geneva Convention, the Germans couldn't shoot anyone wearing a red cross on his helmet. But the first time Crouch was in combat, he saw a helmet with a red cross lying on the ground. When he turned it over, he saw the top of someone's head still inside it. "I took mine and smeared mud over that red cross," he said. Medics weren't supposed to be at risk, and so they weren't supposed to carry guns into combat, but many did. "Yes, I carried a gun," Crouch admits. His weapon of choice was a German Luger. "Where your life's concerned, it's only you that's going to take care of it."

Crouch said he saw General Patton many times. He wasn't impressed. "He's someone you wouldn't want seconds of. I think he hated his mother." Patton, he said, would make his men stand for review even in combat areas. He would pass along the lines, standing up in his jeep, holding onto the windshield. If a soldier so much as moved, Patton had him pulled from the ranks and disciplined. "He was tough," Crouch said. He recalled the time an all-black tank battalion was assigned to the Third Army. The tank crews had put sandbags around the four-by-six-inch peepholes to protect themselves from German sharpshooters, but Patton ordered them removed because he felt they were unsightly. Crouch said few people know it, but the reason Patton liberated so many prison camps on his trek through Germany and Austria was because his son-in-law was in one of them. It was one of Patton's obsessions. "He'd just go to any extent to get that son-in-law back," he said.

Crouch was never wounded, but he had his share of close calls. Once he went to pick up the mail in a jeep, and on the way back, while he was cutting across a field, the windshield of the jeep exploded. A bullet had come from behind him. Later, some soldiers went back to investigate, and they found a German sniper in a church steeple. "They aren't all good shots 'cause they missed me," he said. "We got him."

He remembers what used to scare him most were the harassment mortars, or "screaming meemies." A high-pitched screaming sound was caused by the rotation of the projectile as it fell toward its target. Crouch said when you heard one, if you looked up, you could actually see the round spinning. "That was when you tried to stretch that old steel helmet down to your knees," he said. "Anybody who wasn't scared, wasn't there."

After the war, Crouch eventually went to work for Fruehauf Trailer Company. He retired in 1980. He still has his old army uniform and looks fit enough to still wear it. However, he's had more heart attacks and strokes than he cares to admit, and despite two open-heart surgeries, he has totally blocked arteries on his right side. He walks two miles a day—"I do that as regular as I eat"—usually between 9 P.M. and 2 A.M. because his heart pain is worse at night.

The Seventy-first Infantry was involved in some of the most ferocious fighting of the war. After crossing the Mainz River south of Frankfurt, in early April 1945, the division tangled with the Sixth SS Mountain Division, the elite Nazi troops who, until late in the war, were used as bodyguards for the top Nazi officers. The battle lasted three days. Many of the SS troops fought to the death. When one of them was about to be captured, he often removed his patches and tried to cut out or burn off the distinguishing blue-ink lightning tattoo on the inside of his forearm to avoid being recognized. The SS had a reputation for ruthlessness with Allied prisoners. "We had no mercy on [them]," Crouch said.

Crouch won two Bronze Stars for heroism, both involving the rescue of wounded men under fire. He downplays the awards modestly. "I thought it was the normal duties of the assigned job you had to do," he said. On May 7, Crouch's unit met the Russian Fifth Airborne Division outside Steyr, Austria. No American division got farther east in World War II. On May 8, V-E Day, one of Crouch's wars ended. The other one, the one in his memory, lives on.

V-J Day

Sun over Nagasaki

IWO JIMA, AUGUST 6, 1945—Marshall Whitmore remembers the beginning of the end. That morning, the twenty-two-year-old airman was told to watch for a special B-29 with five stars on each wing, which was scheduled to fly over the island. The Superfortress carried a super bomb, he was told, the likes of which the world had never seen. Whitmore said when the bomber flew over at about ten thousand feet, a squadron of fighters took off from Iwo Jima to escort it to Japan. The bomber, which was nicknamed "Enola Gay" in honor of pilot Col. Paul Tibbets's mother, had taken off before dawn from the tiny island of Tinian in the Marianas. In its bomb bay was a nine hundred-pound bomb with a twenty-two-pound uranium core. The bomb's nickname was "Little Boy."

At 8:16 A.M., Little Boy was detonated 1,870 feet above the port city of Hiroshima, Japan's eighth largest city. Seen from the air, the purplish fireball, 1,800 feet across, blossomed like an angry flower. Enola Gay copilot Capt. Robert Lewis stared in disbelief at the boiling cloud mushrooming to 40,000 feet. "My God," he said, "what have we done?"

At ground zero there was, according to author John Hersey, "a noiseless flash . . . a sheet of sun" that burst across the city. The temperature at the center of the blast was one hundred million degrees—three times hotter than the interior of the sun. Five square miles of the city were totally obliterated. Packing the destructive power of thirteen thousand tons of TNT, the explosion pulverized brick and melted steel. Human beings were vaporized. Some left their oxidized shadows burned into stone; many simply vanished from the face of the earth without a trace.

After the blast would come the firestorms and then the insidious death—the radiation poisoning that was to be the enduring legacy of this first use of atomic weapons against a human population. But that was still in the future. On that late summer day in 1945, all most Americans knew was that their country had a new secret weapon that, it was hoped, would hasten the end of the war. As Whitmore said, when they heard the news about Hiroshima, "we were tickled to death."

Three days later, Kermit "Tex" Behan, bombardier of the Superfortress "Bock's Car," saw a break in the clouds and released "Fat Man," a ten thousand-pound plutonium bomb, over his secondary target, a port and manufacturing center on the southern tip of the island of Honshu. At 11:02 A.M., a sun exploded over Nagasaki.

On August 14, 1945, Japan surrendered. World War II was over; it was V-J Day. Those were heady times few veterans will ever forget. Petty Officer First Class William Hoy was aboard the attack cargo ship USS *Stokes* in the North Pacific when the crew was told to return to Pearl Harbor. The twenty-year-old shipfitter was surprised by the order. "We didn't expect it at all. We thought we were going in," he said. The *Stokes* was carrying a load of marines and equipment for the invasion of Japan, which was planned for November.

"We did the same thing at Iwo Jima and Okinawa. We put 'em on the beach," he said. But he admits he had a bad feeling about invading the Japanese home islands. "I didn't figure I'd come back alive," he said. Pharmacist Mate First Class Richard Brown was on an aircraft carrier headed for Kyushu when the war ended. "We'd just finished with Iwo Jima and Okinawa," he said. "Just wiped 'em out." For the invasion of Japan, he said, they were to provide air support for the marine landings on Kyushu. Instead, they ended up escorting the occupation troops to and from Japan. The crew installed sleeping racks on the carrier's hangar deck so they could transport additional men.

The twenty-year-old visited Nagasaki a few weeks after the blast, which had killed thirty-five thousand people and leveled much of the city. "Anybody that wanted to go to see it was allowed to go," he said. "We [just] couldn't leave the trucks. The center of the blast was just rubble." The few steel-reinforced buildings still standing were "just twisted like wire. . . . There were people pickin' around in it. The Japanese people kept their heads down. They wouldn't look at you," he said. "That was pretty much a pitiful-looking sight."

But despite the dreadful toll taken by the bomb, most veterans defend its use. "I still think it was a good thing," Whitmore said. "I think a lot of us wouldn't be here today . . ." Brown, like many World War II veterans, knows it kept him out of an invasion of Japan. And that's good enough for him. "I wouldn't want to go over there on another mission like that. No way."

Sources

Most of the stories in this book first appeared in one of the three newspapers that I worked for during my journalism career. Two of those newspapers—*Shopper News Publications* (Liberty, Missouri) and the *Antioch Publication* (Kansas City, Missouri)—are no longer in existence. The third, the *Lee's Summit Journal* (Lee's Summit, Missouri), is over 120 years old and still going strong. This chronological listing includes the newspapers in which the stories originally appeared, the civilian's name or the veteran's name and branch of service, and the date of the published story. In cases where a story appeared in more than one part, only the date of the first installment is listed. The few interviews that were not published are listed at the end.

Shopper News Publications

Robert Barackman, U.S. Marine Corps (5/9/84)
James Farmer, U.S. Coast Guard (5/26/84)
Harold Meyer, U.S. Army (4/20/85)
Nadine Meyer, U.S. Marine Corps (4/20/85)
Stewart Kluender, U.S. Army Air Corps (4/24/85)
Oscar Pruessner, U.S. Army (5/4/85)
Ronald Hollingsworth, U.S. Navy (5/25/85)
Tudie Brisciano, U.S. Navy (6/8/85)
James Bennett, U.S. Marine Corps (6/29/85)
Jim Campbell, U.S. Army Air Corps (8/10/85)
Pat Flanagan, U.S. Navy (12/7/85)
Richard McBratney, U.S. Navy (12/7/85)
Les LeTourneau, U.S. Army (12/7/85)

Antioch Publication

William Hoy, U.S. Navy (8/6/86)
Marshall Whitmore, U.S. Army Air Corps (8/6/86)
Richard Brown, U.S. Navy (8/6/86)
Pat Flanagan, U.S. Navy (12/3/86)
Warren Anderson, U.S. Army (1/20/88)
Sam Crookshanks, U.S. Army (1/20/88)
Eddie Epperson, U.S. Army (1/20/88)
Louis Degginger, U.S. Army (1/20/88)
Ralph Saunders, U.S. Army (1/20/88)
Joe Crouch, U.S. Army (7/20/88)

Lee's Summit Journal

Leo Burrow, U.S. Army (7/21/89)
LeRoy Dir, U.S. Army (9/13/89)
Jack Young, U.S. Marine Corps (11/24/89)
John Michael Garber, U.S. Army (2/14/90)
Everett Browning, U.S. Army (5/9/90)
Russell May, U.S. Army Air Corps (11/26/90)
Leonard Jordan, U.S. Merchant Marines (2/1/91)
Kenny Winburn, U.S. Army (3/22/91)
Bob Grimes, U.S. Army Air Corps (5/10/91)
Stayton Parr, U.S. Army (10/23/91)
Bob Sommer, U.S. Army Air Corps (11/13/91)
Louis Truman, U.S. Army (12/6/91)
Buddy Stagner, civilian (12/6/91)
Dee Nicholson, civilian (12/6/91)
George Rhodes, U.S. Army (12/16/91)
Harvey Wilson, Seabees (2/28/92)
Paul Hoover, U.S. Army Air Corps (4/27/92)
Robert Peck, U.S. Army (5/13/92)
Mike Norris, U.S. Marines (5/27/92)
Betty Norris, U.S. Marines (5/27/92)
Ed Henry, U.S. Merchant Marines (6/10/92)
Dean Stringer, U.S. Army (7/17/92)
Mary Eble, U.S. Army Nurse Corps (8/31/92)
Karl Wagner, German Kriegsmarine (10/26/92)

Hans Massmann, German Kriegsmarine (10/26/92)
Wendell Fetters, U.S. Army Air Corps (4/9/93)
Milton Shalinsky, U.S. Army Air Corps (4/9/93)
Paul Shull, U.S. Army Air Corps (4/9/93)
John Weaver, U.S. Army Air Corps (4/9/93)
George Kolb, U.S. Merchant Marines (5/21/93)
Edward O'Connell, U.S. Merchant Marines (5/21/93)
J. B. Shackleford, U.S. Merchant Marines (5/21/93)
Dale VanLerberg, U.S. Merchant Marines (5/21/93)
Alfred Taylor, U.S. Merchant Marines (5/21/93)
Mat Oglesby, U.S. Merchant Marines (5/21/93)
Paul Ceynowa, U.S. Marine Corps (8/6/93)
Bob Wood, U.S. Army Air Corps (9/20/93)
Bob Lucas, U.S. Army (10/15/93)
Bill Thompson, U.S. Army (10/15/93)
Elmer Kreeger, U.S. Navy (11/10/93)
Charles McGee, U.S. Army Air Corps (3/28/94)
Kenneth Woolford, U.S. Army Air Corps (3/28/94)
Travis Hoover, U.S. Army Air Corps (4/11/94)
Charles McGee, U.S. Army Air Corps (4/15/94)
Bob Layher, American Volunteer Group (4/29/94)
Bob Maier, U.S. Navy (6/3/94)
Mel Schneider, U.S. Navy (6/3/94)
Alvin Hammer, U.S. Army Air Corps (6/3/94)
Vince Baker, U.S. Army (6/6/94)
Marvin Boyce, U.S. Army Air Corps (10/24/94)
Harvey Wilson, Seabees (2/17/95)
Mel Schneider, U.S. Navy (4/7/95)
Harvey Wilson, Seabees (4/7/95)
Josephine Clark, U.S. Army Nurse Corps (11/10/95)
Isabel Fritchie, U.S. Navy (11/10/95)
Fran O'Brien, U.S. Navy (11/10/95)
Mamie Mulligan, civilian (11/10/95)
Ken Morton, U.S. Navy (7/18/97)
Bob Seek, U.S. Marine Corps (11/10/97)
Jim Daniels, U.S. Navy (12/5/97)
George Rhodes, U.S. Army (5/27/98)
Don Wood, U.S. Army (6/2/99)
Gene Rigney, U.S. Army (11/8/99)
Thomas Begay, U.S. Marine Corps (5/26/00)

Albert Schultz, U.S. Army (1/19/01)
Wayne McMeins, U.S. Marine Corps (4/4/01)
Finis Saunders, U.S. Army Air Corps (5/21/01)
Raymond Johnson, U.S. Navy (7/25/01)

Unpublished interviews

Bill McMullen, U.S. Coast Guard (interviewed 1992)
Byron Banta, U.S. Army (interviewed 2001)
Larry Kellar, U.S. Army (interviewed 2002)